Gall

Five Years of Unfettered Christian Exploration Somewhere Between Youth Group and the Rest of Life

To order additional copies, please contact us.
BookSurge, LLC
www.booksurge.com
I-866-308-6235
orders@booksurge.com

Gall

Five Years of Unfettered
Christian Exploration Somewhere
Between Youth Group and the
Rest of Life

Pete Gall

2005

Gall

Five Years of Unfettered Christian Exploration Somewhere Between Youth Group and the Rest of Life

CONTENTS

For my family, who love me.

I.

Idle Bullshit

I'm the fat blond guy on the corner, in the African print shirt, squeezing himself into the yellow taxi.

"Burritoville on Addison near Wrigley." I direct.

It's 7:15, Wednesday night, August 3, 1994. I work late most nights because my ad agency buys cab rides and dinners for people who work past 7:00. Once a month my boss complains that as a man I'm taking politically incorrect advantage of a loophole in a politically correct policy intended to protect the safety of female employees. He says that I should be taking the bus and buying my own damned dinner. All I know is that I get four giant chorizo burritos and four Mountain Dews a week for free, and I don't have to deal with the bus. That, and we both know the extra hours I'm working are spent making him look like a superhero.

"Long day at work?" The driver asks in a Russian accent.

"Yeah." I reply, sizing the man up. Lately I've been exploring the power and joy of lying to strangers. "I write for an advertising agency."

This part is true. The world's largest agency, in fact. A fact, as a matter of fact, of which I am quite proud. It wasn't an easy time to get into the ad world, last year, and somehow I landed a great job with big name clients and am earning more than any of my old college drinking buddies.

"Anything I see?"

"Ever read your shampoo bottle?" I ask. "The directions on the back?"

"Yeah."

"I revolutionized the hair care industry with one word." This is the lie.

"How?"

"I added the word 'repeat' to the end of the directions. My client increased profits by 150 percent in a year." I make the number up at random.

"Interesting." He is clearly not all that impressed, and we return to silence as he weaves heart-stoppingly through traffic for a few blocks. Then he asks, "Even if every person washed their hair twice, that would only be double. Why did profits go up even more?"

"Good insight." I say, practicing my client skill of congratulating people's intelligence when they show even this slightest mental effort. It's a cheap compliment and an insult at the same time, but polite social rules mandate that we always ignore the second half. I think it's funny that some people actually receive such feedback as a true compliment. "At first our goal was just to increase sales— you know, get people to use more. And it worked. In consumer research we found that people quickly learned that they were supposed to shampoo twice. And while fewer than half of them did, some shampooed three times. The net effect was an increase of 20 percent. Then the shampoo makers did some testing and realized that using twice as much shampoo was actually very hard on people's hair. So they diluted the stuff, which made it a lot less expensive to produce." I lean forward, locking his eyes in the rear view mirror to force him to listen, just to see how the trick will work, "And that's when things really took off. People who were only shampooing once needed conditioner because the shampoo wasn't working on its own, and people who were following the directions needed conditioner because the shampoo was frying their hair. All told, my client improved its profits by 150 percent, and the rest of the industry followed suit." I sit back in my seat. "Of course, that was just the first year—I've been working on other projects since then."

"This is what you do, write tricky words?"

"That's my job. We call it 'creating a need.' I write the songs that make the young girls sing. I write the songs of love and hair and shiny things." I sing, and he seems to have no idea what song I'm parodying. I write the songs, I write the songs. It's Mr. Manilow to you. Most nights it takes a couple of hours and at least a couple of beers to slow the free association.

"What others?" He asks.

"You mean what other needs do I create?"

"Yeah."

"All of them, my friend." I say, practicing the trick of familiarity with a stranger to build power. "They're all made up, and there will always be new ones. Things you don't even know about today are things that I'll make sure you won't be able to live without tomorrow."

He scowls a little at the cliché, and the dark truth behind it.

I continue with my little cool kid spooky truths. "Don't think of it as a bad thing. Or at least don't think of me as the bad guy; it's the nature of man. We're all after something to tell us about ourselves. We all want to be on the right teams. We don't care much where the things that identify us—in the sense that they give us our identity—come from. In fact, the easier they come, the better. Take Coke versus Pepsi for example; do I see myself as more of a loyal traditionalist with family values, in which case I buy Coke to remind myself about it, or do I see myself as more of a hip fun member of the next generation, in which case Pepsi is my shorthand drink of choice? Exactly the same thing with McDonalds and Burger King, Ford and Honda, IBM and Apple. We build a whole world around that sort of stuff, and it's a ton easier than picking a religion, which, by the way, we do in about the same manner."

"Hmm."

We drive the rest of the way to Burritoville in silence. I tip him big and ask for a receipt for my expense report.

2.

Happy Birthday, Sweetheart

I walk the three blocks from Burritoville towards Lake Shore and my apartment, carrying my dinner in a brown paper bag. As I enter the courtyard of my building, I see Betsy outside my door waiting for me. Before she notices me, I turn and duck back around the corner of the building, where I sit on the sidewalk with my back against the wall and unwrap the burrito. She can wait.

Twenty-four hours earlier we were out for my birthday dinner. Hancock Tower, 85th floor. Window table facing north. I wore a tie. She wore a low-cut black spaghetti strap dress over her perfect body, pearls resting proudly on her delicate collarbones, with double French braids in her chestnut hair. She owned me. My birthday was also our four and a half year anniversary. I'd been shopping for engagement rings for weeks. Before we'd even ordered dinner she dropped the bomb.

"You said there was nothing there, Betsy."

"I was lying."

"How long?"

"Six months."

"So the roses did mean something."

"That was at the very beginning."

"And last Thursday?"

"I've been with him."

"What?"

"Every Thursday. I've been with him every Thursday."

"Does he know about me?"

"He thinks we broke up."

"Why didn't we?"

"I love you."

I was staring at her with my stunned mouth half open when the waiter breezed up and asked for our orders.

"I'll take the lobster and another Glenfiddich." I said.

As she ordered, I looked out the window towards my apartment. My stinking Chicago apartment, in stinking Chicago. I hated Chicago. I hated Chicago people. I hated Chicago sports teams and sports fans. I hated the Chicago accent and the stupidity it highlighted in the people who had it. I hated her ancient south side parents, her brother who would live at home forever, her nurse sister with her addiction to self-improvement books and dreams of the Miss Fitness America pageant, forever with her clumsy attempts to tempt me, to beat Betsy. Was that why her sister had been walking around the apartment naked, to trip me into ruining our relationship without actually telling me about Betsy? Was it mercy all along? What the hell? Freaking life in Chicago. I thought this was going to be it. I thought Betsy's insane family with all of their arguing and drinking and anti-Semitic Catholic bigotry was going to be my family. I thought I was going to be in Chicago forever, because that's the only place Betsy could see herself. Suddenly it was all unraveling.

Outside the window, a thousand feet up in the night air, a spider clung to a strand of web, a strand of hope spun from itself. Were there even bugs up this high for spiders to catch? How the hell did it get so far from the ground? How long would that take, to climb all the way from terra firma? Four and half years, maybe? Maybe the spider had been blown to its current place. Or maybe it had taken generations to get to this height—maybe it was from some family of spiders bent on moving ever skyward. Did it have any idea how far it was from the ground? Did it have any fear, dangling a foot from the glass? I have never experienced a moment I wanted to escape so badly, and it's the only time I've ever wanted to trade places with a bug, if only the bug could have been convinced that it wasn't getting the short end of the exchange.

What would my family say about the end of the relationship? What would I even tell them? My friends were easy; they had all hated Betsy for years and would immediately take me out drinking to celebrate. My co-workers, Brett and Tony in particular, would be angry; they found it absurd that Betsy and I had never slept together, and were hell-bent on finding the right scenario for it to happen. They had all sorts of suggestions and how-to advice. I told them we hadn't because I wasn't sure I wanted to, and because I knew it wouldn't be worth dealing with her after the fact if we did. She already cried every time she reached orgasm, and that was just from...not actual sex. It all felt dirty to her unlivable pleated skirt schoolgirl rules. I quickly cataloged our last six months to compare her behavior in that arena to how she'd always been. It was about the same, though she'd definitely had moments where she had been more aggressive than usual.

"I do, really."

"Love me?" I asked, raising my eyebrows sarcastically.

"Yes."

"You've always said he was such an asshole."

"He is."

"So..."

"So that's what makes it all so hard. So confusing."

"You're confused because you're cheating on me with an asshole?"

"Yeah."

"Have you slept with him?"

"That's none of your business."

"What?" I did one of those coughing/laughing things on the *wh*.

"I'm not going to talk to you about our sex life."

"*Our* sex life. What the hell?" I stopped and took a sip of my scotch because I could see that she was about to cry, and the last thing I had the patience for was crying from her right then. After a long pause and the preparation of a dinner roll, I tried again.

"I won't make you say it, Betsy. Can I ask you this, though: do you and I have a sex life?"

There was a candle on the table, and her skin looked so perfect in the dim yellow light. Her eyes were wet and red.

"No." She answered, and for a moment I thought the collapsing inside would kill me.

On television shows there is a major blow-up. The audience and the characters seem to know something like this is coming, and someone always storms out of the room. But the last thing I wanted to do was walk away from her. I loved her. I was stunned and I wanted her to make sense of what I was experiencing. I wanted her to be with me far more than I wanted to claim the lame high ground of the victim. But I knew I was supposed to react with some sort of anger. I ordered the lobster because it was the most expensive thing I could think of. This is my idea of being a man who won't be pushed around? Cost her an extra twenty dollars? I didn't leave the table, never raised my voice, and took a long time before the snide jabs began. The rest of dinner was a blur, and I spent a lot of time looking out the window at the spider, numbly wondering what in the world would come next. I didn't cry, but I did use my begging voice, my wounded sensitive guy voice. The one I'm so self-conscious about. The one that makes me feel boring and safe and makes me wonder how much her choices are a reflection of my weakness.

She came back to my place with me. We ended up in my bedroom. She slipped out of her dress and stood before me in her black lacy panties and pearls. From the outset of our relationship I've been completely intoxicated by her beauty and her body. She can do the splits against the wall standing up. She has a washboard stomach. There's this perfect tendon that traces inward from her hip. We spent our college years flirting with sex in a myriad of silly and even pathetic ways, and we both knew that after all that time, now that she had slept with him, she was about to sleep with me.

And that would be it. We were not going to survive as a couple. She wasn't going to choose between us. She was going to keep poisoning her options until she made her choice without really ever making her choice; she would orchestrate what would happen to her, and we both knew it.

A better man would have sent her home with a kick in the ass. A lesser man would have gone at it vigorously, selfishly, with an effort to cross her into new low places. I denied the obvious relational truth facing us, and hiding behind some lame and spineless rationalization about hope or romance, I stepped forward. And then she changed her mind. She shook as she put her dress back on. Here I cried. Here I begged. Here I took dirty shots. And then I repeated the process like it was a cheap shampoo, too weak the first time around, and enough to piss her off the second. And then she was gone.

So she can wait while I eat my damned burrito and drink my motherfucking Mountain Dew on the sidewalk, a wino to my food on the street as a couple walks past, holding hands. I hate Chicago lovers.

I'm still on the sidewalk, wiping red chorizo oil from my hands with the paper bag, when Betsy gives up and arrives at the curb to hail a cab. She sees me and drops her shoulders.

"What are you doing?"

"Don't you recognize fine dining when you see it?"

"Didn't you see me waiting for you?"

"Do you think I usually take my meals on the sidewalk?" I answer her questions with questions because she hates it.

"Why are you avoiding me?"

"Uh, because you're screwing another guy?"

"Can we talk about it?"

"Will you quit screwing other guys?"

"Can we talk?"

"How about you screw me then, right now?"

"Please?"

"No? Then how about you just screw off?"

"Don't do this." She's crying now. Again.

"You don't get to decide a thing about what I do anymore."

"I don't want to lose you." She's shaking. Again.

"Go home. Or go find another corner to work if you're looking for love. I'm done with you. I say, and I know this immediate gratification will be followed by tearful apologies later. We both know it. We both know this is pure ugliness. And we both know we won't end well.

Betsy stops and stares. She inhales a sobbing stuttering gasp. I am ice. Furious, venomous, profoundly hateful ice. She turns and runs with her hand over her mouth to Lakeshore to catch a taxi. I'm a complete wreck by the time I get to my apartment.

3.

Truth in Advertising

In other news, I'm about to leave the agency, if I can muster the courage. In the year that I've been there, everything I've touched has turned to gold. I've been invited into every account the Chicago office has, and New York has asked for me on others. General Motors, PowerAde, Johnson & Johnson, 1-800-FLOW-ERS, Time Warner, and a host of pharmaceutical accounts make up the bulk of it. I hear from all sides how well things are going. The ultimate battle, though, is whether to believe what I hear, or to admit the truth.

When I was leaving high school my pastor took me aside and said, "I think you should consider the ministry. I believe you have a calling on your life." Such words don't come cheap in white suburban Presbyterian churches, or from him. And there was something that felt true when he said it, like I already knew it somewhere. At the time, though, that was the last thing I wanted. A pastor? No way. Pastors drink tea with old ladies and have a creepy, fretting predilection for the health concerns of strangers. Not my deal.

I spent my first two years at Indiana University taking prerequisite classes for IU's top-tier Business school before switching to English when it became clear that my grades would fail to land me a job where I'd ever need a calculator. During my sophomore year I took an Accounting exam on a blustery gray autumn afternoon, and I remember the walk home. I wasn't sure I'd passed, and rather than looking to the fact that I knew more about where Miller Lite was bottled than I did about FIFO, LIFO or any other Accounting principles, I prayed that God would "let me prove myself in the real world, and then you can have me."

After graduation, I sent letters and my hammy portfolio to 125 agencies around America and the Caribbean. I got two interviews (both in Chicago, where Betsy had already assumed a position with a bank), and one job offer, which happened to come from the perfect place for me. At my agency there is none of the underdog attitude of a boutique shop. There is none of the truly creative bravado of a more artistic place. My agency is flat-out big, with big corporate clients and pure, soulless results-based marketing agendas. It's been the perfect place to experience a sense of playing with the big boys, without the sense of yearning that comes in a smaller place, and none of the sense of artistic elitism that congratulates people in other agencies. The circumstances of my employment, of my situation with my job, and with the results I've experienced here have simply been too perfect, and I often think of my prayer the day after that Accounting test. I'm beginning to see that I've been shown the end of an empty path, and that maybe I'm being drawn to something else, something God has in mind.

There is something inherently immoral about phrases like "create a need." Likewise, there is something inherently immoral about using a gift or ability for the good of something in which you don't believe. It's a prostitution, really, and people in Advertising talk about it all the time. And the more I consider my job, the more these truths about the immorality of it all strike home. And the more they strike home, the more I think about my prayer after the Accounting test.

And then comes the Conceptrol account. Conceptrol is a spermicidal gel that adds less than one percent to the efficacy of birth control. As far as I can tell from the data available to me, it's a nearly worthless product. And they want to market it to teenagers. So, if I do my job well, I'll help derail the lives of girls who are no match for the power of my message and my thinly veiled invitation to foolish, sinful choices. Not everyone is offered such a clear-cut opportunity to choose the right path, and the clarity of it makes me think about the second half of my prayer on my way back to my dorm room after the Accounting test that blustery autumn afternoon—the part about "then you can have me." And I know, deep down, that the truth of my success is that God let me walk with my idol until I could see it well enough to put it down and head in the other direction.

Somewhere at a similar depth, I know Betsy is another idol, but she's one that I would never have put down on my own, so she's being ripped from me by a God who's claiming what's his.

It's mid-afternoon, and I've been waiting all day to talk to my boss, Buzz. He's made a study of being a creative weido, collecting and taping to his office door instances of 666 from parking lot stubs or rosters or what have you, obsessing about a toy robot, collecting magic tricks, spamming really outlandish porn, etcetera, and today his insanity is killing me. He has to step through my office to get to his—his being the corner office and mine being one that was originally designed for a secretary to the guy in the corner office—and I'm not allowed to close his door or "alter the conditions" of his office. He has been gone in meetings all day, but he likes to return to the same setting as he left, so he hit "repeat" on his CD player. For almost three hours I've been listening to Ted Nugent's "Stranglehold" while the smell of baking yeast wafts its way into my office from the bread maker on his windowsill.

On my birthday Buzz filled my office with balloons and Nerf toys and really did the day up right. My office is still cluttered with child-friendly toys. He's also invested well in me, offering one of the seminal bits of direction in my life. It came after I presented one of my ideas to him, and was sent back to the drawing board with, "Okay, can we all agree that you're funny, and try to figure out if you're any good?" It's not every day that someone seeks to learn that about another person, and it was a big deal to me. He takes the writers out to lunch and makes us play games where we have to continue the story told by the person beside us. He loves to buy Sambuca shots and pass the flame from co-worker finger to co-worker finger all the way around the bar. What makes Buzz especially fascinating to me is the way he uses the word "should." I was taught not to use it because "should" is "too bossy," but he uses it in an intimate way, and works the word as the lynchpin to moments where he claims an authority over someone else's world—always their personal world. When he says, "You should do that," most people do. They call their mothers. They have another drink. They sleep with people from the office. They trust him and give him more power. Used well, "should" can be as potent as "they," which is a great word for telling lies:

"*They* told me inside that I wouldn't have to pay for parking."

"They did?"

"Yes."

"Okay, if they say so."

"Thanks. Have a great day."

In many ways my boss and I are birds of a twisted feather, and I know that two things will be certain when I tell him about my plans to leave: he'll be hurt enough to try to keep me, and then he'll be angry enough to bludgeon me and make me choose to completely burn the relationship if I reject his efforts to keep me. The fact that our talk is coming two days after he decorated my office doesn't help.

There is a game of Frisbee going on in the hallway when he returns, and he joins in for a couple of tosses, pushing the limits and adding some random wrinkle to the game that I can't understand from where I'm sitting. He is consistently the one who takes things right to the edge of their ability to be controlled: there is a tiny hole in his eighth floor window where a dart hit it when we were all playing from 20 feet away. It wasn't a big deal, but it sure could have become one. He's wearing jeans, a gray dress shirt, and sneakers in which he always walks buoyantly on the balls of his feet. He's athletic the way someone who could have played sports but chose the drama club is athletic. His hair is a black horseshoe gripping his skull from ear to ear, and the early baldness tortures him. Julie, the gorgeous production assistant, wanders into the hall and tells him how great the bread smells. He invites everyone to come grab a slice.

The party moves into and through my office to his, and then spreads into both. He's perfect for his job because he's just a little more of everything than everyone around him. He's little more devious, a little more disciplined, a little more curious, a little more insightful, a little more seasoned, a little more gifted, a little more connected, a little more aware of where everyone's careers and lives are heading. It's all part of a well-crafted persona—the persona that lets him use the word "should." The other creative director insists that Buzz is a little bit more of all of those things because he is nothing but the one-up—there is no base substance to the man. That could be, but every loser argues for substance, just like every ugly girl thinks she must have a great personality.

I stick to my work, making only small talk with people like no-memory Margo the epileptic, or Benny the designer who's been fired from every job and always made more money on the next one, or Rex the ambidextrous multimedia guru. I'm trying to be rude, trying to make sure they feel like an intrusion and hurry through. I'm the wet blanket. I rifle loudly through my metal desk drawer to find my headphones and plug them into my stereo. At one point Buzz makes a face and a palms-up gesture to ask if I'm okay. I respond with a gesture that I'm busy and my shaking vertical fingers complain about the chaos he's creating with all of these people. Half an hour later everyone's gone and Buzz is back to work in his office. And then, after all of my previous eagerness, I don't move. I listen to my mix tape and hide behind Pearl Jam and Urge Overkill, not at all eager to quit my job.

Is this really what I want to do? Is this God's leading, or is this me guessing what God would say? Am I making God my imaginary friend and playing the roles of us both? Is this me running away from success? Fearing failure? Is this my inability to stand the pain of my ordinary world, suddenly in burning tatters with all the junk going on with Betsy? What else will I do? If God wants me, where does he want me? It must involve the skills I've gained in advertising, right? He wouldn't just throw away the time, would he? A whole year? What might he want me to do instead? Advertising is all about creating a need, and the only need people really have is him, so maybe what he wants is for me to create marketing materials that help people feel their need for God. Maybe? And then what, send them to church? Right. I hate church. It was fine for high school cutesy stuff, but I have no idea why adults attend, except that it's what they feel like they're supposed to do. It's another "should" argued by people who have been told by some nameless "them" that this is how God wants things. It's just a holy rubber stamp, and it's more fake than any beer commercial could ever be. A leftover tradition. A group masturbation. A dead end. I'd feel better about selling motherhood to a teenager than church to a person looking for God.

No, the God I know is not the God who wants to hear a prayer of confession read from a program. The God I believe in cares about real lives. He makes use of talents—he even gives us those talents in the first place. The people my God would point to as heroes are not the weirdoes hiding in churches, but the people who actually do something because they believe in him and care about the things he says to care about. The God I believe in will experience tremendous grief with each soul consumed by the fires of hell, even if the church people clap and dance and giggle with each sizzle and pop. He would choose to be known. He would choose to love and be loved. He would choose to be chosen. He will break out some major ass-kicking for church people who become barriers to people who seek him more honestly. He will have little patience with the church people who have not shown mercy to sinners, who have stepped over their brother on the street, who have lied to them and made them feel uninvited until they got their worlds in order. The God I believe in will punish people whose "good, healthy boundaries" are not based in truth and love, but in selfish, gluttonous security and safety rather than faith, and who would let their sister bleed to death before they'd let her bleed on their new carpet.

I've been reading about Habitat for Humanity, and I've seen stuff on television about Promise Keepers. What if the two groups could get together for a week or two—a million men swinging hammers across the country to do something helpful for thousands of people with little other proof that Christianity is real to the people who profess it? I can see people watching TV at the corner bar noticing the news article about that one, and having to admit that for whatever else a person may say about the people of God, they certainly are making a difference and displaying acts of loving generosity. That's a "brand" people would join, would want to be associated with, would use to tell themselves and others the story of who they are. That would be a need worth creating, worth pointing out, worth creating a hunger for. Maybe that's something God would have me do?

Or at least stuff like that. There are all sorts of places where Christians are doing good things, where people's needs are being met by Christians who offer their services in the name of Jesus. Maybe all the world, or at least the church, needs is little more than a new way of being seen, a new way of expressing itself. A new and better PR campaign.

4:00. Time is ticking by and I'm still frozen in my fear. Buzz is not going to be pleased. It's going to be ugly. I'm going to feel stupid. Maybe I am being stupid. I don't even know what I'd do. I don't know where I'd live, or how I'd pay for anything. I haven't even gone to church the whole time I've been in Chicago—maybe I'm totally screwy. Maybe I'm being rash. Maybe what I really need to do is sleep on it—for a day, or maybe a couple of weeks while I sort through all of this stuff with Betsy. Surely there is some way to be a Christian in the advertising world—it's not like the industry is explicitly set against God, it's just that the approach doesn't work around a felt obligation to respect Him. There must be a place for me to stay, right?

4:07. Russ Taff's song "I Still Believe" comes on my stereo headphones, and I have *a moment*. I do still believe. And more than that, I *want* to believe. It is true that my world is a mess. It is true that things with my job are going well, apart from the crisis of conscience. It is true that I have no idea what I'd do, or any idea how well I'd do, or any clear sense that the Habitat-Promise Keeper marriage has any potential. It is true that I am not a church person—and I certainly don't talk like one anymore. It is true that I am about to commit professional suicide. But in the face of all that, some things are even more true, and they boil down to the fact that I *want* God to have been calling me all my life. I *want* there to be more than money, flashy work, and lying to cab drivers. I *want* there to be more than sex with a beautiful wife who has settled in to be my roommate. I *want* this whole God thing to be real. I *want* William Blake to have been right when he wrote about there being more than our five senses. I *want* to know a truth that transcends the system; that transcends the truth I already know. I *want* to be about something more. I *want* to believe, and I want it to show. Freakin' Russ Taff. I rise from my chair and *I know that I am about to choose an entirely different path for the rest of my life. Right now.* Right now. Everything changes, right now. My world's apocalypse, right now.

I feel like I've just stood up in a giant lecture hall and screamed "bullshit!" at the professor. All eyes are on me, and my words are distant—I can't hear them and I can't tell if I'm making any sense; I'm just flowing, clumsy and flush with adrenaline.

I knock on the door, right on the 666 of a dry cleaning receipt.

"Buzz? Got a minute?"

4.

Bravado Runs Away

"I don't know what's happening to me, David." I'm sobbing into the phone with the sort of gusto men allow each other only once in their relationships. "Everything is falling apart, and I don't know if I can handle it."

David is my best friend from before college. We were in youth group together. He's two years older and is at seminary in Denver. He got married three months ago. Our mutual friend and I flew in for the wedding together. We had passes that got us upgrades to First Class for $30. People flying Coach pay $3 for a beer, but in First Class drinks are free. We broke even somewhere over Nebraska. We had the seats nearest the curtain separating the plebes from the patricians, and every time someone would pass by on their way to our lavatory, I'd turn around, shoot a dirty look, and snap the curtain closed again, laughing. I stole the oxygen mask the flight attendants use to demonstrate the safety procedures. We thought we were pretty hot shit, coming from the big city ready for a bachelor party and a weekend of drinking with the seminarian we'd love to get drunk at the strip club. He picked us up at the airport and excitedly told us how he'd made it all the way from Denver Seminary to Stapleton International without having to stop for a light. The bachelor party turned out to be a campfire in the mountains with a group of guys. One of them even brought a veggie platter. The only nudity was a cupcake with boobs on the top, which competed with the cigars and one beer apiece for the most debauched part of the night. But that was three months ago; tonight there is a sweeping drama unfolding and David was the guy who picked up the phone to hear about it.

"I feel totally adrift," I blather. "I gave six weeks' notice, and last night Buzz took me out for a beer and offered me a raise to a senior copywriter position that would focus on new business projects with him. I'd wondered if he'd do something like that, and I knew that if he did, he'd wait until time was running down before he made his move, waiting to see if I'd change my mind first. It's been a tense four weeks."

"I bet." David is working on his Masters of Divinity in counseling, and is diligent about practicing his active listening. "It must be hard for you."

"It has been. Buzz's boss told me she'd miss watching my career. She said that with everyone else in the agency she could tell how far they'd go, but she didn't see a ceiling for me and had been looking forward to what I'd do. I know she was probably just doing the white bread praise thing, but it felt good, you know?"

"That's really cool. And I'm sure she wouldn't say it if it wasn't at least partly true."

"I don't know. The whole job thing is just part of it anyway. I'm totally twisted up about Betsy, and I know it's crazy, but I feel like I'm being attacked spiritually, like demons and stuff. This neighborhood is full of gay people and young people, and we're all so obsessed with our own sexual junk—it feels like it's everywhere, pressing in, and my brain is swimming. I can't sleep. I'm afraid that someone's going to break through the window from the fire escape. Everything feels chaotic and frightening. I don't know who I am, and I don't know where I'm going, and I can't believe I made this choice because I wanted to do public relations for *God*. What the hell is that?"

"It's not crazy. There is a spiritual world, and you've just made a choice that makes you show up on the radar of a war that's going on. You're stepping out in response to God. That's going to make you some enemies."

"I made one with Buzz today. I told him I wasn't going to take his offer. It was so weird the way we left things last night, too. We were at the corner of Saint Clair and Ontario, a block off Michigan Avenue—in front of that place where I took you to lunch when you were here—and the streets were empty, no people and no cars. There was a fog and the streets were wet. It felt for all the world like a meeting outside of time. The orange flashing of the Don't Walk lights and the green from the traffic signal were in the puddles, and I felt like I was making the choice they represented—that there was a green light to go forward, and a warning not to go any further with him. I said goodbye at the corner and walked north a block before I got a cab. It was creepy, like there were angels and demons around us or something."

"So what happened today when you told him, then?"

"He told me that he hoped I knew that he would never give me a recommendation and that he didn't ever want to talk to me again, and that I should leave the building immediately."

"That had to be hard after how close you've felt to him."

"Yeah, it was. It wasn't a surprise, but I hadn't thought about how much it would hurt."

"And you're not someone who deals well with having people mad at you."

"I guess. It was just so sudden, even though I knew the end was coming. I stuck my head in a few offices on my way out and told those people what had happened, and that I was on my way out right then. No real goodbyes at all."

"Man."

"But here's the part that really got me." I have to take a minute because I start crying too hard again. I blow my nose on my shirt and continue. "Diane, the office manager who's spent six months of weekly lunches telling me about her marriage being in trouble, was one of the people who was in her office on my way out. She knew I was leaving, but asked me to tell her again why I was going. I told her about the Christian PR thing, about Habitat and Promise Keepers—I told you about that idea, didn't I?"

"Yeah. Has Habitat responded to your letter yet?"

"That's right. No, they haven't. But today; when I told her about it, her response was 'Huh; I didn't know you were a Christian.'"

"Oh, ouch." David empathizes.

"I've spent a year with this person, and I've spent six months in intimate confidence with her, and after all that time and all that depth I'd never given her a noticeable clue about me and God. I thought I was being 'salt' in the agency, was being some sort of example or witness or whatever, and she had no idea. And so now here I am, walking away from the industry with all these bad feelings about it, and about my part in it, with my boss cursing me, and it feels like a complete waste because I don't even get the caveat of 'at least I was a visible Christian who did a great job before he left.' I have no credibility, and this whole thing about doing work for God must sound like it's coming completely from right field to them. I've spent a year as a total sell-out, and I have nothing to show for it."

"A chasing after the wind."

"What?"

"It's from Ecclesiastes."

"And I don't know a damned thing about the Bible, either, it seems. Shit David, what am I going to do now?" And the tears come.

"I think you need to get away. Get on a plane and come spend a long weekend with us. You're too close to the mess, and you're torturing yourself with everything. If it's God calling you, your best bet is to get away where you can be still and know he is God."

"Is that scripture too?"

"Psalm 46:10."

"Do you have the whole thing memorized or something?"

"No, just the popular ones on the cheesy art from the Christian bookstores."

"Do they really have those?"

"You should come out this weekend. I won't make you go to a Christian bookstore, but it would be good for you. Getting away, I mean."

5.

Waking to the Dreamer's Dream

Before there was time, when everything was still simply an eternal mingling of God pulsing in a boundless warmth of lightless vision, there came the dream of creation. In the dream there were stars and planets and galaxies and their gravities. There were comets and asteroids and black holes, and space enough to soar and to laugh and to dream without end. On one planet there would be green and blue and yellow, trees and water and dirt with worms and grass vast and tickling. There would be mountains heaving up through the plains, and there would be butterflies and birds and deer and bears and wolves and trout. In the winter things would go white and freeze. In the spring they would melt and splash and shoot green and bright-eyed into the world, and the summer would make everything strong and would pour out luxurious moments of joy and definition to the world. And as the summer felt the satisfaction of its work, yellow would rush into the aspen leaves, drying them and clapping them together in the raucous applause of a billion thank yous from creation. And in the middle of one river in the mountains of Colorado one plump young man, previously lost and lonely, would nap on a rock, waders on his feet and a fly rod in his hands, and he would daydream about nothing but the place and the moment where he lay, surrounded by dancing diamonds of sunlight in the rushing copper-bottomed water, staring up through the yellow applause to the deep blue eternal canopy. The perfect moment of praise from creation would sigh gently through the heart of the dreamer who conceived it all and who drew it all from bits of his own eternity. And because he saw this moment in his dream, the dreamer set to work for six days of brilliant labor, and Himself saw that it was, indeed, quite good.

6.

Confessions of a Nice Guy

I spent five days in Denver, and have decided to move there. I've returned to Chicago for my things and to say my good-byes. My lease runs through the end of September, which is perfect, and I think again about the agreement God and I made after my Accounting test, and how all of the details are working out so that all of my potential excuses to back out on things with God are being cleared from my path.

It's my first night back in town. Betsy and I lay on the pale blue carpet of her apartment and let the evening fade to night without adding to the streetlight that dapples the room through tree branches and open rolled glass windows. We listen to the sound of people out on Wrightwood, and we let the band-aid pull from our hearts slowly, exquisitely. We cry. We kiss. We talk. We hold each other, and we open our hands to the years and dreams we've had together, letting them slip into the current of life around us. Our life together drifts away, sinking. It feels so grown up, so sad, like a movie from the 70s. College is really over now, and in the chill of the real world, so is our time together.

I don't know if it has to be this way. Does this come down to choosing jobs over each other? Lifestyles? Chicago? Denver? Pride? Fear? I don't know why it's ending. I don't know why she's been with the other guy. I want to ask why she's with him, and how she sees me. But the whole subject is too loaded, too volatile for both of us, and I only make one ginger attempt before I lay my ear back on the warm skin of her stomach and watch her chin move as she whispers to me. The wound she has inflicted is profound, but she is tender towards me, and somewhere in my heart I conclude that she doesn't know why this is happening herself. I will take the trade, the pain for its gentle delivery, and I will be okay.

Besides, there is Denver. There is a whole new adventure coming. I still haven't heard from Habitat for Humanity regarding my idea, but that's up to God anyway. David said it's my job to provide the momentum; God will provide the direction. And maybe His plan still involves Betsy. Maybe if I succeed at this, if I can learn to be more exciting, without becoming a workaholic; if I can bring in a great salary; if my prayers wake something up in Betsy; if I lose some weight; maybe if I learn to ski, even. Who knows? It's a whole new world. And we do have a history together. God wouldn't throw away four and a half years, would He? God redeems some idols, right?

For nice guys there is always a list of maybes. Nothing is ever exactly in a nice guy's control, because everything comes as a response to the sugar with which he lures the objects of his desire. It's never overtly about him, but the sensation he creates in others. And with that comes a tremendous sense of insecurity. Here's the thing about the sensitive voice, the fearful regret of playing the nice guy, the worry that I am too boring or safe: this role has been my salvation for 15 years now, and I don't know what else there is to me. I can do the cocky thing, and I do play that role, but it comes from an insincere and frightened place. It comes because I'm a doormat with no place for my frustrations to go, except Burritoville. I'm clumsy with anything but the doormat role, but being the nice guy is simply a dishonest persona; it's not who I am. I'm stuck there, hiding my inconsistencies in places that feel impenetrable to me, but I know they're plain to anyone who bothers to look. I live on the social meniscus that is the unspoken promise to politely ignore each other's foibles.

When I was a senior in high school I dated a girl from a different school, a girl from my youth group. Back at my school, though, I was known as the guy who kept a count on how many days he'd been dating his girlfriend, who was known to lay roses on her doorstep and run away in case she didn't feel presentable. Who would leave notes on her car. Who once pulled alongside the school bus in which her marching band was traveling with a sign asking if people could believe how cute she was. I did the things that made the girls in my high school gush, though it got to a point where my girlfriend asked me to lay off on the flowers. It may not have been overt, but it was all about me. I'd stumbled onto a way to seem desirable without having to be great looking. I'd discovered the bribery of apparent love, assured service, and for years it's worked. During my senior year, I had "friend dates," after school outings of bowling or pool or movies or a walk through the park, with maybe 40 girls from my school. I was the nice guy. And sometimes we'd make out.

I'm thinking about this as Betsy and I lay on the floor of her apartment, saying goodbye and feeling full of emotions, feeling tortured about the end, though part of me is quite interested in one last effort at coitus. Somewhere along the line my real reason against it learned to hide behind her reasons, and now we've come to a place where neither of us has spoken about the truth for over a year.

I was still dating the girl from the other high school, who is a year younger than I am, when I went to college. It was my freshman year, and I'd begun my intensive study of Miller Lite. On Fridays everyone from the floor of the dorm where I lived would gather in my neighbor's room at noon, beer in hand, and we'd play Jimi Hendrix's version of "The Star-Spangled Banner" from Woodstock, and then crack open the beers and begin the weekend. We'd drink all afternoon and all evening until we all pretty much passed out. It was a tradition with which we were quite impressed. I still have a photo from that day in which I'm wearing a blue and black plaid flannel shirt, open over a white t-shirt. I'm also wrapped in a long ribbon of white trash bags I stole from the janitor's closet. The bags are tied around me like a toga, and then knotted in a giant bow on my forehead. In the photo I'm holding a 32-ounce Hardees cup in a salute, and smiling for the camera about the way I guess I'd expect somebody drunk and wrapped in trash bags to smile.

I finished my 23rd beer somewhere around 11:00 that evening. When I spilled on my flannel shirt, I returned to my room to change into another one. The place was full of my roommate's friends, including a girl named Melissa. I'd seen her around, and I knew she was a hometown friend of the bearded guy across the hall we all called Jesus. She'd been drinking, too. I was between flannels, at my open closet, when she approached me.

"You know, I've always found you attractive." She said, putting her hand on my chest.

I made the motorboat sound with my lips in a laughing response to the moment and to her approach. And to her. Sexy. Classy. Suave.

I remember being led to the beanbag chair. I remember her putting my roommate's cowboy hat on me. I remember my roommate and his girlfriend ushering people out of the room. I remember the condom package my roommate tossed at me landing on my shoulder. I remember talking. I remember her crying about her father, who I think worked for the same pharmaceutical company as mine. I remember Kate Bush on the stereo. I remember her complaining about gagging. I remember my super-lover pseudo-masculine response as we switched places:

"You're going down."

I remember looking for another condom a little while later. I remember not being able to find it in my roommate's closet. I remember calling his girlfriend's number to ask him where they were. I remember still not being able to find one. I remember telling her I'd let her know before I came so she could move off of me. I remember forgetting to tell her. I remember telling her to sleep on my roommate's bunk because I wanted more room. I remember her saying something about wanting to be held. I remember telling her we could talk from separate beds. I remember her crying again. And that's all I remember.

Before I woke up I could tell someone was beside me, right by my face on the top bunk. It was my roommate and his girlfriend, grinning and teasing me out of my sleep. Melissa was gone, and for a moment I didn't remember what had happened, or at least hoped it had been a dream somehow.

"Tell me—" I began to ask, but they pulled apart and gestured to Melissa's bra, which they'd laid on the back of the chair. And then they scurried out of the room to tell all of the guys on the hall.

I was heartbroken. I was absolutely disappointed in myself. I wanted so desperately to escape the fact of what I had done, but of course with such moments, or with any sin considered honestly, there is no escape. It was there, and so was that reflection of my own failure. I had a ferocious hangover, and the tearing inside of my heart joined right in. I spent the first morning of some portion of my soul's honeymoon dry-heaving into the dorm toilet where someone else had previously done similarly, with horrendous aim. By the time I returned to my room there was a group of guys standing by my door, to which they had already applied a hand-made "Player of the Week" poster, with Melissa's bra thumb-tacked to it. I cut the bra up and put it in the garbage. By the next morning the poster had moved to someone else's door.

The desire to find a loophole for what I'd done was overwhelming. I hadn't pursued it, and a case could be made that I was in no condition to make such choices. I tried out the date rape line of logic on one of the guys from the hall. It didn't fly at all. Still, I was incredibly angry with Melissa. I felt like she'd stolen something from me. I certainly saw her as a reminder of my failure, and I certainly wanted to have nothing to do with her. She knocked on my door the next night after I'd gone to sleep. I opened it a few inches without getting out of bed. She asked if she could take my picture. Somewhere there may still exist one of me with messy hair, my chin on the frame of my bunk bed, and an icy stare. Then she asked if I had her bra. I told her I'd thrown it away, which of course I knew would hurt her, but not as badly as the whole truth. After that, I never spoke with her again, except once towards the end of our senior year when I passed her between classes and said hello.

I prayed. I repented. I cried. And I swore to God that I would not have sex again until it was with my wife. I told Betsy about all of this, and as our relationship was growing, that promise started out being the thing that stopped us. It fit nicely into the fear and guilt she'd learned growing up Catholic. And somewhere I'm certain that I taught her she would bear part of the responsibility for my breaking a promise to God if we let things go all the way. It was easier to tell friends, co-workers, and even myself that the reason was her, but it was probably even more my thing, even if I'd weakened so much that she was the one keeping the promise anymore.

And so we find ourselves five years later, curled up on the floor, skin on skin, soft kisses and broken hearts, with my promise kept in spite of myself, and both of us more than a bit confused by the whole experience.

How much of the time does it work that way with God? How much of the time does He orchestrate the keeping of the covenants we make with Him? Is the promise of a fallen man worth anything at all? There have been times where Betsy has wanted to, has asked to, and I've refused. And there have been plenty of times when the reverse has been the case. My promise has been fleeting and forgotten and flat out fought against. It was worth nothing, when kiss came to tug. Still we haven't physically broken it. Is that God intervening somehow? Is that some sort of mercy from Him, something protecting me from feeling double the despair I felt the morning after Melissa, or from learning to ignore the disappointment altogether? Is it help from Him to stick to a wiser gameplan? Is it Him showing me that I can only keep promises with His help? Is it Him telling me how foolish it is to make or trust promises at all? Or maybe it's Him saying that the only promises I should make are ones that include Him in their keeping? Or maybe this whole five-year flirtation with temptation has all been in my head, and the internal and relational crap has all been inflicted by my Protestant performance-oriented faith? Maybe if we'd been intimate the whole time we both would have invested more, would have had some different kind of balance in our worlds, would have stuffed less down, and wouldn't be avoiding conversations about a sex life we don't share. Maybe if we'd been more free we'd not be laying here right now, letting it all go.

This is what the nice guy thing gets me. This is why the sensitive voice scares me, and why safety and trustworthiness seem like such bullshit traits. I can't control how things turn out, and I'm not giving other people honest information about myself by which to draw conclusions. The facts are different from the façade. I'm not safe. I'm not trustworthy. I'm not sensitive or nice. I'm the guy who had a one-night stand with someone he then shunned, soon thereafter broke up with the girl to whom he'd never been exactly loyal or disloyal until the one-night stand, and then spent five years twisting the next girl into the convoluted rules and logic he'd come up with in his wrestling match between the vague heavens to which he dreamed himself worthy, and the all-too concrete damnation to which he suspected himself wed. Oh, and the high school girlfriend? I told her about Melissa a year later. And when she wrote back confessing she wished we'd slept together to see what it was like, I tried like hell to make it happen, even though by then I was with Betsy. And now here I am playing victim and claiming some high road when Betsy tells me about another guy. She'd be shocked to know the truth, though, because I'm the nice guy, the safe guy, the trustworthy guy with the inescapable conscience. I'm the guy she's wounded so, so deeply and will forever feel guilty about; the one spinning out of control and moving away; the one gently beside her, feeling the depth and the gravity of the end of our time together. It's all bullshit; I'm the guy with his tongue on her nipple. And it's not sensitivity; it's cowardice.

7.

Kool-Aid or Calcutta

Two days later I'm in Indianapolis, with Betsy, passing through my parents' place on my way to Denver. There have been questions, and concerns, and both my pastor and a woman I've never met have asked for time together before I head west. Betsy's with me because we couldn't quite muster the last goodbye, and because I still have hopes she'll throw caution to the wind and move with me. The rental truck broke down in Gary, and by the time a replacement arrived and we got everything transferred into it, we ended up too exhausted to drive the whole way. We spent the night in a motel near Lafayette, aggravated, smelly, and both too emotionally saturated to feel anything but the funk quickly settling over us. In the morning she wanted to sleep in and I had to drag her out of bed. I don't think she wanted the process to move forward, and I know she was nervous about the reaction she would get from my mother, who knows that we're splitting up, but doesn't know why.

By the time we get to town, I'm running late and drop Betsy off at my folks' place and rush to my meeting with my pastor at the Friendly Tavern on Zionsville's cobbled Main Street. The pastor is the one who told me to consider the ministry when I was in high school. Glenn. I prayed "the prayer" for salvation in the bed next to his when I was fifteen and we were heading to a work project in Juarez, Mexico. I have a framed 8x10 photo from that trip with all of the kids from the youth group standing in a trench we'd dug for the foundation of a church addition, and Glenn is beside the trench with a shovel and a canister of grape Kool-Aid; part of his alter-ego from the trip, the Reverend Biff Jones. When I was dating the girl from the other high school, I'd gone to him for advice about sex. He'd loaned me a book entitled "Controlling Your Hormones." I guess it was helpful. With Glenn there is a book for everything, and a large portion of his identity comes from knowing exactly which book applies in each situation. It's easier for him than trusting the value of what he has to say of life himself. A tight bibliography beats practical wisdom any day, it would seem.

"What do your parents think?" He asks.

"They think I'm nuts." I answer.

"Probably not a surprise."

"Do you think I'm nuts, too?"

"No. I think God is drawing you out of your ordinary world." He sips his iced tea. "But you have to understand how weird all of this will be to them. And to you, for that matter. This is not part of the game plan any of you had in mind, and it breaks all of the rules."

"I don't know that it does. It's not like I'm going off to live in some rat hole in Calcutta." I insert.

"Not that you know of." He's toying with me, skirting way too near to the whole limp-wristed pastoral image for me.

"No, I'm pretty sure about that. Besides, I can probably do the PR for God stuff on the side, if I have to. I don't see any reason I have to be poor to be obedient."

He grins a little bit like he doesn't believe me, and then asks, "So, you've told me what you'd like to do, but you haven't told me why."

"Good question." I say, intending the insult, and putting on my client tone to reclaim some sense of control. I think it's obvious that the Church has been failing in managing its reputation, and that he's part of it. In selling, or in pitching agency services, this is called the *probe and disturb* portion of the program. "I think the Church has become a toothless lion. And the teeth have been pulled by church people who don't really believe what they say they believe. They don't serve the people they say they've been called to serve; they don't trust the truths they say they trust; they don't love the people they say they love; the don't keep the promises they say they'll keep; and they don't point to the sort of God they say they point to. People from within the Church have made errors in judgment, like the televangelists, and those errors have diminished the Church's credibility, and the more that credibility has been diminished, the more people within the Church have capitulated with society's efforts to relegate the Church to some quaint, outmoded superstition, and the more that has happened, the more the Church is left with little to show for itself but the chanted arcane bromides of its small, dark existence."

Glenn grins the same way again. "I think we'd probably describe things a bit differently, but I understand what you're looking at. And you've already told me some of how you'd envision addressing the problems. But why do you want to give your life to addressing them?"

"Well, right now it's still just an idea. I don't know that I necessarily want to spend my life addressing the public perception issues of the Church."

"Let's say you had drawn that conclusion. What's the desire in your heart that you'd be addressing?"

"God is real. I've felt Him, and I've known both life paying attention to Him and life ignoring Him, and I know that life paying attention to Him is better. I also know the Church was his idea, and for however messed up it is, it must be the best vehicle for his purposes. I'd like to show non-Christians something about life with God being better than life without Him, so they could also experience it. And for people in the Church, in this God-designed vehicle, I'd like to be a part of helping them get back in touch with the incredible power and potential of the Church; of the Church when it spends its life paying attention to God."

"So what's in it for you is the satisfaction of helping other people experience God."

"Yes. And it would be great to be a part of reshaping church so that it was a place that was relevant for me, and people like me."

"But at root what you're after is the changing of lives, right?"

"Ultimately, yes. Though the first step is shifting some perceptions, and redefining the Christian 'brand.'"

Glenn the pastor pops a couple of ketchup-laden fries into his mouth, nodding with a thoughtful grunt.

"What are you thinking?" I ask.

"I think you may be working with unsatisfying tools."

"Huh?"

"If your desire is to change lives, and you want to change the culture of the Church, I think you may be disappointed going the route you're talking about." He folds his napkin beneath the lip of his plate. "Nobody has ever become a disciple of Christ through impersonal means. You may see hundreds of people come down front in an altar call at a Billy Graham event, but that's just the first step. What is always necessary, at least in my experience, is another person, a relationship in which the new believer can learn and ask questions and experience love. If what you're wanting to see is a change in lives and in the Church, I don't think you'll see it with mass media." He studies me for a moment. "And if it makes you feel any better, delivering a sermon usually feels about as impersonal and ineffective as mass media."

This, of course, is a load of crap. This is Glenn having given up on telling the truth, and instead telling only the stories that sell in church. It's his version of the old parental cliché of "we did the best we could." That's not true; we don't do the best we can do, pretty much ever; we do the best we're willing to do. I absolutely believe God can be made fashionable, and real relationships with Him can be presented in ways that are compelling enough for people to act. Shit, people buy bottled water. They buy Starbucks coffee for outrageous prices. Some rental companies have satellite guidance systems in their cars that tell the driver how to get to their destination, even though the driver already has a map. There are a million things to which people upgrade, even though they don't feel like they need to, because demand is driven by the hungers created on Madison Avenue. You can't tell me people won't buy God if the Church decides it actually cares about moving its product.

"Thanks, Glenn. That's a lot to think about. I hope you're wrong, but I'm eager to find out for myself. Thanks for lunch, too."

"I'll be praying for you." He answers. I know he means it, which feels good, for whatever that's worth.

8.

Tattoos Don't Sell in Mayberry

I drive past the cutesy shops of Main Street, through the Victorian part of town people call the Village, and out past the football stadium the school built after our first state championship. Zionsville has been home since my freshman year of high school. It's affluent, Anglo, and has to be as homogenized as anyplace on Earth. There was one person of divergent ethnicity in my high school, from a secular Jewish family, and I remember kids rolling nickels and pennies at him in the hallway. He'd pick them up, shrug, and laughingly say, "Hey, I'm a Jew." It's a bedroom community, populated largely by employees of the pharmaceutical giant Eli Lilly and Company, the makers of Prozac. On my first day at the school I was asked repeatedly if I was a "Lilly Kid," and everyone knows who's meant by the term "Uncle Eli." The existence of Zionsville, with its gazebos and parks and Mayberry charms—its undying desire for a bit of idyllic Heaven on Earth—is proof to me that we have a collective memory of Eden. Zionsville's proximity to, and utter disregard for, the poverty, crime and abuses found beyond its gates is proof to me that there was a reason we were expelled from the garden.

My parents are at home in Zionsville. Maybe they even are Zionsville. Dutiful Lilly executive and nurturing housewife, secure and polite and apparently in full agreement with the rationalizations embraced by the community of which they are a part. My choices have them at a complete loss. Mom is indeed a warm and caring, loyal and insightful woman of indefatigable sacrificial nature, and Dad is truly remarkable for his abilities, discipline, wisdom, and ability to wield power. Both are wholly sincere. They brought their 1950s North Dakota worldview with them as they raised me and my two younger brothers, climbed the corporate ladder, and weathered the storms common to most marriages; I think their parents would be very proud of them. They have lived the American Dream, at least the one articulated by the "Haves" to the "Would like to Haves," for generations. They have worked hard, invested well, and dream of a nice long retirement.

I ended up majoring in Victorian Literature in college, and someday I'm going to write a book about the new Victorian world of leisure and privilege and social rules and controlling familial bribery that exists in places like Zionsville. There was a time when my mother was reading the police blotter in the local paper and saw my friend's name there. "I'm glad that's not my kid." She said, meaning how embarrassing it would be, and how people may think her a bad mother if our family experienced similar problems. Not to worry, though, she raised three good boys. Nice guys, with sensitive guy voices.

Mom's terrified, which she'd say is the appropriate response when one's eldest son quits his job and decides to move across the country, with no housing lined up, to do who knows what, especially right as a four-plus-year relationship with a perfectly nice, polite, very presentable girl is being thrown away.

Dad thinks I'm a fool, which is about as easy a conclusion to reach as the one my mother uncovered. I've tried to explain, but I have to give them room for their conclusions. I sure can't make a great case for what I'm doing either, at least without falling back to the whole prayer to God after the Accounting test story, and while my parents have been active at church for years, they simply do not do things "because God said so." Ever. So far the closest thing Dad's come to support, which also seems to be his final word on the subject, is, "I guess you gotta do what you gotta do."

Loser. Moron. Dumbass. You gotta do what you gotta do. If you're a complete idiot. If I've taught you nothing. If you want to make your mother worry. If you want me to be even more confused by your foolishness than I've always been. If you want to throw away everything you could gain otherwise. You gotta do what you gotta do, but I'll make a point of throwing my hands up in exasperation.

I've been taught that I always have a choice. It's a phrase my brothers and I have joked about with Dad for years. The catch is that every choice has a consequence, and the choices that don't agree with our father's preferences tend to have the heaviest, and most inscrutable, consequences. Even if he's not the one in actual control of the consequence, his celebration of any pain resulting from choosing a path different from his own is loud and clear and endures forever.

That's not to say he isn't a warm and supportive man. There are dozens of lives and careers that are better for having known my father on a personal level. We played catch in the back yard when I was a kid. We go fishing in the summer. We play chess in the evenings in his study. The rub is this: he requires distance and fears intimacy above all things. So long as a person is in a subservient position to my father, preferably one where ailments can be readily resolved through the application of his wisdom, that person will find my father to be attentive, generous, and correct. So long as a person is clearly the weaker party in the relationship, that person will be encouraged to express intimate vulnerabilities, which my father will goad and about which my father will prompt action in the weaker party. Intimacies will not be rewarded with intimacies from my father, though he will admit to the occasional matter of fact foible, so long as the other party remains in a weak position that does not return the favor of his call to action or accountability. As a person moves from being weaker to being more of a peer, Dad begins to size the person up as a competitor. And Dad may not always win, but he sure as hell isn't going to give a competitor a clear shot. Once a person becomes stronger than my father finds tolerable, amicability will remain, but it will be under-girded by a continuous jockeying for position in the pecking order, and because to my father vulnerability equals weakness, and nothing is so deserving of punishment as weakness, my father is able to hide behind his own brand of wisdom to distance himself from intimacy with people by whom he may otherwise be challenged. On the rare instances when my father seems to conclude that he holds the weaker cards in the relationship, as I've seen happen with pastors, he tends to ball up so that only the least vulnerable, most polite parts of himself can be seen, and then when he's no longer in the immediate company of the person he sees as a threat, he will find some way to say that their specialty is not his specialty, and that somehow their interest is silly or unmasculine. I've adopted at least enough of the same way of thinking that it's taken me years to admit that my pastor was right about the calling on my life. And now that I'm showing signs of strength enough to choose my own path, to stand up and possibly even be a challenge, my father's response has been about what I'd expected.

Or I could be totally full of crap. In Zionsville, my father's ways sure seem like the facts of life. His way has worked; there's no getting around that. I'm twenty-three, and I know that means I have a lot to learn. But man do I hope it doesn't turn out he and Zionsville have been right about relationships and careers and priorities all along.

9.

Beyond Here Be Monsters

It's Sunday morning and I'm supposed to meet some woman named Sue in the church parlor. She called and said it was about my career choices. Of course I assumed that she heard about what's happening through the incredibly efficient Zionsville Presbyterian Aunt Bea network. Mom says she didn't say a word, then asks if I know anything about Sue's history. When I tell her I don't know who the heck she is, Mom tells me that her father started a major technology company and that now a significant portion of her money goes to influencing media towards more Christian morality. She and a small group of other people like her are responsible for funding much of the "spiritual" programming on network television. She personally funded some Christian kids' program I'd never heard of, but is supposed to be some big deal. She's a prime supporter of a large Midwestern family values film festival, and of a film school in California. Mom doesn't know what else she supports, but assumes the connections range far and wide. As my mother tells me about all of this, I do recall hearing of her in the past. I remember someone whose Midwestern wifely feathers she'd ruffled referring to her as a "bear for Jesus."

So that's what I watch for as I wait in the parlor, sitting amidst the uncomfortable granny furniture, not certain that I'm allowed to be drinking lemonade in this room. Sue enters, and I'm suddenly scared. Think blonde German schoolmarm. With tenure. And a penchant for corporal punishment. She's extremely matter of fact, very blunt, and it's clear she doesn't see the utility in humor. Maybe the result of spending a life being worried about being kidnapped half the time, and being courted by people who only see her for money the other half?

"You need to return to Chicago and stay in advertising. That is what God would have you do."

I start to explain that I've already left. I start to explain that the industry is immoral. I start to explain about Promise Keepers and Habitat for Humanity.

"No. Your job is to perform in the advertising world, rise as far as you can, and affect change from there. I've been watching you since you were writing for the high school newspaper, and this is simply what you're meant to do. Anything else is a waste of the life God's given you."

I tell her that I'm interested in finding a parallel track, maybe a Christian advertising agency.

"No. You are meant to be a roaring lamb." A reference to a book by a friend of hers that teaches Christians to do things like claw to the top and then be good stewards of the power they've earned. "You are meant to be a healthy cell in an otherwise cancerous body. You are not meant to drop out and be a part of the Christian subculture. You are meant to impact the general culture."

I tell her I don't want to be a part of the Christian subculture. Then I ask what about the shows she's funded? Did that reach beyond the Christian subculture? I tell her I want to show a more real, more desirable faith. I want to stand for the right things. I tell her I don't know exactly what this will look like, yet, but that I do know it doesn't include going back to Chicago.

She tells me about William Wilberforce's protracted, but ultimately successful, efforts to end slavery in England. She tells me we are in a similar battle. She tells me that she's funded some very highly rated shows, and that they offer a far superior alternative to the other stuff on television. She tells me that the more people produce shows of moral character, the more that will influence the culture, the same way negative shows undermine the culture. She tells me that it is my duty to do the same thing in the advertising world.

I ask her what she thinks about Glenn's comments—about the relative value of mass media and interpersonal communication. She tells me that all interpersonal communication happens within a context, and that the single most powerful voice in the shaping of that context, at least in America, is the combined voice of mass media. She says that Glenn may be right in terms of the reaping, but that my calling has everything to do with sewing, and that my job is to shape a context in which truth and love and community are properly understood and valued. And then, before I can ask or say another thing, she tells me that our time is up, rises, shakes my hand, and she leaves me alone with my lemonade.

10.

For Those About to Rock

Betsy and I said our goodbyes when I dropped her off at the airport. There were tears, but we'd also spent way too much time talking about everything and we were both ready to be done with each other for a little while. We shared one last kiss, and when she closed the door to the rental truck she pressed her hand against the window where it left a print. I watched her go inside, and then I drove away, shaking like the time when my friend and I hit a cat and had to decide whether to feel horrible about it or high-five and turn up the radio like it didn't matter at all.

I wore my fishing hat like a man heading for the mountains until the middle of Illinois, the tinny dashboard radio turned up enough to screech over the sound of what is obviously some sort of unwanted white elephant truck earmarked as a replacement to one-ways going cross-country. I sang. I cried. I sang and cried. I did the math and figured Betsy must be home and pulled over to call her from a pay phone. No answer. I stopped to try again every 100 miles or so until just after 2:00 this morning, west of Topeka, when I finally realized she was at the other guy's place.

So that's that.

But I have more pressing matters to consider right now. Outside it's pitch black and raining. Really raining. And windy. I've had to slow to about 40 miles an hour a couple of times, and I've learned that even a fully-loaded Ryder truck can hydroplane. But I'm not about to stop. I've turned the radio up even further—AC/DC right now—to keep me awake and to compete with the sounds of the rain and the wipers. With the nasty crosswind and the lousy visibility and the emotions and the lack of sleep and the loud music grating its way through the blown speakers, this is as white-knuckled as things get.

I'm terrified. I may well die on the road tonight; I'm getting pushed all over the place and spending half my time on the rumble strips. Everything in the world says to stop, to turn back. Betsy asked me to reconsider. My parents are against this. Glenn and Sue both think I'm being a fool. A few minutes ago there was a tornado warning on the radio—but I don't know what county I'm in so I've kept going. My ego wants me to turn around, to call this off. I really have nothing to gain, and besides, I only have one year of professional experience; who cares how well it went, it won't be worth anything to anyone in the real world. What the hell am I doing? Why am I doing this? Maybe I should head home. The tears start again. And then, another *moment*.

AC/DC: "for those about to rock—BAM—we sa-lute you!"

That's me! I'm that. I'm about to rock. I have no idea what that means, but that's where I'm going. Screaming headlong into the storm in the middle of the night, I mash down on the accelerator. This night will be my birth—if I survive it. Swerve. And even if I don't. Rumble strip. I have no idea what I'm being born to; just a sense that I want to get away from all that is behind me, all that is outgrown, over-stayed, and wrong. I want to be born! I want to be born! I want to be born!

It feels great to challenge death like that, for a while. But for every AC/DC song, there's a Bryan Adams coming. *Oh—thinkin' about all our younger years. There was only you and me, We were young and wild and free. And love is all that I need, And I found it there in your heart, It isn't too hard to see, We're in heaven.* I don't care, there is no way in hell I'm going to die in a high speed crash in a Kansas tornado in the middle of the night with Bryan Adams singing me into eternity. "Heaven" my butt. So I decide to slog through the rest of the storm at a more reasonable speed, thinking about one core curiosity.

I knew nearly nothing about God when I signed up for a life with Him. I was a kid, 14-years-old, when I decided to trust Him. I pictured myself hanging from a trapeze on a cloud, and imaged myself letting go. I had no idea what I was getting into. I had only a vague understanding of what sin was. I certainly didn't even begin to understand how some guy dying on a cross could have any impact on me. Prayers were the not-quite rhymes we said before dinner, or the fluffy stuff pastors in black robes intoned with their hands raised over the congregation before they let us go to lunch. Worship was droning through more not-quite rhymes in the hymnbook and trying to figure out how to sing along with the impossibly high notes of songs clearly written for old ladies with broaches and blue hair. I didn't know a thing about what I was doing when I prayed for God to take control of my life.

All I knew was that I felt something missing. Or I felt something to be gained. Or I knew there was something real being articulated, something of an audacious truth I'd never admit to on my own, but was able to respond to with an unexamined sort of shrug. And that's all that was requested of me. Glenn told me that all God needed was a little nod towards the question of "Do you want to give your life to someone who loves it, and you, more than you do?"

I nodded. I needed a friend. I wanted to belong. I was part of a mass of people who needed an opiate. All of the things that are said of Christians by people who belittle the gullibility of Christians were true of me. But it was the one time in my life where I was offered something real, not just some vaporous product, posture or placebo, and there was something real, profoundly real, about the thing I encountered and to which I gave my nod. The fact of the matter is that I was not solid, I was not strong, I was not even all that real, but that has no bearing on the existence of the thing to which I was responding. In truth, the very fact that someone knowing so little, with so many obvious needs, could have such a moment is the best evidence I have that I was interacting with something real. And if God is real, then, well, that changes everything.

Or so I thought. But I was wrong. It turns out that we're already living in God's world—he doesn't offer the welcome package like we get when we first arrive at Disney World. I thought my prayer would change everything, but it didn't. I suppose I was a tiny bit changed right away, mostly just in that I had a different sense of self-description and an absolutely elementary claim to a different life trajectory. But in no way did everything feel changed. I still did the same things I'd ever done, both good and bad. I still couldn't see through walls or tell the future. I couldn't read minds or bend spoons by staring at them. I couldn't make a mountain throw itself into the sea like the Bible said I'd be able to do if I mustered faith the size of a mustard seed. And frankly, I was a bit thrown by this.

I didn't know why things hadn't changed more. I didn't know why I wasn't happier, or why I didn't feel some huge liberation, or why I didn't feel absolutely sure about the reality of the God who'd been real enough for me to give my life to Him. But it turns out my problem wasn't that things hadn't changed; my problem was that I didn't know how to tell that they'd changed.

In college I smoked pot a few times. I remember saying, as is stereotypical, that I didn't think it impacted me, but then one time I was in the back seat of a friend's car, high, and there was this riff from a John Mellencamp song that came around. *Da-da, da-doop, do-doop.* Wow! I thought, of all the sounds in the world, what are the odds that those three would be put together? I began to ruminate, my mind in awe about what I'd experienced. And then the riff came around again: *da-da, da-doop, do-doop.* Unbe-freaking-lievable! All the sounds in the world, and those three were chosen once, and then a second time! Amazing! Staggering!

And that's the moment I understood that pot did, indeed, impact me. But it was a different experience than drinking, with no obvious physical evidence for me to point to. It took a moment of altered perception for me to see that something had most certainly changed for me.

I think things with God are sort of like that, and to tell the truth, there are a great many times when they feel about as rational as being blown away by the miracle of music. I think they're supposed to feel that way, though. And it makes sense that they would. If God created everything, that would include the ordinary world—the mundane, corporeal stuff to which firm rules and understandings apply. But creation would also have to include all of the stuff that doesn't fit neatly into our 18 or so hard fast rules about the world. Things like love, or forgiveness, or peace, or endurance, sacrifice, obedience, submission, conviction, sin, holiness, authority, salvation, damnation, time, eternity, heaven, hell, souls, union, hope, grace, moments with Russ Taff or AC/DC—all of this needs more than what the rational world can make sense of. And it all sounds a lot like some stoned Hoosier in the back of a Caprice Classic listening to John Mellencamp on the way to Big Red Liquors. That's just the way it is, and you don't know you've slipped the bounds of the very small rational world until the moment when some bit of eternity tackles you, blows your mind, and refuses to travel with you back into the world where God's ways seem more than a little bit weird.

And in the moments where you're tackled and your mind is blown, there is no question that what you're experiencing is worth the cost of being a weirdo. In those moments there's no question that what you're experiencing is anything but the truth about the world, and that the truth goes beyond what's shown on the 6:00 news or taught in textbooks. It's absolutely preferable to the alternative of staying in the smaller world, and it's absolutely worth being seen as a weirdo some of the time.

I'm on my way to Denver, to start a new life, because over the course of several months there was a needling sense of invitation to more. When things fell apart, I knew exactly where I'd turn, not because I had any idea about what I was turning to, but because I'd been feeling the invitation. It doesn't make sense. It just is. I know things work this way—from the job search to the job placement to the circumstances surrounding its dissolution. Same with Betsy. Same with the reactions I received in Zionsville. Same with my own doubts. But beyond the reality of such things lies an even greater reality, where just a hint, a hunch, or a vague invitation is worth more and is more compelling than all of the rational stuff I could have instead.

What exists in the kingdom of God, meaning the world and the reality that are larger than the small mundane world, is a richness of life that is too much for us to take in large doses. Or at least it's more than I'm willing to take in large doses. We're not meant to pursue chaos, or holy goosebumps, or to let the rest of the world burn. We're called to expand the world by forcing the larger reality of the kingdom of God into the smaller skins of ordinary life. And this process involves pain. Life is always a mix of joy and pain, and we need them both or we will forget the truth, which is that we are created beings who depend upon a creator for every breath we take. I remind myself about this by remembering that I cannot control the fact that I'm alive; I can kill myself, of course, but I have no exact sense of what makes me live. I don't know where the batteries are. And further, I have no positive control over my continued existence. I don't know why I exist, which tells me that I exist because of a choice beyond myself. If I did not feel the pain—either physical, situational, or simply the fact that I'm at the mercy of something beyond myself, I would soon forget that I am not God, even for myself.

And it's the experience of joy and pain meted out together in mixed helpings that makes me hesitate to take too large a dose at once—there is too much rawness to life with God for me to process. I can think back about my nice guy persona and the lies that surround it, the sins and gluttonous horror I've forged there, but all of that by no means represents the darkest truths about me. There are moments where my ability to stand and face the truth of my own monstrosity, where I used to flee, proves to me that I am indeed impacted by God. I've been changed. And there are moments where my ability to experience joy about Him or about what he has made, including myself, show me the same thing. But so far what I've seen has been that a big dose of good news makes it very easy to forget God, and a big dose of bad news makes me wish I could. I haven't found a way to experience too much of Him at once without losing my grip on my life completely.

That said, I'm still struck by how very little I knew about God when I gave my life to Him. I know hope now like I never knew then. I know a different perspective. I know more about my own sin. I know that I'm called to engage with this world as a matter of fact, not as a matter of measuring myself. I know that it was a Stoned Hoosier moment to quit my job, but I know that it was real, and that I am going to Denver because I've been *called* to Denver, patiently but persistently, for some time now.

Good. Fine. So how to measure it? What am I called to? What is my mission? For what purpose am I being called there? Is it really about PR for God? Habitat for Humanity and Promise Keepers? Was Glenn right? Was Sue? Was my dad? I don't know. The fact of the matter is that the calling feels like one of those things whose source is outside of the rational world. I feel a hunch, an invitation, but it's not specific, and I don't know how to translate it back into the ordinary world without putting some objective detail to it. It seems like the PR stuff could be an application of the calling, but it's not necessarily anything. Mostly the specifics that come to mind are ways for me to draw my brain back into the rational world by arguing for a sound, reasonable trajectory. And maybe it's just me, maybe other people are actually given specific purposes and callings, or maybe the invitations they receive from God fit better into their understandings of the world. Or maybe other people are less timid and can handle larger doses of truth about where God is calling them. Maybe they can picture traveling the distances from Chicago's Miracle Mile to a random rat hole in Calcutta, but for me it's too much to take in at once. All I can handle is that I've been asked to move, that I feel a desire to take God at his word and see what happens, and that I want to share some living experience of Him with other people. I want those things to happen in a context with which I'm familiar, but I know that the context is my filter, not the truth, and that I'm going to have to get comfortable with responding to invitations that don't always make sense to me. I guess that would be my goal while I'm in Denver; to learn to recognize and respond to invitations not because they make sense, but because of who's offering them and because I believe that the best I can do with most of life is to nod in response to the greater reality when it asks if I want to come along. And if I survive the tornados and the storms tonight, maybe I'll change the world.

II.

The Deal About Scaffolds

"Your problem isn't that you're gay. It's that you're an asshole." This is my version of tough love truth and renegade honesty. Sitting across from me in the beautifully decorated living room of his 1920s bungalow, on the chaise before the fireplace, is my landlord, Stephen. I've been in Denver for almost six months and am finishing up my first quarter of seminary, and it's already clear that the biggest problem regarding the continuation of sin in the world is the way people tiptoe around it and let themselves be defined by their favorite-flavored spiritual maladies.

"What the hell does that mean?" Stephen is in his mid-30s, but is still in good shape and is very fashionable. He tends to be somewhat bitter for my tastes, and it drives me nuts that he can't just submit to truth in his life. He has been active in the homosexual world on and off since college, when the whole gay thing surprised him. It wasn't exactly the popular thing to discover about oneself as the leader of the traveling choir for his small Christian school. He believes it's nurture, not nature, and he believes his homosexual behavior is sinful. He's been in counseling about it for some time, but he also has a boyfriend. The boyfriend, to his credit, is really a great guy, and if homosexuality wasn't so obviously a mortal sin, they'd make a wonderful and complimentary couple.

"I don't think your struggles with homosexuality are the real problem. I think of sin like a well that narrows as we go deeper into it, and as we fall, we carry with us these boards, these things we call sin, and we only fall until the board jams into the sides of the well. Those boards make the scaffolding of the sin we're willing to admit. We stand on a board and we say, 'this is my worst sin—there is nothing darker than this about me' and we swear that the board we're on is not a board, is not a scaffold, but is really the bottom of the well. You think your gay tendencies are the worst thing about you, that they're what force you to the bottom of your well. You seem to think that if you could clear up that struggle, you'd be okay—or at least you'd be able to work your way up out of the well by cleaning up other things." He takes a swig of his margarita rocks, looking at me dubiously as I continue. "But the truth is that if you could remove that board, the board of your gay junk, you'd find yourself falling downward because there are still many things that are darker and more odious about you than that particular issue. Your problem is not that you're gay. Your problem is that you think your gayness is the furthest extent of your problem."

"Do I?"

I realize that I'm making the face I'd make with Betsy if she got upset over an honest reply about a new haircut. "I'm not trying to make you angry, Stephen. I'm not trying to hurt your feelings. I'm just saying this because I see you hurting, and fixating on something that is a worthy struggle, but is not more important than you are. And the more obsessed you become with fighting it, the harder it is to let go of, and the less aware you become of the other areas of your life where you could use a little attention and where some success could do you good."

"So maybe I'm defining myself too much by my sin, as you say?" He asks.

"Exactly."

"Hmm. So, when you go to church and they ask for prayer requests, what do you ask people to pray for you about?"

"I don't want to get into a fight, Stephen. This isn't about me."

"Humor me."

"What are my prayer requests? Well, right now the biggest thing has been my crumbling. I want to be torn down and rebuilt. I also pray for patience. I ask for prayer about school stuff and about wisdom in speaking the truth in love."

He grins, nods, and gestures with his glass, a sweeping inclusion motion. "All pretty noble things, aren't they?"

"I don't know—I don't think most people understand me or what I'm talking about when I tell them I'm seeking to be crumbled or downwardly mobile."

"I think they do. But even if they didn't, if you explained it, you'd earn their praise."

"No. Most people feel threatened by someone taking God seriously. They seem to think that what I'm pursuing includes some insistence that everyone should do the same thing. There's a reason Jesus called us sheep—it's that we're timid and want to move in a herd, and people in the herd don't like it much when someone asks new questions or wants to explore actually living like the Bible describes."

Stephen gins. "Okay, try this one. This morning I stood in a circle holding hands with the other people from the praise band, doing prayer requests. The pastor's wife asked for prayer for her kids. She said they have such rebellious spirits. The kids are 2 and 3 years old!"

I laugh.

"I'm not making this up! She's the pastor's wife, and she's pretty guarded, I'll admit. But the next person was the drummer, and he asked for prayer about the minivan he and his wife are thinking about buying. He said they wanted to honor God with their choice. Honor God with a minivan choice? Come on! Is this really the pressing issue in his life—the one that's so overwhelming he needs to call in prayer reinforcements?"

"You don't know what all is entailed in his purchase, or what baggage he may be sorting through about it. It could be a valid request. It's pretty dangerous ground to critique other people's prayers very closely, Stephen."

"Would you have shared your prayer requests with them? Would you have risked talking about crumbling with them? Or not being sure about what you're doing with your life? Or being a month late paying me your rent?"

"Probably not." I answer. "But maybe. I don't know, I might have. Yeah, sure, why not?"

"Here's my prayer request. I went to counseling Friday after work, and prayed for freedom from my sins there. Again. For like the millionth time. I cried myself to sleep that night, half drunk. I took a walk with Marty yesterday and told him that I couldn't see him anymore, because I believed that what we're doing is wrong. Which means that I think he was wrong back when he made the choice to leave his wife and kids was wrong, and so is the hope he's had for his future. I came home feeling like I'm the only person in the world actually still fighting this battle—everyone in the gay community thinks it's leftover bullshit from an outdated society of mutilators. I ended up getting drunk, by myself, and passed out covered in my own spew from masturbating to gay porn. The closest I came to telling anyone at church about it was when someone noticed I was chewing a piece of gum—which is a major league rebellious thing to do on stage, but I was doing it to cover up my alcohol breath—and they asked if I had an extra piece." He's angry and red-eyed. "What do they teach you in seminary about sharing that kind of prayer request? Would you share that one? It's not like you can explain the parts people don't understand and have them see what a noble pursuit you're on. I'd be kicked off the praise team immediately, because my sin disqualifies me from worshipping God. Rebellious toddlers and minivan selection—those things are good to take to God, and are clean enough to keep a microphone in your hand—but I'd lose the one thread of connection I still feel to this fucking God who won't answer my prayers! My gay crap may not be my definition, and it may not be the bottom of my sin, but fuck you if you think I want to go deeper, or if you think it's something that I can carry with me into church as a matter of fact, or if you think it's something that isolates me because I don't trust God enough to be honest with it. I know what it would cost me. Look at what it already costs me!"

12.

Salesmen and Witnesses

So that's my roommate, Stephen. He also has a small collie puppy named Maggie. We live in the gay rich artsy part of town in a three-bedroom place, and we have God talks pretty often. I'm the third seminary student in a row to live with him, and he still goes to church, so his deal is more that he can't choose between his idol and his God I guess, so he keeps both of them torturously close to him. It's not unlike me and Betsy in some ways—it's been six months and we still talk pretty regularly. I pray for her to be stirred by God, for her to see the error in her ways and to choose me. I feel like it's supposed to be finished with her, but I can't give up on her. It's absolutely left-over nice guy stuff—my idol.

Habitat never responded to me, and I can't get past the sweater-vests and calling each other "brother" that's everywhere with Promise Keepers, so I've let that idea go. I'm doing seminary because David was doing it, and it seemed like it would be a good thing to have some extra letters after my name no matter what I did. I moved out here with cash in the bank, but after buying what has turned out to be a less than serviceable Jeep, and paying a quarter's tuition at seminary, and not making any changes to the way I live, things have gotten very tight.

I haven't known what sort of career type stuff I'd like to do, so I've been looking for plain old jobs—something I can do to make some cash while I'm in school. I left an application at 7-11 and never got a call back. Same with Church in the City. Boston Market called me in to take a personality test, and then they didn't call back. That felt like bottom. Really, how screwed up do you have to be to not be Boston Market material?

It doesn't look like I'm going to end up back in seminary next quarter. I don't want to take out student loans and then try to do ministry with big debts over my head. Glenn said he thought Zionsville Presbyterian would be willing to pay, but by the time they wrote to make it official, I'd already run out of time to enroll—and had decided I didn't really want to go back.

Seminary is a lousy place for Christians, I think. At least in the short-term. If you're someone who's really strong about what you believe, seminary will unravel that for you. The fact of the matter is that there really aren't many, or maybe any, airtight arguments to make about God. There is enough to justify faith, but there is certainly not enough to eliminate doubt or make disbelief an untenable conclusion. For people who come in not knowing this, seminary can be crushing and can take away that sort of faith. I was fortunate in that I didn't know any complicated arguments and didn't have much of a firm stand regarding the basis for my faith, so when I was told that there were no airtight arguments, I sort of shrugged and said, "Okay." I've learned something else in seminary: the only thing more wimpy and tragic than a pastor is a theology professor. Take all of the nerdiness and uncoolness of a pastor, cram that into a wrinkled corduroy blazer with elbow patches, knot a full Windsor in a 1950s tie, smudge up some thick plastic glasses, and then remove the ability to shave a moustache evenly, and you've got a Denver Seminary professor. That said, the only people I've ever met who live more seriously submitted to God than Glenn are those same professors. Not auspicious in terms of making a person want to convert, but I suppose that's another example of where the arguments aren't airtight: is the life lived by those people worth how it'll make you look?

Seminary is also bad for people like me; people who see additional schooling as a hoop to jump through on the way to actually doing something with their faith. I can't think of a single practical course available there. Even the Hebrew won't help—it's outdated the way Shakespearean English is outdated. Seminary offers tools, and that's good I guess; it keeps people telling a more consistent story. But the actual content a person learns in seminary is all presented as though it will amount to a grand airtight argument, even though we've already decided such a thing doesn't exist. So what it comes down to, instead, is an education that leaves seminarians knowing how to go a few steps further in their arguments than the people with whom they argue, but they can still never close the deal.

I think the real question Christians need to ask is whether they're called to be salespeople or witnesses. A salesperson knows the features and benefits matrix, and can show you the chart where the "Heaven" column is checked in Christianity but not Judaism, or where "Eternal Individual Existence" shows up for Baptists but not Buddhists. A salesperson enters every interaction looking, by definition, to sell something. They stand for something outside of themselves, some product they want other people to want. But the problem is that the salesperson selling Christianity can't ever sell the faith on the chart alone. Like the car salesperson, Christian salespeople rely on the new car smell, or on how a new convert will look driving Jesus (complete with a little silver fish on his butt). The sale only comes when the salesperson can answer one question more than the consumer is willing to ask, or when the consumer gives in to a desire to buy for some reason beyond pure empiricism.

The other option is to be a witness. Witnesses don't have to explain what they've experienced, at least not beyond the best of their understanding. They only have to be able to talk about what they have experienced. Where a salesperson represents something beyond the salesperson, a witness will speak of something beyond the witness, but represents only the witness. The Bible is full of talk about witnesses. Seminaries are full of salespeople in training.

We need both, of course. It's a foolish thing to expect the God who created everything to need us to stand in a single file line. What I guess I'm finding frustrating, and what has me planning to do something else after this quarter, is that salespeople tend to try to build arguments to prove that their way is the best or only way. And it's hard to be near that sort of gravity without getting sucked in by it.

What I have learned at seminary, however, is that we're called to be servants to everyone and that there is work for us to do in the world. Mostly that consists of pointing out the reality of God in this place. I'm excited about my role in that. It answers questions with questions: Who am I? Who would God have me be? It's an answer, but it's fluid. I dig that.

13.

Hypocrisy and Naked Seminarians

Another pretty cool thing is what's happening on the relationship front. Betsy and I still talk maybe once a week; there are a lot of questions and leftover emotions for both of us. It turns out she's seeing two guys—the guy she was seeing behind my back, and another guy she's seeing behind his. I have to think that means her choices had more to do with her than they had to do with me, but that only lessens the suck factor by a small amount. She's not the cool thing. The cool thing is that Buzz's counterpart creative director at the ad agency in Chicago was talking to a representative from one of my old clients about my departure, and she was impressed enough to ask for my contact information. We've been talking a lot lately—sometimes for hours. It's the drippy, flirty type stuff, wrapped in layers and layers of Christian protocol and musing. Her name is Lisa, and she lives in New York. When we eventually mailed photos to one another, we both sent older ones, from when we weighed less.

She's the opposite of Betsy. Not just because she probably can't do the splits against the wall. She talks. And talks. And talks. But it's refreshing because I've spent so long playing both parts in my romantic relationships. She calls me. She leaves cute messages. She sends me flowers. She's a mother bear about her younger brother and single mother, and me if I'll let her. She says she's a bit of an altar hound, which means that she likes to cry at church and go down front to have people pray for her a lot. It means that she's emotionally open. She comes from a charismatic tradition and has lots of scars about men and women, about leadership and submission and truth and worth and all of that. She always wants to pray on the phone. I hate that. I still don't much like praying out loud, especially with other people, but especially on the phone, and especially *especially* as the tidy summation of a flirty conversation. The other day she let it slip that she'd told some of her friends that I was *the one*. I told her I thought we should actually meet before we started using terms like that.

I don't know what I think. She seems like a good idea in many ways. We have overlapping beliefs and passions. We have similar levels of openness to our personalities, and to the choices we make in life. It would be easy enough to just go with it—to shrug and let her lead me away to whatever house and life she has picked out. I think a whole lot of people do that, and I can see the appeal.

She makes me wonder if that's what I was like with Betsy or the girl from the other high school. I know I must have been, but it sure feels gross to think so. I don't want someone who says they know me so well, or who gives herself to me so readily that there's nothing left for me to pine for or find my own attraction towards.

Stephen's pissed about the whole thing because I spent over $200 on long distance last month, which I paid, but which left me short on rent. I ended up going to the bank and getting a cash advance on my credit card. That's not the first time I've done that, and my bills are piling up. Thank goodness the credit card company agreed to extend my credit limit.

Stephen is pissed about another woman, someone I met at seminary. Mindy. She's from Minnesota, and she says she knows her way around a man. She also plays guitar and has a very lovely voice. She's also big into a mystical sort of faith. How to describe her? Not pretty, but aware that a man will trade beauty for access? There's nothing wrong with how she looks, exactly, but several details are off in a nearly creepy sort of way. I know that's not a kind way of describing her, but what's so striking about her is that she seems to have a firm understanding of the positives and negatives she brings to the table, and she sort of leads into a relationship by being very clear about the trade she's willing to make. Utilitarian beauty, it could be called. A scrapper. An underdog with heart.

She's also not all that stable emotionally. When I was telling Stephen about her, he ended up referring to her as "The Psycho Sex Girl." Now whenever she leaves a message, Stephen sings, "Are you ready for the sex, girl?" I stop by her apartment on campus to hear her sing, and there are always three or four guys already there. Seminary is a ripe place for utilitarian beauty, for usury fumblings and tortured libidos and learning experiences. Repression squeezes temptation into the light.

What Stephen's pissed about is that a few days ago Mindy asked if she could come over to write a paper on my computer. I told her she could. I was very guarded during the entire evening, because I assumed she had ulterior motives. She dragged out the paper-writing process until about 3:00 in the morning. I watched TV in the room with her while she worked. By midnight I was frustrated with her and was feeling like she was taking advantage of the situation. By 1:00 I was ready to shut her down rudely if she made her move. By 2:00 I started to watch the way her bra strap pressed into her shoulders. At 3:00 the printing was complete and we decided she may as well stay the night.

Here's the thing about seminarians in bed together: some sin is regrettable, more is lamentable, another step turns things uncomfortable, one more makes it condemnable, and if you go around the world you'll end up with such a crisis of conscience that you'll quit on ministry. Thankfully, seminarians live almost entirely in the mind, learning to split hairs and tread semantic arguments like goats on mountain cliffs, and at 3:00 there are so many extra rationalizations at play that it's hard to tell right from wrong. My best effort at sorting them out goes as follows. She took off her shirt, and that was right. But her deodorant had expired, and that was wrong. She kissed me, and that was right. But when she opened her mouth to pass her tongue across with enough spit that I could have gargled, that was clearly wrong. She sucked my finger, luxuriously, and that was right. But when she said, "in literature they call that foreshadowing," it was such a corny line it couldn't have been anything but wrong. And my laughing at the line and ruining the moment could go either way. In the end our actual behavior probably warranted a label somewhere between regret and lament, but a couple of hours later, when we awoke, I told her it was a horrible mistake and sent her home. She felt like it was the beginning of something great, and was hurt that I felt differently. I called Lisa and told her I felt like I had cheated on her, which gave her the opportunity to forgive me and take her daydreams to the next level. I called Betsy and told her I felt like I'd cheated on her with both Mindy and Lisa, and she said she knew how I felt, but had to go because she and a co-worker were on their way to get frozen yogurt.

Stephen said the whole thing was bullshit, and that I was a fool and a hypocrite with no discipline and an addiction to the affirmation of women. And he hasn't sung the Psycho Sex Girl song since.

14.

Waiting for Air Force One

I keep thinking about the fact that if I die, I will go to Heaven, but so long as I'm alive I'll know the pain of life. My credit cards are taut with burden. Betsy and I haven't spoken for a few weeks. Lisa is high pressure, but is trying to get me to make the first move, to her specifications. Mindy moved home at the end of the quarter. I didn't re-enroll and have been doing mostly church stuff for the past couple of weeks. I don't know where the hell I'm heading. In a phone call home the other day my mother mentioned that she misses being able to brag about me. Being alive is hard. I've given up hope that anything I assumed I'd experience here will actually happen; it's clear to me that I'm destined for something much closer to the rat hole in Calcutta than I'd expected. So at night sometimes I put on my cross necklace and go to the roughest parts of town hoping to get shot. Suicide by carefully chosen wrong place at wrong time.

Tonight I only made it a few blocks, to the corner of Colfax and Josephine, in front of the 7-11 that never responded to my application. I was planning to drive to an area near Five Points, where the risks are greater, but I saw this one-legged black guy in an Army coat in the bus shelter, and I stopped.

His name is George, and he's drunk as Cousin Roscoe, to use the parlance of southern Indiana. He's wearing an Army Buzzet, and his left pant leg is folded up to his knee. His metal crutches are on the ground at his foot. He wet his pants and smells like it, and sweat, and alcohol. It's cold enough that I wonder if his pants will freeze. He tells me that Air Force One is waiting for him out at the airport, and he wants me to take him there. I ask about his world, but he is so far gone that he can't report on anything but his immediate surroundings. I ask him if he's hungry, and he is. I buy him a ham and cheese sandwich from the 7-11 cooler. He doesn't have any teeth, so he can't bite through the ham. I'd noticed his missing teeth—I should have thought to select a different sandwich. What he can bite off, the bread and cheese, he gums without swallowing. He fishes a hooked finger across the roof of his mouth and flings each bite to the ground, and then wipes his hand on his wet pants. Clearly his drinking has reached the point that he's given up food for booze. His coughing makes me think of the news report I heard today about a tuberculosis outbreak that has the firefighters and paramedics concerned about the people they pick up.

I try to make conversation with him for an hour, with little progress. He's still far from sober, but his stupor is clearing, and he asks about me. I tell him about seminary and moving from Chicago. I tell him about Betsy and Lisa and Mindy.

"Bitches." He blurts in slur. Then in whimsical free association follow-up, "I loves me some bitches."

I tell him about how I go out at night with weird thoughts of getting killed and escaping the pain.

"I hear that. Air Force One's going down one day, and that'll be that." He empathizes.

For a long time we just sit on the bench, him taking and scraping bites of cheese sandwich from the roof of his mouth. He puts the ham in his coat pocket.

I don't know why I'm sitting here with this guy. I don't know what I can do for him. Frankly it seems pretty clear that he's not long for the world. I ask him if he'd like to pray with me. He offers me his hand. My hands have been pulled into my sleeves to minimize my exposure to his coughing and fluids. My first thought is to recoil, to protect myself. But my first action is to push my hand out from my sleeve and take hold of his, which happens to be the one he favors for fishing bites from his mouth. I pray and he coughs and shudders. I say Amen. He says Amen.

And he doesn't let go of my hand.

So I don't either.

And we sit that way for about another hour, fat white do-gooder and one-legged wino near the end of his tour, holding hands in the bus stop on Denver's main drag for sin and vice.

This is what God had in mind instead of shaping culture with the power of mass marketing like Sue would have had me do. This is what was more important than my dreams with Betsy. It's what was more pressing than my parents' plans for my life. George. He is more important because if I hadn't shown up he'd have spent the night alone and forgotten. The world is full of such people, and such moments, and they make sense of all the questions that can never be answered by seminarians and people who live in ivory towers of rationalizations and convenience. My mom would be horrified, and could never brag about such things to her friends over coffee, but my heavenly Father is proud.

Maybe an hour before sunrise I put newspaper down on my Jeep's passenger seat and drive him to the drunk tank he tells me about. I go home and sleep for a few hours. When I return to the place to offer him breakfast, he's already gone. I conclude that if I get tuberculosis, it was worth it, and I get my wish to escape my pain.

15.

Thieves Hate DC Talk Too

"First, it was not a strip bar, it was an erotic club. And second, what can I say? I'm a night owl."
– Marion Barry, Mayor of Washington, DC

Last week my Jeep died around the corner from the house. There had already been problems with it, which I'd looked into. Among other things, there is silicon floating loose in the radiator, which I'm told is not a particularly good thing. It also won't pass emissions, so I won't be able to renew the plates anyway. I don't have the money to fix it. I don't even have the money to move it, or to pay the ticket I found on the windshield. Someone stole the radio and tapes from it—though they left the Christian stuff. You know Christian music is bad when thieves who are in enough of a rush that they'll break a window take time to reject some of the tapes they find inside. I visited the scene of the crime to duct tape some cardboard into the missing window and then slogged home along the uneven sidewalks trying not to break my neck in what I hope is the last snow of spring.

My world feels about like that on all fronts. Broken down, broke, and stranded, with what remains inside proving absurd and unwanted even by desperate people. And outside all is treacherous and inhospitable. I've been in Denver eight months now, and what felt so exciting, so promising, so worth risking for, has turned out to be a lemon. When I call home, I still talk about how much more beautiful the scenery is here, and how the weather is better, and I still have experiences with God that I try to shape into stories to placate my mother's fear for my safety and my sanity, but most of my energy seems to go into simply coping.

I talk to Lisa a lot, but never about feeling dissatisfied; that would sound too much like a lack of faith. We talk about my Bible studies or moments with one-legged homeless guys, or about faith in the workplace or about her participation in New York's war on pornography. She uses terms like "tremendous man of God" to describe different leaders in her Christian world. My impression is that people who are doing "mighty things for the Lord" tend to be real assholes, with a singularity of meritorious focus that justifies them in the eyes of the masses, who in turn are kept always at arm's length, too far from the details of their heroes' lives to see what's really going on. In advertising I learned the bromide "the masses are asses." What's meant by it is that the lowest common denominator is what sells. Blaise Pascal talks about majority opinion being the one that rules because it's the one with the numbers to enforce its will, but that the majority opinion is, by definition, the opinion of the least clever. That's why, for preventative reasons, America has a Representative Republic instead of a Democracy (but to keep the least clever appeased we nevertheless persist in calling it a Democracy). It's what keeps decent movies from being blockbusters, and is why decent scripts are generally left untouched by big studios. The same goes with selling based on brand image instead of features and benefits. People don't want substance—they want an identity by proxy or proximity. They'll drink Coke even though Coke will kill them, because Coke tells them something about who they are. Or Budweiser, or most any product—in the end there is only one god that won't choose your death over its own. The masses will re-elect Marion Barry mayor of the Washington, D.C. even after he's found guilty on drug and corruption charges because they want to be part of a culture more than they want what's best. They'd sooner cheer for a football player who gets away with killing his wife than experience the discomfort of losing a hero. Masses make the hero, make the brand, and will roll with whatever the hero or the brand does so long as the pellet still comes when they press the lever in the Skinner box. Lisa is part of a church culture that makes heroes of people who too often seem willing to trade upon heavenly gifts—assuming they are not complete frauds—that were intended for the betterment of the church, not the person with the gift.

But it's not entirely the fault of the hero, and even when it begins as such, heroes are hard to reach with reality checks; there's too much at stake—for hero and follower alike—to listen honestly. Not that it can be much fun, really, to be a hero. It's a horribly isolating thing. You can't be yourself—people won't make room for it. And when you insist on showing the world the life you lead behind the Wizard's curtain in your own private Oz, the bile that comes from robbing them of their idol is intense. The very last thing we want is to be left alone in front of God with nothing to cover the truth about who we are. And we expect those around us to live likewise, and we expect to hide behind them too. We are the rabid gatherers of fig leaves, and it's been so long since we've seen ourselves without them that even we have no idea who we really are without our coverings anymore. We've become utterly dependent upon our false selves and our heroes, and of course it is anathema to question the addiction.

Beyond all of that, there is something that feels really good about Lisa's world. There is something cool about the term "tremendous man of God." There is something about it being a never-ending adventure. Something about a mission, a challenge, an identity. And a holy "attaboy" at the end sounds good. Plus there is the safety net of it being God's deal—so ultimately He's responsible for how we look, how well we do, whether we're on the right track, and even for picking up the tab for our failures along the way. For example, I'm amazed at the choices, and at the way God picks up the tab for the choices, when the Bible's Abram and Sarah go into Egypt during a famine. Abram tells Sarah, his wife, to tell the king that she is really his sister, knowing that because Sarah is beautiful the king will want her and would kill her husband to have her. Abram knows that if he's going to eat—along with the people counting on him—he's going to have to put Sarah on the corner, so to speak. Talk about an Indecent Proposal—only in the Bible version, as opposed to the movie, it's like Woody and Demi are homeless and they show up at Robert Redford's country club and set Redford up to unwittingly sleep with a married woman. I don't see the Bible story as making Abram look like a genius or a man of remarkable character for this particular choice, even though he is clearly the father of the faith elsewhere, but in Lisa's culture of "tremendous men of God" there seems to be an over-willingness to take such shortcuts and then reject any hint that such choices may conflict with hero status. There are far too many "pimps for Jesus" in Lisa's church world.

But again, there is something that feels really good about the idea of being a holy man. Maybe not a public hero, but maybe a quiet hero someone else talks about some. I could be a quiet holy man, where the benefits of that holiness are experienced by at least some people who know me. I heard about an old man in Boulder who is retired from his job, but who donates his time to meet one-on-one for an hour each week with 40 college students. It's said that he loves so well that any time one of these 40 students expresses even a bit of self-doubt or self-condemnation, the old man cries for them. He sees them the way God sees them. He sees their beauty and their promise, their pain and the truth that lives beneath the pain. He is a simple man, out of the public eye (though I heard about him in a stadium full of people). He quietly loves 40 college students, and that is his full-time work. That seems pretty cool. That seems like something I'd expect a holy man to do. That seems like something I'd like to do. I could see that man being a sort of hero for me—as he is already a sort of role model. Does that make him a "tremendous man of God"?

In reality I think what's going on is that I want this deal with God to pan out. I don't want to have to admit defeat in my choice to move here, or to go to seminary, or to drop out of seminary to pursue real ministry work, or any of the other wacky decisions I've made and slapped a "Jesus" label on in the past several months. I want people to clearly see that He was calling me from Chicago, and the best way for them to see that is for there to be really cool results—fruit, the church people call it—from my obedience.

But I don't know what He wants me to do exactly. I can hold hands with homeless men all He wants, but what drives me out into the night is not love for them, but a desire to encounter my death, or some adventure, or some great story, or something that allows me to escape my own ball of worries and gluttonous pride for a comfortable, but not transformational, period of time. I want there to be something I pursue for positive reasons, because I love it or desire it or because the need so captures me. Right now I'm a tourist who's been reading way too many travelogues and is eager to spend evenings practicing the language of the people I'm visiting. And I want them to find me fascinating. I want them to feel amazed and grateful that I've given up so much, that I've traveled so far, to get to know them, and maybe to help them out somehow. I am, after all, a servant, and what's mine is theirs. Of course the fact is that I've burned through pretty much everything of mine, and what I have remaining died around the corner last week. Maybe you'd care to have me regale you with some of my new thoughts about Pascal and how man is but a worm? Would you care for a ham and cheese sandwich and some quality time at the bus stop? Maybe you could say something negative about yourself and let me cry for you? Or, better yet, perhaps I could interest you in some used Christian music tapes?

16.

A Change of Scenery

It's June and I'm sitting on the hip roof of a bright red barn surrounded by the scrubby buttes, alkali gulches and jagged green mountains where a bunch of John Wayne movies were filmed, watching a canary yellow crop duster cut through the blue sky, popping in and out of view as it dusts the fields of lettuce and Olathe sweet corn. Behind me is the window into the apartment I've been calling home for the past three weeks—one bedroom, a small kitchen, a tiny bathroom, and a space for a chair and my radio. The room comes with the job. The rest of the giant barn turned church turned residential treatment facility belongs to the good men of Teen Challenge, a drug and alcohol and whatever else you've got rehab program. Among charismatic believers, it seems that the best way to get name recognition is to mention the Eric Estrada movie *The Cross and the Switchblade*, which told the story of the original street gangs that inspired the birth of the program. It's a year-long program built around discipline and Bible study and church attendance and physical labor to pay the program's bills. I'm part teacher, part cook, part counselor, part driver, part prayer warrior, and part low-level staff. Most of the time I feel like the guard with the mirrored sunglasses in *Cool Hand Luke*. I'm the morning shift; another person with a similar job description takes over in the afternoon. The description includes getting up at 5:00; starting breakfast for the 10 men in the program; waking the men up at 6:00; making sure they're bathed, fed, prayed, and in class by 8:30; grading their work; preparing lunch; dropping most of them off wherever they're working that day; running the donated expired food that goes too bad for our use out to a nearby farmer's pigs; and venturing into town to pick up replacement expired groceries from the City Market. On Wednesday evening, or Sunday both morning and evening, my job also includes driving the guys to church—either the Assemblies of God in Olathe, which is small and friendly, or the Assemblies of God ten miles north in Delta, which feels like the big city compared to everything else along the Colorado/Utah border. There is also a couple who are administrators and something like house parents, and there's an executive director who does a lot of fundraising around the state, and Norm, the white-haired gentle spirit who takes meticulous care of everything—down to having special carpet on the dashboard of his Toyota Corolla to protect it from the sun. Norm's primary role seems to be to pray for the men and to be around for them after they leave the program. The fundraiser doesn't live on site, but the rest of us do. It's hot and dusty and there's no air-conditioning, but it's a dry heat, as they say, and it's been fun living in a setting that feels like a country music video.

Lisa was thrilled that I'd taken the job—she knew about Teen Challenge in New York and believed they were "doing tremendous things for the Lord." I found out about it in the newspaper classifieds, and was hired on the spot. The way it works is that I stay here for three months and then decide whether I want to commit for the rest of a year. They say it's important to the men in the program—all 18 and over, even though the program is called Teen Challenge...insurance liability reasons—to maintain as consistent a staff as possible. My pay is $300/month plus the room and my share of the donated expired food. And the cash part won't kick in until July, so for June all I'm getting is the room and food.

Most of my stuff is still at Stephen's house, in his basement in case he decides to rent my room to someone else. I was able to get the Jeep to start and stay running long enough to get it to a dealership described by one of its own salesmen as "the bottom of the barrel." I paid $3,000 for the heap in October, and because I knew what it was supposed to cost to repair, and because I'd read something in the Desert Fathers about making sure to lose just a little in every financial exchange so you're sure not to take advantage of the other guy, when the salesman asked how much I wanted for the Jeep, I told him $600. He wrote me a check immediately, and later said he'd be able to sell the thing for $1,000 the next day. I felt a little foolish, but at least I was able to pay Stephen the rent I owed him, and my credit card minimums too. With Teen Challenge not paying me this month, I'll miss a month with the credit cards, so in July my entire check will go to the minimums and the late fees I'll incur. I keep thinking about my dad's line of, "losses are a part of life, but you can't make them up in volume." My financial situation makes the gulf between us that much wider, and growing.

But the work here matters, and that makes me feel like I do, too. The men are here because their addictions have defeated them. Judges have given them the choice of this or prison, or wives have made them choose between this and divorce, or parents have said it's either Teen Challenge or the streets. The men arrive absolutely tied to their sin, both in terms of how they go about their average day, and in terms of how they view themselves. They have become their addictions. They are at the end of their ropes, unable to distinguish between who they really are and what they've been doing, and they are desperate to glimpse a bit of hope running contrary to the expectations left them by their addictions. What I say to them, and how I treat them, and whether or not I spend time praying for them—to impact them and to prepare myself to be with them—matters. Lives hang in the balance, literally.

GALL

There is not a lot to do here, though. I don't have a car, and I can't just borrow the Teen Challenge van anytime I want it. When I'm not on duty, I either hide, sweating, up in my room, or I play chess with the guys. I've played Rolo, a Mexican guy in his late 20s who's here to kick the bottle, maybe 50 times, and he still hasn't won. But he keeps coming, which is really cool. I've actually only lost once, to 18-year-old Jarrod, who attacks with every piece with no regard to good or bad trades, and whose insane approach overwhelmed my defenses. A person can only play so much chess, though, and the guys have other obligations here, so that leaves plenty of time to sit out on the roof and journal or read or pray.

And all of that time on the roof, plus all the time at church and how serious things are for the guys in the program, combine to make life feel a lot more about God than it can when there are more distractions. I've started praying kneeling beside my bed at night, the box fan cranked up all the way in the window and blowing noisily onto me. I've never been all that much into prayer, and I've certainly never been one to literally kneel beside the bed, but it didn't take long to realize the value of physically submitting myself to God, whether I felt the hocus pocus of it or not. There are conflicts in the lives of the men here every day, and as much as anything I realized that I was going to have to find some way to hand those issues over to God, or else they would eat me up. But here's the real thing: it feels good to pray. It feels good to make the time to be quiet enough to sense the reality of God. It feels good to sense that the spiritual balance of the place changes as men enter or leave the program, and that my prayers contribute to the stability of the place somehow. It feels good that in some way I'm able to partner with God. That's a pretty big thing, really.

I had a cool experience because of all this time and prayer last night. I was thinking about how we're supposed to love God and Jesus. But I don't think a person can love God without the help of God. I mean, I'm grateful that I've been born. I'm grateful that God loves me. I'm grateful that I've been forgiven my sins through the atoning work of Jesus on the Cross. But love? Not really. I didn't ask to be saved, and for that matter, I think it's a pretty bum deal that I was born into sin in the first place. The whole interaction is pretty coerced, to tell the truth, and Jesus asking to be loved seems a bit much. What are my choices, really? I want what God offers me, and I want to experience a life with the Holy Spirit, but I've never quite been able to get to the point of saying that I love Jesus. Besides seeming too high pressure to be sincere, people talk about having a "personal relationship with Jesus," which is fine and good, but I've never had a personal relationship—let alone a loving one—with an invisible friend, or a person who wasn't willing to be present with me and communicate in ways that I understand without some sort of scrunch-eyed concentration on my knees in submission. I've felt guilty about not being able to honestly say that I love Jesus—the person, not the concept or the principles or the subculture people seem to mean when they talk about loving him.

Last night something changed. And nothing changed. Mostly the thought occurred to me that I do, indeed, love the man, the person, of Jesus. He is my friend, and I will recognize him when we meet. We will embrace as long-separated brothers, or better, and in that moment I will finally feel the depth of my yearning for him, my missing of him. I sat on my bed and said it aloud.

"I love Jesus."

"I LOVE Jesus."

"I love JEsus."

"Aye luuv JeSUS."

"Se amo Cristo."

And it made me laugh, happily, gratefully, joyfully, finally. It was a Stoned Hoosier moment, a moment when an altered perception highlighted that changes were, indeed, taking place within me. It was not something cool about me. It was not a reflection of my efforts. It was not something I was making up. Somewhere, over the course of the past several months, my heart has been changed to a place where I understand previously impossible—even annoying—concepts like loving the God who first condemned me, then saved me, then played coy with me when I was hurting. What I hadn't understood before was that he loved me, and that he was willing to fill me with his love until it was only natural that of course I would love him too. Isn't that what I was wired to do? It was another moment where I saw that all covenants are God-initiated and God-fulfilled. I love Jesus because God has been working a change in my heart. Very cool. And it makes me want to pray more, to see what else is out there.

17.

When Scaffolding Collapses

When you're a 30-year-old Cajun grade school dropout with a vague history of pedophilia, and have been interrupted by one of the other guys in the rehab program while you were masturbating with Colgate one morning, and with your own feces another time, you start your day with a bit of a credibility challenge, even if it is your birthday. It's a lonely life, and mercy gets used up quickly, with little extra given for being a good cook or being able play the piano like the best of the old time tent revivalists. In the face of such odious failures, even a big heart, and a sincere—if sputtering—desire to find freedom from your demons is difficult to trust. And though everyone argues that sin isn't graded on a curve, grace feels especially stretched when you pray knowing that even among people whose worlds have been ravaged by their addictions, you're the biggest freak in the bunch, by a long way. Even further than the other guys would ever begin to guess.

So it wasn't a complete surprise that Ed pulled the stunt he did today. He came to dinner after receiving a birthday phone call from his mother. His eyes were red like he'd been crying, and as he spoke, through the crooked teeth that always look like they could fall from his turtle-ish head, he began to choke up.

"My boy died last night." And he had everyone's attention. Someone asked what happened.

"He was with his mama, and they was on their way back to my mama's house, where he lives, and they got hit by a truck. He died in the helicopter on the way to the doctor's." He started to shake.

Someone immediately suggested we pray with Ed, so we had him sit in a chair and we all stood around him, with hands on his shoulders or his feet or his greasy brown hair, and we prayed for his family, and for him, and that he would not abandon his rehab work at Teen Challenge. For a few moments Ed wasn't a disgusting pervert; he was a father mourning the loss of his only son, from whom he has already been separated for months.

"Tammy wants me to come on home. She's tore up pretty bad and she don't want to go through this alone. I'm fixin' to leave, y'all." Which of course everyone urged him not to do. Even Rolo, who almost killed Ed this morning for something he saw Ed doing but refuses to talk about.

When the administrator, Dale, called Ed's mother to convey his sympathies and to discuss what Ed should be encouraged to do next, he learned that not only had there been no accident, but that Ed doesn't even have a child. And Ed's mother has no idea who Tammy might be.

Dale, white-haired Norm, and I called Ed into Dale's office and told him what we'd learned. Dale was a rancher for years. He speaks plainly but has given his life to the ministry of Teen Challenge because he believes in what he sees happen in the men's hearts. It was time for Ed to "come to Jesus," as Dale says.

Ed was defeated. For the longest time he just sat still, gripping the wooden arms of the office chair.

"I don't know why I done it." He finally whispered.

"Son, you're out of slack." Dale said. "I think maybe we've done about all we can do with you."

Norm's eyes darted back and forth between Dale and Ed. He knows what's at stake in the lives here, and he knows how one man bent on self-destruction can drag down the rest. But there are few things as wrenching as dropping a man off at the bus station in Montrose, knowing you're releasing him back into the world that has already nearly destroyed him, and with your throwing in the towel you call him a failure at what seemed like his very chance at redemption. None of us wanted to hurry to kick Ed out, angry though we were. Ed said nothing.

"What do you think?" Dale asked Ed.

"No, sir."

"No sir, what?"

"I don't want to go. I got no place else to go."

"Okay then. We'll give it overnight to pray on it, and we can talk again in the morning."

"Yessir."

"In the meantime, you can't leave the lie hanging out there. You have to make it right with the other men."

At this Ed's face twisted in on itself, and he looked like he may vomit. He turned white and his eyes looked as though he couldn't make sense of the pain he felt inside. There was no anger, not the slightest indication that he was going to try to bargain his way out. He knew what he'd done, and all I could think about was that in his soul the scaffolding that he'd mistaken for the bottom of the well of his sin was collapsing, and he was shocked to be hurtling down further into the dank, despairing blackness. Bottom is always, always lower than we think it is.

Ed nodded. "Can I have a few minutes first?"

"Yeah." Dale answered, rising.

"Would you like me to pray with you?" Norm offered. And Ed began to sob. Dale and I left the office.

GALL

While Ed and Norm prayed, Dale and I gathered the other guys and told them what had happened. There was no telling what would happen if Ed broke the news to them himself. It would be better to give them a few minutes to digest the news, and then let Ed apologize. Duncan, the other staff person with the job description like my own, except that he's a big-talking graduate of the program himself, and about as hard-core military about it all as can be, immediately rose from his chair and left the room when Dale said he was not intending to send Ed home.

A 19-year-old named Josh just arrived yesterday, furious with his parents who tricked him into being here. There are no locks, no bars, on the place, but it's a very long walk in any direction if a man wants to leave, and Teen Challenge is a major shock to the system on a normal day. Josh was visibly freaked out by what he was experiencing. The rumors he'd surely heard about Ed already. The story. The prayer. The lie. Duncan's response. And now a public confession. That's quite a first full day in rehab. He watched it all happening, and he studied the other men when Ed finally entered the room.

Ed already knew what the men think of him. Their opinions are actually probably more generous than what Ed thinks of himself in his more honest moments. But there is something weird about sin, something about the way we battle with it, that makes us somehow embrace the struggle and find something like a glory in it. Among the men at Teen Challenge there is a real temptation to tell stories about where they've been—war stories—and even to bring some of that battle-based paradigm into the way they relate to one another. There are rules against it, and we make every effort to shut down those sorts of conversations because all they do is feed the wrong dog in the fight between hope and despair, but it's nearly impossible to eradicate. Serial killers will always have their place in prisons, and people with Ed's issues will always find a parallel niche in rehab facilities—that's just part of how the world looks when people work to earn the praise of their sins. For as much as Ed hates himself for his addictions, and for as much as he hates being shunned by the men in the program, there has always been a certain pathetic and soiled security blanket of evil comfort he finds in his position as chief freak.

Today he broke. He was as small a man as I've ever seen, and he let go of his security blanket. It's nearly impossible for me to imagine how terribly frail and insignificant he must have felt. When your last shred of comfort comes from being the guy whose reflection in society comes from getting a reaction for being the one who masturbates with your own shit, and you let even that shred go, you are about as stripped bare as you can be. And then to have to confess and beg forgiveness from a group of men who are already panicked about seeing their own tattered pieces of self-delusory comfort being ripped from them—men to whom you've lied and whose mercy you've already taxed beyond its normal measure when they prayed for your lie only a short time earlier. How awful. May I never live the moment Ed lived this evening.

"There ain't nothing I can say. I lied to you. I wanted to feel normal for a while on account of my birthday, and I lied to get it. What I done was wrong, and I'm sorry."

The room was silent long enough that I started paying attention to *Forrest Gump*, muted and playing on the television. Nobody made eye contact with Ed, who stood looking at the carpet in front of him. Finally Dale broke the reverie.

"The van's leaving for church in ten minutes. Let's get going."

I didn't hear anybody say a word until we were loading into the van, when Jarrod the insane attacking chess player said to Ed, "It's your birthday—you should take the front seat." And nobody protested. Maybe Ed got the seat because nobody wanted to have to sit next to him. That would make sense. But I prefer to believe Jarrod demonstrated the right kind of mercy for an addict rebuilding his credibility from zero.

18.

Intercession

It's still the night of Ed's birthday. We went to the tiny double-wide trailer turned church in Olathe. Old Sister Rose played an electric guitar laid across her lap, and Norm played the piano. We sang "I'll Fly Away," which has a particular charm in the orange-carpeted, flimsy-paneled room with its ten non-Teen Challenge congregants and their tambourines. Pastor Cordell wished Ed a happy birthday, and the church people clapped for him. By the last song Ed was singing along. His southern accent—and the fact that he was the only one there who could sing—made him easy to pick out. He was smiling as we climbed back into the van. As we drove home he watched the last shades of red and purple fade over Utah, and a couple of times I saw him close his eyes.

That was earlier. Now I'm on my knees beside my bed, feeling the wind from the fan blow the hair on my back. I think of shaving it. Then I think of my mirror, covered for three days now in dried shaving cream so I won't be able to see my reflection. I'm fasting. I don't know how long I'll go. Maybe 40 days. I want God to take my life. My preference would be that it would be taken literally— that I'd die. Same reason as what drove me onto the streets in Denver—I want to escape. And if I don't die, I at least want God to take my life and do something with it. I don't want to be in charge of it anymore—I don't know what to do with it, and I feel like it's not amounting to anything. I want to be a holy man.

I try to pray. I concentrate. I petition. I think about the day with Ed's breaking, and I pray for his safety among the men during the night. Not that I think anything would actually happen to him, but every morning as I make my way from room to room to wake the men up, I brace myself that someone may be missing, or may be hanging from the ceiling. I try to pray, but I can't get into the groove.

The groove, when I get into it, feels like a conversation, except it doesn't work with words so much. It works more with images or whole chunks of satisfying reply—as though God answers not with sentences, not with sequences of letters streaming from left to right across my mind's eye, but with paragraphs. And not always with answers to my questions—it's more like he answers the question behind my question. I don't know how it works for other people, but for me the question behind my question seems to always be something like, "Are you real? Do you see me? Do you love me? Will everything be okay? Daddy?" I know it's pretty far out compared to the world I knew in Chicago—I know how this would sound if I talked about it on MTV—but it's hard to think of a more beautiful thing than when I wait beside my bed, covered in the noise of the fan, and somewhere in the emptiness within me I feel the sweeping answer that wraps me in, "I am. I do. It will. I am. I am. I am."

But tonight I can't get into the groove. When Lisa and I talk on the phone she likes to pray about angels camping out on the roof of the barn to protect us from demons and such. I don't know how all of that works, but I do know that I can feel a certain "disturbance in the Force" when a man enters or leaves the program. So I pray about Josh the new guy and for strength for the angels who protect us. Still I can't click into the groove. So I pray that if God wants me to pray, he'll need to clear the fog between us. Then I tell him I'll talk to him tomorrow and climb into bed.

A few minutes later I feel him speak, which for me feels like one of my own thoughts, except that I can tell it didn't originate with me—plus it feels benevolent. "Try again now." I return to my knees and feel a real clarity and ache regarding a need I can't identify. The sudden and dramatic change is remarkable, and on a hunch I leave my apartment and head downstairs. I listen outside of Norm's room and hear him praying. I knock.

"Were you just praying for me?" I ask.

"A few minutes ago." He answers, not at all surprised that I'd show up at his door to ask such a question.

"I think maybe I'm supposed to join you—I was blocked and then God said to try again. Is there something in particular going on with you?"

"I'm worried that Shane is relapsing. For the first month after he graduated he was strong and stayed in touch, but he hasn't returned my calls this week, and I'm concerned that he's hiding from me."

"Okay. Do you want to pray together, or separately?"

"Stay here, but let's pray on our own for him, and we'll tell each other what we hear."

"Good." I answer, and as I kneel down with my elbows on a chair, I think about how very far I am from where I was a year ago.

I pray in tongues when I pray for other people. I can tell from the sound and tone, and from something inside of me, what I'm praying in a general way, but it's sort of like the groove type responses I get from God in that I don't feel like what I'm praying is as narrow-band as words. I'm praying something more communicative somehow. Something more accurate. Something that, frankly, I can't explain. And even though the prayers feel more accurate and more led by God, I have a frustrating tendency to listen to the words and try to figure out what language I'm speaking, because it sounds like a real language. It doesn't take long before I start noticing that there are a lot of Qs, but far fewer Bs in my language than I might have expected. It's nearly impossible for me to pray in tongues without getting overly distracted by the sound of it. So I've learned to quietly sing my prayers rather than speak them. The tune and tone changes depending on the person for whom I'm praying, and I can tell a great deal about the prayers based on the song. One time I was praying for a friend's wife and the song turned into something like a Native American dirge chant, and I knew that I was praying for healing for the sexual abuse she'd experienced in high school. That was the first I knew about the abuse, and I cried and cried for her as I sang, as I believe God does. Later I told my friend about my prayer experience, and he confirmed the things I already knew from the song.

I'm confused by the people on television who pray in tongues in front of huge crowds or the cameras. I have a very strong sense about when it is and is not appropriate to pray in tongues, and in my case it feels like such public displays would be about the most sacrilegious thing I could do. The other thing that seems fairly obvious is that I only get the insights into people's lives that I can handle responsibly. It's not like I get to read someone else's mail, or tell their fortune or something—it's more like I'm able to tell something about the load I'm helping to carry because I can tell what it feels like loaded onto my shoulder. And the secrets I can feel when I help carry a prayer load are as sacred as praying in tongues. I can't imagine a more safe confidence than what is shown to someone as they pray for someone else. The only real challenge is that in the light of Heaven, all sin is pretty matter of fact, and sometimes it can be hard to remember how desperately the person with the sin wants to keep the sin hidden in dark places. That's a horribly foolish strategy, of course, but not as foolish as it would be to break someone's trust by letting the world know about what you've been shown in prayer. It's a delicate thing, and I think it's exactly the delicacy of the dynamic that keeps God telling me to keep my big mouth shut. The gift is a lot to handle—at least it has been for me.

I also don't know what to make of the way the gift came to me. After spending the first three years of college convinced that Christianity was nothing more than the cutesy crap I'd seen so much of, in my senior year I encountered William Blake. He blew my mind, as did the professor who introduced me to Blake. I spent the year on a sort of quest, following from Blake, with his line about "if the doors of perception were cleansed, man would see everything as it is: infinite," to Aldus Huxley's *Doors of Perception*, to Jim Morrison's band The Doors. I read a ton of Native American spirituality stuff. I learned about, and moved away from, the Gnostics. I dove into ancient Chinese Philosophy. In fact, it was Chuang Tzu who played the most significant role in pointing me back towards Jesus. He had the system figured out—he had the lock. But he was missing the key. Meanwhile I'd been walking around with the key tied on a shoestring around my neck, with no real idea what sort of life it was meant to unlock. The confluence of all those people brought me back to the intellectual conclusion that Jesus was the way after all. And then a friend from high school called out of the blue to tell me he was getting married and that he'd become a Christian. A loony, raving, charismatic Christian whose world was far bigger than he'd ever believed it could be. He caught me on the right day, and over the course of a couple of conversations, I caught the bug too.

I fixated on tongues. It seemed to me that speaking in a prayer language had to be undeniable, unquestionable proof about God. And unlike other gifts, which come and go, I was told the prayer language would be there whenever I choose to pray that way. I concluded that any time I had doubts, I could pray and experience again the undeniable proof of God's reality. I wanted to pray in tongues maybe even more than I wanted to experience God. I begged and pleaded, and for months nothing came.

There's a Far Side cartoon where a young man is at the front door to the School for the Gifted, pushing on the door that says, "Pull." That was me with tongues. On the retreat weekend where the gift was given to me, I learned something important about God. He is the pursuer, the initiator. It is my place to ardently desire him, but it is not my place to obsess about what he can do for me. When I refuse to see that, he's willing to let me beat myself against walls, or push doors marked "Pull" until I wear myself out. I didn't yet know that the doors of Heaven only open outward. Finally, nearly in despair, I relented in my pursuit enough to give God room to open the door; and then he gave me the gift. With it he could have said, "Here—now try to explain this to people."

I can't explain it. And it isn't final and ultimate proof about God any more than the rest of creation already screams of his existence. It won't come with me back through the filters of rationality so I can pin it to a board and dissect it. It's a satisfying gift, and one I'm glad to have been given, but it is no real measure of anyone's position with God, and it doesn't take away the gap I feel between myself and Him. And as soon as I got to Chicago after that weekend retreat, I stopped going to church, didn't pray much at all, and spent a year with people who didn't guess I was a Christian. Tongues isn't anything more than one tool, one gift, and there are dozens of others I'm just as good at ignoring.

Tonight I'm singing quietly into the chair for Shane. Quietly, but ardently; there is a great joy in feeling like you're laboring in prayer—that your efforts are having some sort of real impact someplace else in the physical or spiritual realm.

"I feel like we're supposed to pray for him to wake up." I say.

"So do I." Norm answers.

"Maybe we should call him on the phone." I suggest.

"I don't think that's what God has in mind. Besides, I'm feeling like we're supposed to be praying it—it means something different from what the phone can do."

"You're right." I answer, and for another hour we return to our respective prayers.

I have no solid theological understanding of what tells me that our prayers are finished, and that we've been successful. In fact, it sounds more like Rastafarian "I and I,"—meaning "me and the spirit within me"—than Christian doctrine. As I pray, I picture Shane in his bed, asleep. I pray for him to awaken. I sing my prayers. And then I can tell that he is stirring. Not his body—it's still asleep. Not even his conscious self—it's dreaming. What I can tell is that there is a stirring in his spirit. It's more like there was a fire burning in him that he'd let fade to cooling embers, and our prayers have blown them back to a small flame—enough that tomorrow he'll re-engage with his faith. I pray that he will awaken with a worship song in his head, and then I "cool down," amazed at what I've experienced while we've been praying. I thank God for the opportunity as I ask for more of this in the future. I thank him for my being unable to get into the groove before, because if I hadn't been stuck, I may not have noticed when things cleared up, and if I hadn't noticed that I wouldn't have come to Norm's room.

Norm finishes praying at exactly the same time I do. We hug, and say good night.

By the time I get back to my room I'm thinking about how God is making me into a holy man, and I hear the siren song of becoming a "tremendous man of God." Lisa will be so impressed when I tell her about it in a carefully matter of fact way tomorrow.

19.

Yeah, but…

It doesn't make any difference how mind-blowing a given experience is, you'll still have to wipe your ass the next morning. It's been eight days since Ed's birthday, and yesterday I turned 24. I spoke with my parents, and with Lisa, and with David in seminary, and with Betsy. It was the eleventh day of my fast, so there was no birthday dinner. At least the day was better than it was last year.

Sort of. The good news is that God claimed me. The bad news is that I've been left to feed moldy bread to pigs in the middle of nowhere. I don't have any idea where all of this is leading, and increasingly I've begun to wonder if God's response to my offer to give him my life and to be a holy man to his glory has been politely declined. I've begun to wonder if I've simply been shuffled off to perform some mundane chore far away from the action.

That frustrates me, but as soon as I start to compile my list of grievances, I think about how I did tell Lisa about my prayer time with Norm, and I did make sure that she was impressed. When I speak with my mother, I let her be impressed with my abilities to quote chapter and verse from the Bible. I find myself dropping references to seminary with the people I encounter through Teen Challenge—it impresses them and serves as caveat to the role I play here; a claim to some sort of deferred greatness. And for as much as I hate to admit it, it kills me to consider how little money I've earned this year. It's August 3rd, and year to date I've earned $300—and after taxes it wasn't even enough to cover the phone bill and credit card minimums, so when this month's payment arrives I'm going to be in exactly the same position again.

I am a man, and here is an inventory of my desirability credentials: reddish hair, and an inability to tan; glasses; 300 pounds; no car; no cash; no direction; no prospects; no discipline; pride that refuses to submit, and is able to turn the lousy reality of my position into some pie in the sky rationalization about being a holy man; partial education, which leaves me opinionated but uninformed; petty and reactionary, which leaves me still largely defined by opposing my father; lust that I keep barely in check by excessive and warping repression; and capping it all, a refusal to step out of the fire that is consuming me.

I pray that it will take me, the fire. That I will die, or that I will live remarkably. I want God to take my life. Take it. Take it. Take it. Admit some value to it by acknowledging it to end it or redeem it. Stop ignoring me. Stop assigning me to things that are smaller than I want. Yes, I know the inconsistencies are there. I know it's pride. I know it's weakness. I know I'm not God, even to myself. But take my life—play me or trade me.

20.

Alone in the Desert

Same day, evening. I'm on my way to Grand Junction to pick up my date for the evening: Christine, a beautiful woman who recently returned from a two-year mission term in Israel. I saw her sing at the Assemblies of God camp last week-end, and I felt myself conclude that she could be my wife. That would be a good story. After we returned to Teen Challenge, I happened to tell Pastor Cordell about her, and he said she is his fourth cousin and one of his wife's best friends. They helped set up the date. I've been cringing about the card I sent her; with a cartoon drawing of a detective holding a rodent in his hand. It said, "My name's Friday. I carry a badger." Yeah, I'm a catch.

I'm driving an ancient-smelling brown Malibu with a curtain of fabric fall-ing from the ceiling—Dale's emergency vehicle. The engine light is on and Dale warned me that I might need to pull over to let it cool off some. I have doubts about the car making it all the way to Grand Junction, let alone completing the round trip. A card with directions to the church where Christine and I are sup-posed to meet is on the seat beside me, under the brush and deodorant.

It's been a long time since I wore a button-down shirt or my Polo cologne. I wish I'd made time to get a haircut. And I didn't iron very well. And I can't remember if these are my stinky shoes. I don't suppose it will matter—if she's the one, then she's the one, and if not then none of the other stuff matters anyway.

We meet, and she is lovely. I'd really built her up in my mind, and I was worried that I'd be disappointed, but I'm not. We take her car to Pizza Hut, where she eats a salad and I drink water with lemon. I tell her about my fast. She tells me about going to church on the Mount of Olives. I ask about her family. She tells me that father is an engineer. I do my typical joke about, "Oh, really? I love trains." Christine's father isn't the sort of engineer that makes the joke work; he actually drives trains. The joke confuses her and she seems to wonder if I'm making fun of her dad. I feel like a goof.

We go to the amusement park, where we play miniature golf and take a spin on a couple of the rides. She takes me to the national park just outside of town to watch the sunset from a cliff. She's delightful. She's so nice. She smells good. She's interesting. She's beautiful. I'm so pleased that this is the woman God picked out for me to marry.

We return to the church parking lot. She says she had a good time and thanks me for driving up to see her, and then she practically peals out and disappears into the night. It's absolutely obvious that whatever she thought of me, it was less positive than my own conclusions. I drive frantically in the direction where she headed—I want to know if I did something wrong—but I can't find her, and the engine light comes on again, so I grudgingly get out of city traffic and head south back towards Olathe.

What the hell is this? I thought she was going to be the one—I thought God said so. This sucks. I'm embarrassed, and I know Christine will tell Cordell's wife about the date and that they'll laugh about me together. I'd hung too much hope on meeting my wife. But I want to meet my wife, to get that piece of direction figured out. Once I meet my wife, a huge part of the puzzle will be solved. Instead I'm left with nothing. Just this crappy car and a place I don't want to return to in Teen Challenge.

I don't want this life. Why won't God take it? Screw it—I'm not going to wait for him to take it—I'm going to throw it at him. Tears fill my eyes and the oncoming headlights blur out into stars. I pull off the highway to a dirt road that disappears into the desert, determined to have one of those dramatic yelling at God scenes like I've seen in movies—like Lieutenant Dan has during the storm at sea in *Forrest Gump*. I tumble from the car, tears streaming down my face, and I suck in a huge breath as I throw my head back to scream for God to take my life.

And then I see the stars. I didn't know there were so many. And God says to me, in a chunk, "I made the stars. I made everything. And I control the gravities that hold it all together. And I formed your eye and give you the ability to see what I have made. I am in control, and I have you."

And my giant breath comes out in a crippled whisper. "It's yours."

Then I get back in the car and drive home.

21.

Breaking Fellowship

I'm leaving Teen Challenge. The three-month trial period is just about up, and I decided not to sign on for the year. David will be here to pick me up in an hour or so. I've struggled with feeling stuck here, and I've disagreed with many of the harsh choices the program makes, but there were two things that happened at church this week that iced the deal for me.

The church in Delta is having a revival, which is something that starts out being foreign to me. I've always thought of revival being something that happens when God shows up, like Pentecost when he appears as tongues of fire in the room where the disciples are waiting. I've pictured revival being spontaneous. The Delta church has had this event on the calendar for months. There are speakers to book, music to plan, and announcements to produce. People plan their vacations around the revival, and for others the trip to the revival is their vacation. It's probably mostly a semantic thing, when it comes down to it; revival week is really just an invitation to God to reinvigorate people's faith.

Except this. There is such a focus on what I've started calling the "holy tickle" that things tend to get screwy. The gifts feel good, and to some people they're pretty impressive. Lisa's whole thing about "tremendous men of God" comes from exactly that impressiveness. And it is impressive to see miracles—for a leg to grow or for demons to be cast out or to have a prophet speak your secrets out loud. The problem is that the gifts are not meant to function like merit badges; they're not intended to create a pecking order. They're not supposed to be the primary focus of the way people interact with God, or with each other. But in some church cultures, that's exactly what they've become, which means people are often tempted to build their whole understanding of God around the recipes they think will produce spiritual abilities in them. Sometimes the desire for the gifts is good, and sometimes it's bad, but there are huge problems that tend to develop when people fall more in love with the voice than they are with the speaker.

"The Jews killed Jesus," the sermon unfolds, "and look what happened to them in World War Two." It's a path of logic that emanates from the desire to figure out how God works and how to work the system to get the holy tickle. It has to do with innocent blood and God's justice.

"What did you think of the thing about the Jews?" I ask the Teen Challenge executive director later. "The part about Hitler as agent of God's justice."

"That's what I've always been taught. Guess I didn't think much about it at all." He finds my questioning to be insubordinate and distasteful.

I don't have an intellectual category to accept the teaching. My understanding of the theology is that Jesus died not because the Jews called for his crucifixion, but because there was no other way for me to be reconciled to God. I could not make up for my sins, and I needed him. The Jews didn't kill Jesus: I did. And in terms of justice for his innocent blood, I guess I see his resurrection, and mine, and the power his blood wields in the world as something like justice. I think the preacher in Delta was wrong, whether I'm correct or not, and I think his error comes from an ultimately unwise craving to be a Christian hero.

We returned to church for the evening service, and that's where the especially rough moment happened for me. There was music and clapping. There was a guest speaker, introduced as "a mighty man of God much blessed by the Lord." He invited people to the front of the church and blew across the mint on his tongue as he touched their foreheads, and they fell to the ground. Maybe an okay thing, and maybe not. It doesn't float my boat, but I know enough to say that I'm continually amazed that Jesus shows up pretty much anywhere he's invited—often to places where I wish he wouldn't. He still seems very happily wed to his bride, the Church, and until he divorces himself from it, I know it would be foolish for me to do so.

That said, the bride's a freaking mess and could use some serious counseling. Ever since Ed's birthday when he lied and then apologized, a real change seems to have come over him. I think his repentance was sincere, and it's possible that some of his temptations were actually removed from him. The change has brought him extra attention from Dale and Norm, and from Pastor Cordell too. And that's where the rub comes in.

Jarrod the insane attacking chess player saw how things were going for Ed. He saw how to earn the praise and extra goodwill of the Teen Challenge authorities, and he's been asking about what he needs to do to be saved. He also wants to know how he'll know that God has forgiven and saved him. He was told he needed to repent of his sins, which means admitting they were sins and also turning away from them, and he was told he must give his heart to Jesus. He was told that he'd know his prayer worked when the Holy Spirit came into his heart, and he would know this because he would begin to speak in tongues. He was told it usually happens right away.

The evening service rose to a fever pitch, and an altar call. Most everyone present at the revival already believed, but everyone knew who the Teen Challenge men were, and several people pointed when Jarrod asked me to go forward with him. I stood behind him as he prayed with the people on the edge of the stage, and then they asked if he wanted to be baptized in the Spirit. One man placed his hands on Jarrod's chest and back. Another anointed Jarrod's forehead with oil. He got the full package from the prayer helper people. And then he started to speak words. The men all exclaimed, "Praise the Lord!" Jarrod looked around at all the celebration that was going on for what he'd let the helpers do for him, and he started hugging them and also saying, "Praise the Lord." I could tell, though, that something wasn't right. Later I asked about it.

"Did you fake it tonight?"

"Fake what?"

"The tongues thing."

"My prayer was real. The other part they just wanted so bad, and the guy was hurting my chest. They said I should open my mouth and let myself start talking. So I did, but nothing came, so I starting talking like they did."

What to say to Jarrod? The guy has nine months left of deconstruction and reconstruction with his life, faith, and sense of self in the program. What to tell him about the imbalance of the churches upon which he's dependent? What to say about my own experiences with prayer, with my own perceptions of appropriateness? How to be loyal to Teen Challenge, and loyal to what I believed to be true from my experiences? How could I remain a part of this? I decided I could not.

I was angry when I talked to Lisa about the whole thing. I told her what I thought about "tremendous men of God" and the culture that creates them. I told her how painful it was to be associated with the stuff about Hitler and the culture that had introduced Jarrod to what will certainly be a years-long warping experience, if it doesn't turn out to be something that either locks him into a tortured reality or drives him from the faith entirely. I told her I didn't know how I was going to parse through what I'd experienced, how I was going to distinguish between baby and bathwater. I want to serve people—that's what we've been called to do—but there has to be a better way than this. She wanted to pray about it on the phone. I told her I'd talk to her some other time.

22.

On Filling Canyons

It's two weeks later, the last week of August, 1995, and the blue numbers on Jon's car stereo says it's 2:53 in the morning. We're somewhere just outside of Kansas City, heading west on I-70. I've known Jon since about 11:00 yesterday morning, and this is pretty much the first break in our conversation. He looks like a 23-year-old Conan O'Brien, coarse red hair forced grudgingly to obey the part he chisels down the left side of his scalp. He is on his way to Denver to begin his Masters in Philosophy at Denver University. He plans to move into the field of artificial intelligence and the study of how people learn. We've spent the time discussing heady God stuff and things like harmonic theory, comparing notes on his understanding of Kant and my understanding of Blake, leap-frogging each other enthusiastically with the next mind-blower. I can tell he'd be a great teacher, and I know I'm a provocative sponge as a student of this sort of thing. It's been a magical drive, and I can already tell we're going to be friends a long time.

But right now we've slipped into a lull, and I think about the woman in the car in front of us, who is so beautiful that even the taillights of her Saturn look pretty. Rachel. I know her from seminary, where she is one of the few women studying for a real degree—not just the counseling MA. Last week she called to see if I wanted to ride to Indy with her on her trip home to see family in Cincinnati. She and Jon both went to college at Miami of Ohio and know each other from some campus ministry. Jon is from Seven Mile, Ohio, which he describes as "four miles from Three Mile Creek." She looked him up while she was home and learned about his plans, so they decided to caravan west together.

When I first saw Jon, in the parking lot of the Cracker Barrel where Rachel and I had agreed we'd have my mother drop me, I didn't know what to think. David always left the door to his apartment on campus open when Rachel came over—she was known as a sort of temptation, and he didn't like to have her around, but she is pretty and she is fun, and it's not like you can just kick someone like that out, even if you are married. I assumed Jon was what we'd begun calling Rachel's male friends: the *hom du jour*. The guy of the day. It's mean, but man does she burn through them. I figured she had Jon on the line, which frustrated me about her, but mostly threatened my position.

I'd done the bulk of the driving on the way home, and Rachel spent a lot of time asleep in the back seat. When we'd go under a street lamp I'd look at her in the rear view mirror and say a prayer for her, or an appreciation of the beauty God poured into her. I loved that she bit her nails; it meant that she was down to Earth. Her hair puddled in chocolate wisps around her cheeks. Her t-shirt rode up to expose a milky white hip as she slept. I drove with my hands at ten and two, to be extra vigilant and extra responsible. I thought of Richard Nixon and how he used to drive the woman who would become his wife on dates with other men just so he could be with her. I would do that for Rachel.

On the way to Indianapolis we'd stopped for the night with friends of hers in St. Louis. We were treated like a couple, and we played tennis in the steamy night. I fell asleep aching for her. The next day I told her I thought she was the most beautiful woman I'd ever known. She asked two or three times during the remaining hours of the drive whether I really meant that. "Do you really think I'm pretty?" I was desperate to press home my affirmation of that fact.

Jon laughs. "If you want to know the soul of womanhood—at least contemporary womanhood—in one question, it's 'Am I pretty?'" He throws his girl voice on the question.

"But isn't that the role of a man?" I respond. "To build up a woman and make her strong and confident? Especially in a world where the measure of a woman moves ever more shallow with things like beauty and masculine strength or corporate success?"

"Sitting at the feet of a woman and telling her how pretty she is makes her stronger the way throwing pennies into the Grand Canyon makes it a prairie. Especially Rachel. The abyss is too deep, and too vast, and praise from a posture of submission is so tiny that all it really does is make her see how impossibly insufficient you are."

"I don't know." I contend. "I guess it seems more like one of those things where you just hug the kid until the kid quits kicking and screaming and calms down. I see Rachel more like that—desperate for affirmation from a man who is not just trying to get into her pants, who is strong enough to do better by her."

"Is that what you did with Betsy?" He asks.

"Yeah, pretty much. Except that a certain access to her pants was part of the deal."

"But in the end you weren't enough."

"I don't know if that's what the problem was."

"Okay." And he casually slackens his posture to show me that he's not going to push it further.

I woke up yesterday morning in bed with Betsy. We didn't have sex—we just sort of played house. She drove down and spent the night with me at my parents' house. It had been a long time—and things have changed. I don't think we'll ever see each other again. We went to dinner and watched a movie together, but there was nothing for us to talk about; she didn't want to talk about our past or what happened, or about the other guy and how things were going with him, or about my world in Denver. She just wanted to be with me and hide in my kind words. I hadn't slept much during the previous couple of days, with the driving and the pining for Rachel, and somewhere in the night, laying beside Betsy in half-sleep, I touched her face and told her I loved her. I stopped myself just before I called her Rachel. That's when I knew for sure. Finally, after a year of tortured conversations and neither of us being quite able to explain why we were still talking, but neither being able to explain exactly why we shouldn't, I knew it was done. Whatever we had before is gone, and frankly it's only sad the way never getting to play high school football again is sad. It's just over, a remnant from another time, and it didn't translate forward. The rules have changed. She's not the same person anymore, and neither am I. The people we both were before are gone, dead like anyone else in history, and the whole thing feels more matter of fact than anything else. I knew it, and she seemed to know it to an extent, but it did still feel like she was getting something for free. It was affirmation and appreciation, and I felt like I was giving it from a place of honesty and abundance in myself. It felt like a good thing, even if there was a tinge of drain to it all.

"So what I am supposed to be if not nice?" I ask Jon.

"You know, the opposite of nice is not mean. Nice is all about appearances and saying the right word—it's about offering yourself up for evaluation and critique and rejection from the other person. Especially the way you describe it. The opposite of nice is authentic. That's what you should be. That's what can fill a woman because it gives her something to hold onto, something to choose instead of her own pit of insecurities. If you are authentically yourself, even if you're a mess, it's a ton stronger than being the puppy dog with the soft coat and gentle words."

"I have been authentic with Rachel, and with Betsy. I could see something in Betsy, and can see something in Rachel, that they can't see, and I want to call it out. I want to believe in them enough that they will start to believe in themselves."

"And let you touch their boobs."

"It's not like that."

"Of course it's like that. Have you gotten anywhere with Rachel yet?"

"I've tucked her in at night. I've massaged her legs. We've talked about intimate things."

"Have you tried for more?"

"I think Rachel's different, but I don't really like to make the first move. It's better to let them do it."

"Why hasn't she?"

"I want to say it's because we're friends and that she is afraid of being more vulnerable with me because I know her well enough to hurt her, but I guess most of me assumes it's because I'm overweight. Or broke."

"Bull, bull, and bull. You know why you haven't already had sex and been passed along for the next *hom du jour*, as you call it?"

"No, Doctor. Why?"

"Because you haven't tried. You share the same screwed up personality deficit. You both want other people to make the first move to validate you, and neither of you really cares enough to risk making the move yourself. She'd say yes to you—it's part of the trade she offers guys. It's the same trade you make when you sit there being all nice until a woman makes the first move. She strikes her pose and asks, like all women seem to, 'Am I pretty?' and you strike your pose, usually on your knees with your lips on her butt, and ask with your super nice high-pitched voice, 'Am I nice? Am I insightful? Am I trustworthy and loyal and unthreatening enough that you're willing to use me for a cheap moment of escape?' And you sound just like every guy trained in the talk show generation."

"Shit, Jon. That's pretty harsh."

"Yeah, maybe. And about your being overweight—that's your built-in excuse, not a real reason. You've seen plenty of couples where you've been like 'What the hell is she thinking? She's way more attractive than he is.' I say there are three reasons for that pairing. The first is that they're like you and Rachel, except he cared enough to make the move and she was tired of moving from guy to guy. The second reason is when she's into remodeling men and thinks she can change him. And the third time you see couples like that is when he's man enough to be authentic and let his strength lift her from her stupid-ass fixation on the 'am I pretty?' question. You look the way you do because you've learned it's the best shorthand way to invite women into the nice guy game you play. Rachel's irresponsible and mean, even though she's plenty smart, because she's determined to offer nothing but her looks and perkiness for men to find attractive. You're birds of a feather—or magnets with the same charge, more like it—and like magnets with the same charge, your similarities are exactly what will always create the distance between you. I can tell you now that you may as well walk away because nothing is ever going to happen between you because neither of you, for all of your reciprocal masturbatory compliments, really gives a crap about the other person."

"I don't know, Jon. I have strong feelings —"

"And yet you were with Betsy last night, just for kicks. A cheap compliment that you feel dirty about today. You've chosen the nice guy route because it seems like there's less responsibility with it—less pressure for you to get it right, with fewer people to hurt, except yourself."

"No way. There's far more responsibility dealing with someone's heart than with their ass."

"Don't you believe it—their ass is just as tied into their pain as any secret they ever share with you."

"No, Jon, you're wrong there."

"So you'd rather have somebody be attracted to you for your body than for your heart or mind, since it would be safer?"

"I think it would be far easier, yes. But I'd rather have someone be attracted to me for what's inside than what's outside."

"Again, there is no distinction between them—you're both. But here's a question for you —"

"Okay."

"Have you ever had someone come after you because of the way you looked?"

"There were girls in high school, and I lost my virginity to a girl in college named Melissa."

"What did you weigh then?"

"A buck 80, maybe 200."

"Any reason to hide from future experiences like you had with them?"

I pause, and the pain and anger and sense of failure with Melissa, and the feeling like I was taking advantage of the girls in high school, catches up with me. After maybe a minute I answer, "Yeah."

"Hey, sorry I pushed. Sometimes I work too hard to make a point that doesn't really need to be made." And I can tell he really feels torn up about my response.

"No big deal. Good thoughts." I respond. "How about another Mountain Dew?"

23.

Dipshits and Ping-Pong

Jon and I have decided to find a place together, but in the meantime I've been staying with David and Danielle—on the futon in the living room of their seminary campus apartment. My mom couldn't believe a couple who have only been married a year and a half, living in close quarters on a shoestring budget, would have me stay with them. I guess there have been times when it feels odd, like in the morning when Danielle passes through the living room on her way to her teaching job, or when any of us have to use the bathroom at night—especially after our respective nocturnal episodes. And while I don't have much stuff, it seems like it's never all quite cleaned up, and even though I put the bedding away every morning, the futon looks pretty well slept on. The other day David and I were wrestling while Danielle was at work and we broke the pin that locks the futon in place. We found a one-inch dowel to replace it, but we didn't have any tools to cut it to length. It happened to exactly fit the width of the frame of the front door, so we braced it there and I stood on the motel style balcony outside and did a back kick to break it. The piece just missed David and stuck in the wall about five feet high, in exactly the first place a person would see as they walked into Danielle's apartment. We hung a picture over the hole, made some macaroni and cheese, and turned on the afternoon cartoons.

David and Danielle fight a lot. I guess that's part of getting used to each other, but there are times when Danielle seems uptight. We learned quickly that if we're around when she gets home, we had better not still be watching cartoons, and the dishes had better be washed. One afternoon David and I absolutely scrubbed the place down (we were both janitors in high school and know what we're doing) just to see what Danielle would find to be upset about when she came home from work. We grinned over that day's macaroni and cheese in front of *Animaniacs* as we watched her drop her things and look around the house. Eventually she opened the front closet and emptied it to reorganize the games and stuff. We started laughing and said we couldn't win—that no matter how well we cleaned she'd find something that had to be done and something by which to be frustrated. Danielle called David into their room and they had one of their long talks, and then he and I went for a drive.

There is no way Danielle would have even talked to David in high school.

She was the homecoming queen and is both beautiful and a delight to be with. She's far more socially savvy than either of us, with a lot more experience and an uncanny insight into emotions and heart stuff. Sometimes I think she's skewed too far that way, that she's too emotional and too governed by her feelings, but it seems like for as much of a roller coaster ride as her emotions take her on, she's usually right, and pretty much right away. David, on the other hand, was the tall soccer player whose greatest high school joy was shifting gears in his car without using the clutch. Power-shifting, he called it, and until the transmission on the Honda went out, it was really cool. He was famous for his booming fake laugh and being the most mature kid in youth group, all elbows and Adam's apple.

They're not like what Jon said about Rachel and me, as far as I can tell. I don't see David's posture towards Danielle being one of subservience or some continuous recognition that she could have "done better" or something. I don't know how he was with other women because he never had a girlfriend in high school and I haven't been around him much since, but if he and Danielle started out more like Rachel and me, at some point he definitely cared enough to make his move, and that changed things. He's not offering himself up for beatings or bowing down at her feet like Jon pointed out in me. I think he's just trying to figure out what in the world he has to do to make his wife happy. I think that even though he knows it's ultimately impossible, he's willing to try anything to please or console her. Sometimes I wonder if knowing that he's paying whatever price he can find to pay, and knowing that it can't ever really work, doesn't feed into Danielle's frustration; David can't make her feel better. And maybe after so long thinking her husband would be some knight who would make everything okay, I wonder if she doesn't feel a little betrayed or scared about the whole thing.

There's this, too. Besides the newly married thing, and besides having David's big, needy friend from high school living on the couch, and besides living on a teacher's salary while David studies and often seems to be on vacation, they're living in two distinct worlds. Danielle is surrounded by a life that is actually happening; there are kids and parent teacher conferences and union issues and paychecks and bills and a new relationship to forge and all of the stuff that must make all newlyweds panic about what they've gotten themselves into, plus all of the unknowns about what they'll do when David finishes school, and how far that could take them from her parents. Real world stuff. But David's in seminary, which means that life is sort of suspended for a while yet while he earns his degree. And even though life is still happening around him, David is completely seeped in a world of hypotheticals and principles and is much more in touch with the driver's manual than he is with the steering wheel. They get into an argument and David is thinking about the psychological diagnosis for what's happening, or the doctrinal obligations or principles behind what's happening, and all Danielle is trying to do is express how frustrating it is to leave for work before we're out of bed, only to come home to Dipshits 1 and 2 eating macaroni and cheese with their shoes on the sofa.

I've heard people say someone is "so heavenly-minded they're of no earthly good." I guess that's part of where David's at right now. And I know that I am, too. And I sort of like the comfort of being able to bring intellectual constructs into relational moments to defend my obnoxiousness with doctrinal theorems and formulas. Part of what the Bible calls for is the renewing of our minds. I think this is part of the journey—that there are times when we are in a learning mode, and that makes us pretty clumsy.

In high school David and I played ping-pong in each other's basements a lot. I was okay, and we split games pretty evenly. Then I decided I wanted to learn to spin the ball. I'd play David or anyone else and all I'd focus on was learning the spins. I lost almost every game. But over time I learned to control these killer shots, and pretty soon I was nearly unbeatable. David quickly caught up with his own spin abilities, and we went back to splitting games, but either of us would crush anyone else we played. I think something similar happens in seminary, with David or with Rachel or with me or with Mindy who went home to Minnesota. In fact, I think the same thing happens in any Christian during certain phases of their growth. Usually they're the people who show up on television protesting this or boycotting that, or they're the crazy passive-aggressively aunt who sends dopey Christian gift books to family members in hopes of getting them "saved." We drop a lot of games because we're learning a better way of playing the game, and as we learn it maybe we raise the game of the people around us. I don't think we're very good at admitting that's what's happening at the time, but I hope that's the end result of our awkward phases.

I suppose the danger is that we won't outgrow them. The other day I came across something of Annie Dillard's where she quotes Dionysius, an idea hound who heard the apostle Paul talk about Jesus and decided to believe. She has him say, "You must abandon everything: God despises ideas." This doesn't mean that God hates thinking; it means that God's bigger than the conclusions from which we form our idols, and that we had better be sure not to choose the neat-o parts of experiencing God or theology over the One we're experiencing—the *Theo* behind the *ology*. Pascal says, "Reason's last step is the recognition that there are an infinite number of things which are beyond it. It is merely feeble if it does not go as far as to realize that." When I consider the reaches of space or things like string theory, or even the volumes and volumes of psychology texts, which cover a subject of a more human scale, it's obvious that we don't know it all, nor can we. Pascal continues, "If natural things are beyond it, what are we to say about supernatural things?" God is our Lord, our master, our maker and the one who holds together each molecule of our universe by constant choice. God is not our bitch. And in the end the marching orders we've been given are very simple and straightforward: Love the Lord your God with all your heart, all your soul, all your mind, and with all your strength, and love your neighbor as yourself. If a person's clumsy phases or spin techniques don't eventually dump them back to that simple edict, what stands before them is an idol and an enemy of the One you absolutely don't want to be allied against. I don't see how extremists or radical fundamentalists have anything but a tight grip on a love of their ideas—everything about God points a follower back to the world, back to people, back to their neighbor. And back to their schoolteacher wives or the schoolteacher wife who endures my overstayed welcome on the futon. It's a horribly difficult balance, and must be one of the core reasons God extends mercy in the world. But it's still a critical one to get right. Tremendous men of God, beware.

24.

As Honest as the Moment Is

For all of my concerns about the culture of Christian heroism, I still very much want to be a holy man. So I'm doing what it seems like a holy man would do. I pray and I study and I go to church, and I've taken a job as the pastor's assistant at Agape Christian Church in Five Points, which is where I used to go in hopes of getting shot. I'm the only White guy for a couple of blocks, and when I get off the light rail I pass crack dealers and prostitutes and homeless people—some of whom I've gotten to know by name. I've been learning a lot about racial reconciliation and about how it takes Black women longer to dry their hair and how urban people really don't want to be White suburbanites. In Indianapolis I always pictured the inner city as a sort of fenced-in free for all zone like I'd seen in movies about life after nuclear war, or after the robots took over. I assumed there was nothing I could do to make a difference downtown, and for the most part that was fine with me because I also believed that poor people were poor because they lacked the character to pull themselves up by their bootstraps, whatever those are, and it seemed like they'd stay poor only until they decided being poor sucked enough to stop being poor. I knew Zionsville was insulated and anomalous, but I didn't realize how far from the real world it is. Zionsville, and really the bulk of the khaki and denim shirt White world, is in touch with reality the way any other fanatic with an idea, an ideal and an idol is in touch with reality.

I have a guide through all of this, for whom I am grateful. His name is Tony and we met at seminary. His mother is White and his father was Black, which is true of his wife as well. Tony is a year older than I am and is the associate pastor for a White church in Boulder. He also does a fair amount of preaching in Black churches around town, and it's happened more than once that I've attended those services and been asked, as a visitor, to stand up and introduce myself so the congregation can welcome me. I always say, "I go wherever I can still hear Tony preach for free," and everyone laughs and he looks good. Tony is also paid to spend a portion of his time at Agape, and we do quite a bit together.

The church building was built by a German congregation in 1892, and its steeple is visible for some distance. Only about 20 people attend services on Sunday, but maybe 150 come for a hot meal every Saturday afternoon, and about the same come to the food bank on Wednesdays. The house behind the church has been turned into a community center, where people come for bus passes or clothing for job interviews, or for help with things like a temporary mailing address, or to connect with other ministry help elsewhere. Pastor Woolfolk is the man over all of it, and I ask Tony a lot of questions about the way he works. The Agape complex is all donated, and most of that is drawn out in this strange dance of White guilt and a laughing, shuffling performance from Woolfolk. Oh, that laugh though. It starts with a rasp like Ernie from Sesame Street, and then bounces its way louder with these coarse hooting sounds that lift his shoulders up to his ears as though the joy he's sharing with his companion is far more precious than the work that surrounds them. He creates something like a foxhole humor with it, where joy will not be scared off by the taxation of struggle and toil and despair at hand. And I suppose that is the truth of it; there really is good news to talk about even in the broken lives that pass through the church all the time. Pastor Woolfolk laughs like that easily, with anyone, but there is something different about the way he does it with a White person dropping off a box of food or something. I can't tell if it's a remnant from a time where submission was expected, or what it is.

"Is he putting on an act to keep the donations coming?" I ask Tony over an out of season plastic cup of donated Eggnog in the dining hall. "Is he that savvy and that willing to do what it takes to bring the best results for the people he serves?"

"What if he is?"

"That would suck. He's either not being respectful of himself, or he's being horribly usury of the donors. And it would mean that he's perpetuating several kinds of horrible stereotypes and roles."

"Whose fault is it if that works?"

"I think blaming White people for being clumsy in their efforts to help and making fools of them by playing a false role makes the gap between Black and White that much greater, don't you?"

Tony is staring absently at the Eggnog carton. "What is nog anyway?"

"It's eggs, and cream, and sugar —"

"But what's nog?"

I decide to play back. "You really don't know?"

"No."

"Well, I guess that's because you didn't grow up near farms. Eggnog is a German drink they serve around Christmas because that's when they also make sausage."

"Huh?"

"You know that sausage wrappers are really cleaned out intestines that are stuffed with meat, right?"

"Yeah."

"Nog is the yellow mucus lining they roll out of the intestines when they prepare them for stuffing." I show him the rolling action with my hands.

He squints at me, his lips coming apart slightly and curling down at the corners.

"Tony, I don't know what the heck nog is." I say, laughing. "Tell me about the thing with Pastor and lying to White people."

"I wouldn't say he's lying."

"He's not being honest."

"He's being as honest as the moment is."

"What's dishonest about wanting to help people?"

"Nothing, if that's what it really is."

"Oh geez." I say, feigning exhaustion. "Is this another complaint about the handout not being warm enough?"

"Beggars can't be choosers, right?" He tips his plastic cup at me, nodding a salute.

"When it comes down it to, that's exactly right." I respond, Republican sensibilities shining through. I can back this up Scripturally, too.

"And that's the gap in the moment. That's the piece that Woolfolk is being courteous about. He's interacting with people in a way that matches their side of the deal."

"What's the gap in the moment? What's he being courteous about?" I'm pivoting my thumbs up like I don't get what makes him think he just scored a point.

"When someone comes here to give to someone they call 'brother' because they're both Christians, the claim is that something better than throwing scraps to beggars is being done. Woolfolk is not a beggar; he's being called 'brother.' And the people Woolfolk helps are called brother too, even if Woolfolk is the proxy for that brotherhood. The gap comes because stereotypical White people don't know the difference between helping a brother and helping a beggar—all need is weakness, and stereotypical White Christians get real uncomfortable around weakness. Woolfolk's willing to work with that discomfort. He thanks people in a way that makes them feel like they contributed something important, and he invites them back. It's the opposite of complaining that the handout isn't warm enough. It's recognizing that some people need the comfort of making sure the handout is cold to maintain a sense of distance from the weakness they perceive. He's not trying to change the attitudes of the people who donate; he's meeting them where they're at."

"But doesn't he have some obligation to do just that—to change the way donors see what they're doing." I take a sip of eggnog, "If what they're doing is really wrong, that is."

Tony knows this ground better than I do. "No. He has an obligation to make a choice about how he'll respond to being put in the role of beggar. Will he take what's being offered, or not? That's the way beggars are choosers. The person doing their drive-by good deed isn't asking what he needs; they're saying, 'here, take this.'"

This is frustrating for me. "Aren't the people who help just doing what they've been asked to do? It's not like they just spontaneously decided to bring groceries to some church downtown without knowing about the church and the programs here."

"Actually, sometimes that's exactly what happens. But you're right, most of the time people come because that's what their church has told them about the needs here. With some churches, that's all Woolfolk tells them about. But you've been here a few weeks now, do you think more than food bank donations are needed?"

"Sure. Though I don't think there's enough of a structure to make good use of volunteers for much else."

Tony points at me with a quick gun gesture, "Exactly. How do you communicate real needs through impersonal structures? It's hard to tell a suburban church, 'We need you to come down and meet some people and see what stirs in your heart. It will likely end up taking more time from your schedule than you were planning, and it may even be enough to upset large portions of your world. And while we can provide the introductions and give you some guidance as you go, we're not set up for you to just come in and volunteer for a couple of hours and then head back to suburbia.' That's too brother, not enough beggar. Beggars say, 'I need a dime.' They offer a binary yes or no opportunity to help. A brother says, 'I feel something's not right in my world.' It's messier, and many times there are no answers, and what matters is who's willing to spend their time sitting beside that brother. If someone who would be a healthy influence doesn't spend the time, there are always unhealthy people willing to hang out. The people who do their drive-by Christian duty are looking to do a good deed, to do something that absolves them of a sense of obligation, and Woolfolk is willing to be friendly and say 'Thank you for the food. Please come back.'"

"You say that a lot of the time there aren't answers, Tony, but isn't that mostly a cop-out for people who don't want to take the common sense steps they need to take to improve their lives? I mean, I see new coats on kids in the projects, or big TVs with cable there. Or all of the young single mothers who go out and leave their kids at home while they go out partying, and end up with more kids. Those are common sense things—obvious answers. It's not like poverty is some mystery."

"There's a story where Jesus is near Jericho and a blind beggar hears it's Jesus passing by. He yells out, 'Son of David, have mercy on me!' So Jesus has the man brought to him in the crowd, and what do you think he does with the blind beggar next?"

I nod for him to get on with the story and say, "He restores the man's sight, of course."

"No. He asks, 'What do you want me to do for you?'"

"Yeah, and then he heals the guy."

"The beggar. He does heal him, but first he asks. It's entirely possible that the beggar could have said, 'I've been blind my whole life, and I get around fine. What I'm worried about is my bad leg, my sick wife, and my son who's been taken into slavery. Can you help with those things?' You're right that there are some simple changes people can make to change a great deal about their lives, but there is a critical difference between the way we treat beggars and the way we treat brothers. The difference between beggar and brother is asking the question."

"But you just said that all Woolfolk tells some churches about is the food bank type stuff. When someone asks what he needs, isn't that like what Jesus asked? Isn't a suburban church asking what they can do to help the same thing? Isn't that the moment when they prove that they want Woolfolk to be brother instead of beggar? Isn't it up to Woolfolk to give the real answer then?"

"Here's where things get even more complicated. For some churches, he does tell them about what he'd really like to see. He'll tell them about more long-term relationship stuff. And most of the time the pastor who's asking the question will say that's more than his congregation is likely to be willing to jump into, so they're left with the lowest common denominator stuff like serving food at the community meal or dropping off donations. Other pastors ask the question, but aren't really asking the question. They're mostly interested in adding to the list of good deed things and good idea partners their church has, and they're looking for a binary sort of help to toss Woolfolk's way, and they don't see much value in the relationship beyond what they can bring downtown. And it's a hard thing to know which pastor is which, and it's a rare thing to have someone be willing to come down here and sit and learn. I'm sure there are times when Woolfolk doesn't give the real answer because he doesn't feel optimistic about the response that will come."

"So he goes with what people assume he'll need because that's the way donors are used to helping."

"Yeah. And he needs food for the food bank."

25.

A List of One Item

"You have such beautiful hair. Don't you think his hair is beautiful, Sister Hazel?" I'm at the community center behind Agape Christian Church, and the center's director, a middle-aged Black woman with long fingernails and cigarette breath has her hands, both hands, in my hair. "It's so soft and so fine."

Sister Hazel responds, "It sure is, Miss Gladys."

"I wish my hair was like this." Miss Gladys gushes.

I finish making photocopies and head back over to the church office. I feel odd. I don't want to stand out. I don't want to have one more thing that a Black person does not. I look around at the world down here and I see so much that makes me ashamed of the world I'm from. I see people enduring each other's pain, finding room enough for it to be matter of fact, as pain and failure truly are. I see genuine warmth and honest sacrifice. I see older women taking in foster children and carefully parenting them. I see grown women call each other "Sister" and "Miss," and I feel the respect that comes with that. I watch the way people who come to the hot meal or to the food bank or to the community center are legitimately grateful for the service they receive. There's a ministry down the street where a man, a white guy with a long beard that inspired me to grow the one that has bushed out red and curly, opens a storefront coffeehouse at 5:00 in the morning because the liquor stores open at 6:00 and he wants to give the homeless alcoholics a place to choose mercy on whichever morning the desire for sobriety finally grabs them. That man keeps the alley behind his storefront swept and clean because he knows the men he serves sleep there. A couple of nights ago one uninitiated homeless man shattered a bottle against the wall and the other homeless men beat him up for it, and then made him clean up the space to show a little respect. I've been at lunch down the street and seen Crips, gang members in their blue kerchiefs, take the kerchiefs off of their heads to pray before they eat. There is something about the pain and the hardship in the world down here that makes it so sweet, so rich, and I don't want to have anything to do with holding up Zionsville or soft blonde hair as something to be envied. I know it's an over-statement to say that something, anything, about the way I'm living, earning less than my rent and eating from the food bank, sells suburbia or will make people down here feel badly about their lot, but there is something in me that wants to be rid of my own connections to my escape route, to the duality I feel.

There is a knock on the front door of the church, which remains closed and locked when there are not services going on. Pastor Woolfolk looks up from his papers and I answer the door. There is a filthy White guy in his 40s standing there.

"How you doing?" I ask him.

"Not so good, not so good. It's supposed to snow tonight, and I'm trying to scrape together some cash to get indoors. Can you help me out?"

He's lying.

"Sorry," I say, "but we don't give cash. I can make sure there's room for you at the shelter if you want, and I can hook you up with a bus pass."

"No, that's okay. But hey, can I get a couple of bucks from you to buy some food?"

He's still lying. He wants the cash so he can buy something to get high.

"I have a token to get me home," I tell him, "and that's all I've got on me. But we do have some food in the pantry and I'd be happy to grab some for you."

"No thanks." He's ready to walk away.

"Tell you what I will do, though." I say. "I'll make you a trade."

"For what?"

"All you've got are those beat up sneakers with holes in them?"

"Yeah."

"That's going to suck when it snows."

"Yeah."

"I'll trade you these new boots for your shoes."

"Yeah, okay. Sure." And he starts slipping them off. He knows not to ask if there's a catch. Maybe he doesn't care. Maybe he knows there isn't one. I untie my boots and we hand each other our footwear.

"Hey, these are nice." He says.

"Good. And they'll be warm. Sorry I couldn't help with the money, but I hope you'll come back if there's anything else you need. You know about the meal on Saturday, right?"

"Yeah. Hey, man, thanks." He offers his hand and we shake hands, White style. I close the door and return to the office, dropping his shoes in the trash.

"What was that?" Pastor Woolfolk asks.

"Just helping a brother out." I reply.

"With your shoes?" He asks.

"It's what he needed." I respond. Pastor Woolfolk grunts a little and returns to his work. So do I, and nothing more is said.

The workday ends in the late afternoon and I lock the door as I leave, coat collar up to my ears. I walk the three blocks to the light rail, watching the ground for glass or needles, but don't encounter any to avoid. People at the rail stop look at me curiously, noticing my socks. The light rail takes me to the transfer station near the college where I catch my bus. People notice again. And I start thinking about how we go through our lives with a certain list of traits or comebacks or whatever that we rely upon to tell us, or others if need be, why we're good enough to be in a certain situation. I usually notice the dynamic when I walk into a physician's waiting room, where other people are already waiting, and it seems obvious that the first thing people try to figure out is what each other's illnesses are. When I walk into those sorts of situations I find myself reviewing a list of things like, "I'm smart. I'm educated. I have some money. I'm kind. I know some martial arts in case I have to fight." Sitting on the bus it occurs to me that all of that is wiped away in strangers' eyes by the fact that I don't have any shoes on. For the first time I see how truly silly every item on my list of qualifications is, how easily they can all be wiped away.

We get to my stop, and people watch me as I disembark. There is glass on the sidewalk in front of the lots next door to my condo, and I tread carefully. And then I stop. The mountains are already white with the snow that's coming, but there is a break in the clouds and the sky is a beautiful red and yellow and purple smear. I have only one qualification, and it's the one I forget about almost as soon as I remember it, when I do remember it. I have no claim to worthiness, on a bus or at a community center, or anyplace else, but the fact that instead of the bottomless well of my sin, I have the love of Jesus, who says I'm okay, who makes me okay. I have only Jesus to excuse me or to make me worth knowing. Everything else is just silliness. I stand and sing quietly to the sunset:

Praise God from whom all blessings flow. Praise him all creatures here below. Praise him above thee Heavenly host. Praise Father, Son and Holy Ghost.

Then I pick my way through the only glass I've encountered since I left the church in the ghetto, this glass here in the suburbs. When I get inside I think about my day, from Miss Gladys and her cigarette breath to the reminder that my identity must, must come from Jesus because nothing else will ever be sturdy enough to trust. I think about how readily I forget that fact. I want to be forced to remember. I want something that will feel sort of like what it felt like to have people see me with no shoes and wonder about what had happened to me.

Half an hour later I'm a fat young White guy with a bushy red beard, and a shaved head to remind me who I am. And whose.

26.

Chocolate, Bible Study & Blowjobs

Jon and I have been going to a cool church downtown—a place I attended while I was in school because the last thing I needed on Sunday was another lecture. Pastor Woolfolk has no problem with my not attending his church on Sundays, so long as I'm on time the rest of the week. I chose the place because the music was good, the dress was extremely casual—even interspersed with a good number of homeless people—and because they were doing "real" ministry, as stereotypically evidenced by walls covered with flags from around the world, each representing a place where they sponsored missionaries. Beyond such clichés, they prayed a lot, did late night sidewalk evangelism where they stopped people on the street and asked them about Jesus, had a food bank and a clothing bank, and the leadership participated in a great many inter-church boards, where they were both the recipients of suburban giving and the White voice from downtown.

What I hadn't seen until Jon and I showed up together was that there is also a large group of people, maybe forty or fifty, who are about our age and place in life, and who meet in what's called the "college and career" class. It's a lame name, but several of the girls are very good looking, so when we were invited to attend a home Bible study, we shrugged and accepted.

The group meets in the upstairs apartment of an old house across the street from Curtis Park, which is a part of town where White people often get profiled and stopped at night because the police assume the only reason a White person would be in the area after dark is to buy drugs or pick up prostitutes. Our first visit started off about the way such events always go; cookies and chips in bags, ice from the store, two-liter bottles of soda to be poured into plastic cups and carried into the mismatched living room of futons, poster art, a television on a crate, and the obligatory single plant fighting for survival in the corner near the drafty window. Jon got a seat on a futon, and I ended up on the floor, shifting my weight as my ass and legs fell asleep.

The people were friendly. The church is big on growth and inviting new people, and Jon's good looks and interesting way of talking brought him attention. I got the double effort; the normal one that strangers extend unattractive strangers, plus the added quick-nodding cheerleaderish enthusiasm that nice people offer someone whose harder-to-categorize bald head and beard make him look like the photo negative of Gordon from Sesame Street. After some mingling, the host, Twan, a guitar-playing struggling actor a few years older than everyone else, prayed to officially open the evening. Then he asked the icebreaker question.

"Tonight we're going to talk about temptation. The Bible says that Jesus was faced with all of the temptations we know, and because he experienced them, he is able to be a better, more understanding judge of what our lives are like. I thought maybe we could go around the room and each share what our own biggest temptations are, and then move into the study."

If I've ever experienced a perfect example of the absolute loss of contact with the real world that exists in much of the Church today, it was in Twan's question. Our biggest temptations? As an icebreaker? In a quick trip around a circle on futons over Safeway grape soda and Chips Ahoy? I sighed. I knew how this was going to go.

Joanie was first, because Twan gestured for her to start.

"I guess it's probably procrastinating."

"Ooo. Good one." Becky said.

"That was mine." Kathy echoed. "I'm so bad about that."

"What about you, Kirk?" Twan continued.

"I think TV takes a lot of my life." He replied. There were nods.

Crissy, the bubbly, granola Meg Ryan-esque nurse who wears her blue hospital scrubs at all times, was next.

"Chocolate. Absolutely chocolate."

That was Loma's, too, though she didn't say so to the group. She turned to Joanie the Procrastinator and their body language made clear the jealousy and bitterness between the two heavier girls towards Crissy and the attention she got from the men in the group. The men, to Loma's point, responded to Crissy with things like:

[Kirk] "If that's your sin, it sure doesn't show."

[Twan] "Better be careful—someone could use that against you." Wink.

[Robert] "You know, chocolate's an aphrodisiac."

And as soon as he'd said that, Robert, who looks like Niles from the show *Frasier*, skinny with thinning blonde hair and the careful walk of a clarinet player in a marching band, shrunk back a little. He's obviously not the sort to say such things. Jon and I may have been the only people in the room to catch what he said, but when he said it we looked at each other and smiled. We've been friends since that first evening.

The next person in the circle was Pamela, a dark haired Swiss woman who looks and dresses like a slender single mother in love with a rock star. In fact, she is a single mother, to a three-year-old, and her ex-husband is in jail for something to do with cocaine. Twan scraped his eyes off of Crissy to turn the question about temptation to Pamela.

"What about you?" he asked.

"I think you are all full of crap," she said. "I like chocolate, and I would watch too much television if I could, but the truth is that what we really want is to be screwing."

There were guffaws and squeals and gasps and furrowed brows everywhere. But she continued.

"I want chocolate, but I want it melted and licked off of me. And so do all of you. Maybe in front of the television. And Joanie, even you wouldn't put that off until tomorrow."

Twan was desperate to regain control of the moment. "Well, I'd say the ice is sufficiently broken!" And he steered the discussion to the notes he'd printed out. As we filed out at the end of the evening, he pulled Pamela aside and told her that he understood it was also her first time to the study, but that her answer had been inappropriate, especially in mixed company.

I'd say that's Christian culture in a nutshell. We have this Bible that tells these horrible stories about sin and depravity and temptation and addictions that overwhelm people, even to death. And we have this God who loves us and mourns for our suffering and yearns to clean us up, set us free, and draw us to him—and not necessarily in that order. And we have Jesus who sought out and spent his time hanging with people who laughed too loudly, who were surely a bit rough around the edges, and who were very often absolutely buried in inappropriate behaviors and lifestyles. Jesus preferred them because they were not the religious "whitewashed tombs," painted and clean on the outside, but dead and reeking on the inside. Christianity has this entire worldview that treats the filth of life as matter of fact, and as impermanent, redeemable, escapable, unable to make the bride too filthy to be loved. But we have this thing in our culture where we don't believe a bit of it. We work so overly hard to make God look good that what we say has no credibility at all; we lie about him all the time. We're such dicks. In our insecurities and arrogance, and our lack of honesty, we demand to see God turn lives around, to do something cool for us. To be our bitch. We want to be able to tell a great story about how well our lives have been transformed by a God who, to our exquisite torture, simply does not do enough flashy stuff for us to let his work stand on its own. We are so desperate to share the good news that we almost always fake it. We forge the miraculous and we promise more than we really experience ourselves. And we are so conflicted about how to be "good Christians"—people whose lives have been turned around and made squeaky clean—even though that's not what we experience exactly, that we have developed a twisted, white-knuckle culture where we are far less matter of fact about sin and temptation and doubt and the profane than are our scriptures, our God, or even the rest of the world around us, where there is no promise of rescue or redemption. We're obnoxious fools, and our dishonesty makes us incredibly vulnerable and weak, and far from trustworthy to people who could actually benefit from knowing the truth according to God.

While it's a frustrating reality for me, I don't think it would be a good idea to abandon the church or these friends. But there are sure a lot of bullshit rules to watch out for. There's no way I'd be able to tell "good Christians" about my life in any sort of real terms, and mine has been exceedingly tame and safe—I can only imagine how people with darker closets must feel. I'd have to make veiled references, using terms that demonstrated that my sins had passed through the evangelical autoclave and been sterilized. It would be important that I didn't use any of the naughty words, and that every evidence of past evil wore a nice pink bow of present righteousness. I'd hear about the passage in James that talks about coarse talk and how fresh water and salt water cannot flow in the same stream, or about Ephesians where Paul writes that it's shame to even speak of the sins people do in darkness. But shit, I'm not interested in being tied up or defined by my sins. I'm not looking to be a hero for them. I don't even want to hold onto them. But certainly there must be some way for me to make sense of them, to learn what is true in the face of the pain and confusion and lack of control I've known. Isn't there? And I can think of dozens of really nasty stories in the Bible, about a woman driving a tent spike through a man's head into the ground, or about a king—a man "after the Lord's own heart," no less—who sees a woman bathing and sends her husband to certain death so the king can cover up the fact that he's already started sleeping with her, or about Jesus taking and eating wheat from another man's field on the Sabbath, when all of the good religious people were scandalized by such forbidden behavior. Beyond those are a whole assortment of stories about rape, incest, adultery, idolatry, murder, everything. If there is a point to the experiences in the Bible, if those stories mean something when held up to the light of God, why wouldn't it make sense for me, or anyone else, to do the same?

I think Pamela was just fine saying what she did at the Bible study. In fact, if there was a problem, it was treading so naively on such sacred ground. If you're going to wander where the cows graze, you're going to step in shit.

And as grazing cows go, the group of friends Jon and I have developed is pretty great. It's a group tortured by a time in life where it's hard to tell the difference between real dramas, like when Kirk's wife of one year divorced him because he wasn't macho enough, or Pamela's experience with her ex-husband, and the petty dramas of romance or social snub that Loma and Crissy seem so keen on acting out to keep clear of the harder stuff, but it's a great group nevertheless. Some portion of the group is always doing something together, and that's become the bulk of my social world. It's nice to have a place to go when the tensions of work or poverty start to get away from me; a place where I can talk about why I'm doing what I'm doing, and have people mostly understand.

27.

Tale of the Pink Toy Bitch

It's an unseasonably warm November afternoon, and skinny Robert has taken the afternoon off to join me for a community reclamation project pastor Tony and I have been doing with the people around Agape Christian Church. The two of us arrived early, and are waiting in the warm grass enjoying the day. Sonny Lawson Park takes up a full block, with a softball field, a basketball court, and a picnic area where the people from the Catholic Worker house go to meditate. Across the street is a burger place called Brown Sugar's Burgers and Bones, which is run by a Black man named George who refuses to speak to me—not even to thank me after the time I changed the fluorescent lights in the men's room. I've always assumed it's because I'm White. Could be because I'm Christian. Could be he just doesn't like me for some other reason. In any case, Robert and I grabbed a late lunch from Brown Sugar's and crossed the street to eat in the Catholic meditation area a couple hundred feet from the basketball court. I'm drinking a cherry soda with my barbeque burger, and am still laughing at the enormous split sausage Robert is squeamishly working on.

"Look, I didn't think to ask why they'd call it a 'Cracked George,'" he says, "and your cackling isn't making it any better."

I jab my chin towards the restaurant for Robert to look, "Is that him in the window, laughing at you?"

"Shut up." He takes a bite, letting the sausage push his cheek out. And then with a full mouth, "George and I will not let you mock what we have."

It's a gorgeous day. Half of the guys playing basketball have removed their shirts. Robert and I are both wearing shorts and sandals. Tevas, not Birkenstocks. Big difference in Denver, and maybe no place else in the world. Tevas mean outdoors and activity; Birkenstocks are for hippies or church. Behind us, at the other end of the park by the softball bleachers, a few elementary aged kids watch as Eights, forever in his headphones and sports jerseys with the number 88 on them, sells the occasional crack rock. Five dollars or fifteen, depending, he told me when I asked one day, whether or not you'll suck his dick. There are a couple of prostitutes I've never met walking along Welton over our other shoulder. Across the street is the restaurant, and then Central Baptist, where the other day the pastor was beaten in his office by a group of Crips who were not at all pleased that he was helping one of their own change his life. The beating was big news around here, as nothing like that had happened before.

"So tell me again how this works." Robert asks, chewing.

"In a little while pastor Tony and some of the other people from the neighborhood will meet us here, and we'll light candles as the sun sets, and we'll spend an hour walking around the park singing civil rights songs so that the drug dealers will have to go elsewhere to do business for a while."

"So the idea is just to make it too much of a hassle for them to stay here?"

"That's part of it. The bigger effort has to do with people reclaiming their neighborhood—standing up for it and controlling what sort of place it becomes."

"And nothing's happened before? It seems like it would really piss off the bad guys."

"Nothing so far. Though the police have heard about it and they've started hanging around while we're here because they think it's a really dangerous idea. Did you see the car already parked over by the church?" I jut my chin past beyond the basketball court to the white cruiser parked there.

"Geez. This is pretty serious stuff, then, isn't it?"

"I don't know. It's exciting, that's for sure, but people do things like this in cities all across the country. It's not a new idea."

Then we both notice a commotion on the basketball court, and it's directed at us.

"What the fuck are you doing down here?" a muscular shirtless black man yells at us as he clamps the ball with both hands.

We don't respond.

The man slams the ball to the ground and starts walking double-time towards us. "You doing a little sight seeing? Down here to watch the poor niggers play ball?" He's coming hotly, with at least a dozen men right with him. Another 20 people pour off of the bleachers to come watch what sure looks to be a beating in the making.

Robert is on the far side of me, and both of us are now sitting with our knees drawn up, leaning back on our hands. Robert sits up to a cross-legged position. I'm too frightened to move, though I know fighting and fleeing are already out of the question; we wouldn't have a chance at either. For the first time the real prospect of being killed downtown crosses my mind, and I realize that something really did change that night in the desert; I have no desire to be killed. None at all.

The young man smacks his chest and throws his arms out wide as he takes the last few steps towards us, screaming about how we would be well served to utilize the tools of photography to capture our adventure among the impoverished indigenous population. I feel Robert absolutely seize up, and it occurs to me that he may cry. There is real threat, and we are in real danger. Mercy may not be a bad card to play. His wife left him a couple of years ago, and he has a young son to think about, if his own skin isn't enough. The man stops and stands over me, close enough to kick my feet. The sinews of his chest flicker up into his neck as he makes one final demand of me.

"What the fuck are you doing down here, you PINK TOY BITCH?" His arms are flung wide, splayed hands pointing downward. Crushing in upon him, and around us, several of his compatriots seem to pose a similar query.

I'm pretty sure this will only end when the policeman in the cruiser calls for backup and drives the block to our aid. I assume that if I cover up very well I may survive with some serious bruises and maybe a concussion. I got one in high school football, and was hoping not to experience it again. There is no possibility of winning this conflict. All I can think of is the truth.

"I work at the church around the corner, and we're meeting some people here to pray for the neighborhood." I respond, surprised by how collected I sound.

And the young baller pauses. He juts out his lower lip and raises his eyebrows, nodding. "Oh. Well. God bless you then." And he turns and leads the group away, a couple howling to us about how close we came to getting thrashed.

I watch them go, the adrenaline pulsing in my neck. I can't move. I look to the police cruiser, and for the first time realize it's unoccupied.

We spend the next ten minutes calming down. Robert has to walk around a bit. I suppose I'm a little more accustomed to the sense of eminent danger than he is, but I also overstate my comfort, telling him such moments are truly rare, and that the safest thing to be downtown is still a White person because while you may get grief about being an outsider, you'll never be confused for competition.

"Yeah, but those were just some ordinary people playing basketball in the park. How much worse will the reaction be when the drug dealers decide to fight back?" He asks.

"That's why it's so important to get the whole neighborhood involved." I reply. "The more people stand up, the harder it is to push them back down."

"So where are they now?" He asks. "And why are you part of getting them to stand up? You don't even live here."

"You'll see in a couple of minutes. And I'm only helping to organize their standing up. I'm just here to add to their numbers."

Right then Pastor Tony and a couple of people from the church arrive. We tell them about our experience. Both of my friends laugh hysterically when Robert tells Tony the part about my being called a Pink Toy Bitch. Pastor Tony is clearly proud of the respect shown the church by the basketball players, and he wanders over to the court to introduce himself around. We retell the experience to a couple of other people as they arrive.

"They wanted to know if we were sight seeing, just down here to see the poor Black people."

"It's not a bad question." A young Black man from our group says, staring steadily at us. We are both so taken aback that we say nothing, and the moment passes.

We light the candles and walk around the park, singing. The drug dealers and prostitutes amble away, and for an hour we do the good deed we came for. I don't know quite where to give credit for our not getting killed, or what to think about the basketball player, or the comment made by the young man from our group. Now that I think about it, I don't know what to say about exactly why we were there, either.

28.

Don't Know What to Say About Poverty

Here's what I've always thought. Poor people are poor because they make poor choices, meaning either bad choices or the immediate gratification choices of the poor. The family may be in jeopardy of having the electricity turned off, but there is a nice TV in the family room and at least one of the kids is wearing some name brand coat, or shoes with Michael Jordan on them. The hand that's trading food stamps for groceries seems to forever have a fancy manicure. Jobs are scarce, but there's always cash for cigarettes and alcohol. Birth control is somehow perceived by a single mother as more expensive than another baby. Being a deadbeat dad sleeping on the couch at a friend's house is no big deal so long as the pager stays on and a man can still get some action at the club. I've always thought poverty comes down to selfish, short-term choices made in the face of wiser options. And empirically I suppose this is true in many ways, but I grew up in a family with means and with a prudent approach to money and budgeting, and today I'm questioning if it's really true that poor choices are the same thing as weak choices. Could it be that sometimes they're self-affirming choices, albeit stolen and taxed heavily by consequence, but noble in their own way? There are times when even people who are being wise about their poverty reach the end of the patience and humility it takes to manage their suffering.

And it is suffering. In a world where having things and being able to do things is presented as the norm, and where so many people nearby have so many more resources, poverty in America comes with a very distinct and oppressive feeling of being a second-class citizen. And actually, poverty is pretty much how we distinguish between first- and second-class citizenship. We're not so concerned with worth, inherent though our Constitution may proclaim it; we measure people by economic utility. If you're net worth isn't worth much, neither are you. Certainly there are places in the world, pretty much every place else, actually, where poverty is far worse. But there are few places where the distinction in lifestyle between people with means and people without are as crisp and tightly spaced as they are here, and the feeling of self-denial that comes with being a good steward of poverty's wages is a huge, numbing weight that is very definitely a sort of suffering.

I've been good about it for the roughly 120 days I've been working at

PETE GALL

Agape—living on few dollars and food bank food. Granted, my type of poverty is a chosen one, and I can push the "No Thanks" button anytime I want and can return to the life from which I've come. I can go get the job, buy the house and car, and walk away. I've probably felt the suffering in a more acute way than people who grow up with it, but I've also felt it in a far more superficial and temporary way, and have certainly not experienced the soul-warping (or refining, depending on whom you ask) weight of chronic poverty. I've eaten the beans, rice and other donated food I've brought home from the Agape's food bank. I've even spent the couple of dollars it costs me to take the bus and train back to the church to get a hot Saturday lunch. When I gave away my boots, David and Danielle bought me new ones from their modest budget, and I felt selfish and silly for playing this poverty game and taking from them. I've felt the desire to be able to buy my own things, or to eat what I want. I've missed Chicago, where I could get a free meal just for working late, or where on more than one occasion I bought new clothes so I wouldn't have to do laundry. But there's a piece of me, a piece that has always allowed me an arm's length buffer zone of arrogant distance between myself and poor people and their poor choices, that I can feel crumbling. And frankly, it's terrifying; I don't want to be like...them.

This morning I woke up five days away from my next paycheck. In the meantime I have one cup of uncooked beans, one cup of uncooked rice, and just over four dollars to my name. I have no room on my credit cards, and once that bit of food and cash runs out, I'll either have to wait or beg for more. It was the first thing I thought of when I woke up, as I would assume it is often the first thing people with very little wake up considering. And I felt it more than I thought it. I felt like I was at the end of my options. I felt weak. I felt as though I had been foolish. I felt as though I deserved to be in crisis, because that is what I've always thought of people who were not heavily entrenched in Crown Ministries or some other stewardship system. Fortunately I'd already purchased my bus pass for the week, so I will get to work with no hit to my pocketbook. I'm standing in the aisle because there are no seats, and I think about my bald head under the mud cloth kufi I've started wearing. I consider my identity in Christ, and I remember that he is my provider, and I cannot forget how much worse things must be for people in real poverty. I pray for them, and I pray about my own stuff, both financially and emotionally. I thank God that he is pulling me through a challenging time and that I am learning something from the discomfort. We pass a billboard for Egg McMuffins and I tear up.

Mrs. Hamilton is at Agape Christian Church today. She's a stout older African-American woman whose first name is Eva. One time pastor Tony greeted her by her first name, and she responded with, "Pastor Tony, I call you Pastor Tony, and you'll call me Mrs. Hamilton." She's old school, the sort who will spank anybody's kids, no matter how old they are. She's lived most of her life in a neighborhood on the decline. She was widowed quite some time ago. But she's a pillar at the church, and she has two foster children with whom she seems to be doing a phenomenal job. The state subsidy that comes with the children makes up a significant portion of her budget, but the arrangement seems like a great solution for everyone concerned. I can't imagine that she'd even have the time of day for what I'm feeling, so I don't mention my own financial woes to her. She inspires me, makes me want to be strong, to be certain of myself without the external comforts of things I'd pursue with poor choices.

All morning I watch the people come and go. I watch the way the pastor has a special place of rank in the community. There's another pastor from elsewhere in the city who drives a bright green Rolls-Royce; for his people. When I first heard that last bit, I thought it was total crap, but what I've come to understand is that in some cultures, unlike the suburban White culture I'm from, the community can feel a certain camaraderie with the person who reaches highest among them. In the case of the Black pastor with the green Rolls-Royce, he represents the community's ability to drive the best, show up anywhere, and wield a certain voice and power that the people from within the community don't have on their own. In many ways he is their proxy, their emissary, their moderating priest in contact with the practical gods of power and privilege and progress. He is the Goliath in their army, the giant who can be sent out to fight to spare the lives of many others. And even with communities or churches where there is no Goliath, as at Agape Christian Church, there is a still a champion, a David, who is accorded a voice and a position of respect higher than that of the people. Champions are one of the few assets poor people have and can hope through that White people like myself simply cannot see, and disenfranchised White people suffer for not having.

Around lunchtime I wander over to the Nation of Islam store on Welton, hoping Brother Jay X will be there. Pastor Tony introduced me to him, and he's been far more courteous and even hospitable than I would have expected. I don't know how far his kindness would extend, and I don't suppose it would be offered at all if I showed up on my own and was in a different place in my life. I think he is good to me because I'm thinking and learning, and am seeing the flaws in the system and the heavy thumb of White culture. I'm something of a curiosity to him, and I stop by once or twice a week to visit briefly with whomever is there. I usually buy a grape soda and head out.

There is a hand-painted sign for bean pies in the window, and the public room of the tiny storefront is painted white and ringed by tables weighed down with Nation of Islam literature. Incense fills the air, and prayer rugs and different sorts of clothing for sale fill the small space. I remove my kufi as I enter. Brother Jay isn't in. Coretha is, with honey skin and a soft, somewhat vacant personality that I know has been shaped in my mind by the smoke that always rises in a wavering stream from the tip of the incense between us. She is draped in pale blue, though her dreamy black almond eyes offer me nothing of herself. Coretha has never been a fan of my presence. She is simply obedient to Brother Jay's choices and manages me with distance.

"*Assalamu 'alaykum.*" I say, which I was taught means "Peace be upon you." Actually, it means more than that. It really means "may you remain safe from every pain, sorrow, and distress," and the included word "*Salam*" is actually one of the words for Allah, so the peace or protection is designated as coming from Allah. I would not greet a Muslim in the Middle East this way, as my Christian standing makes it blasphemous for me to use the term, or so I've been taught. Brother Jay taught me to greet his people this way, though, so I do. At first I was hesitant because I'm neither Black nor Muslim, let alone Black Muslim. Then I was hesitant that I was greeting someone and offering peace to them in the name of a god who is not mine. Finally I came to the conclusion that I know which God I'm about, and I gauge the type of Islamic zeal I encounter in the people I meet based on their reply. My use of the greeting has opened doors for immediate and intimate discussions of faith and doctrine with several people, and now I do it on purpose.

"*Wa alaykum.*" Coretha replies. She does not include the "*Salam*" in her reply because she views me as a heretic, unworthy of respect. She has been taught that the only time she would use "*Salam*" with me, other than if I became a believer, would be if she needed something from me. Unlike some of the other people in the Nation of Islam, she has no interest in a purely Black faith, nor one that mixes a lot of Black Christianity with Islam. Frankly, I find her distinction and precision both admirable and a little sexy.

"How are you today, sister?" I ask her, casually selecting a small book on the truth about Jesus' mother from the table.

"I'm good. How are you?"

"Doing alright. Just taking a break from work. Do you mind if I sit and read for a bit?"

"You're welcome to stay as long as you like."

The book explains that Mary's father went out of town on business, and that Joseph snuck over one night and impregnated her. The story includes fake beards and costumes and the whole nine yards. The whole virgin birth thing was a story made up to save face. At one point Mary quotes Mohammad.

"Coretha?"

"Yes."

"Have you ever read this?"

"Of course."

"Do you buy what it's saying?"

"Yes."

"Do you know when Mohammad lived?"

"When?"

"Around 600 AD."

"So?"

"Do you know when Mary lived?"

"Tell me."

"About 600 years before that."

"So what's your point?"

"Well, how could Mary quote Mohammad if she lived 600 years before he did?"

"That's a lie of the White man."

I have no idea how to respond to this. "That's a pretty big one, 600 years."

"You don't really think the White man never lies, do you? Or that that's his biggest one?"

Pretty much the last thing I want to get into with Coretha is a long discussion about the honorable history of Europeans. But then I can't help myself.

"I think you'd be hard-pressed to find an Islamic scholar who would call the details of this story accurate, especially the part about Mohammad being someone Mary could have quoted. I think you'd end up with an Islamic scholar calling this a piece of cheap propaganda intended to mislead a gullible reading audience."

This is our first exchange of more than a couple of words, and certainly our first exchange where I wasn't completely deferential, and Coretha clearly doesn't care much for it.

"You gonna buy the book?"

"Of course not. When I buy fantasy, I like better drawings of the superheroes. And in color."

She laughs a little. She's letting the tension go. I can't tell if it's because she already knows the book is over the top, if it's because she doesn't really care if we agree, if her distain for me in general is greater than her willingness to engage, or if she really thinks the comic book reference was funny. "You gonna buy a grape soda?"

"I'd love a grape soda, sister, but I don't have the money."

"Jesus don't pay like he used to?" She's smiling now. She is so beautiful.

"He's not the one writing the checks, I'm afraid. I'm pretty much in this for the life insurance plan."

"Are you really running that low?"

"I have about four bucks to last the rest of the week." I shrug, and then grin, "And some beans."

"Oh." She thinks for a moment, and then asks, "You ever tried my bean pies?"

"I've never tried anyone's bean pies. It sounds like something you'd get with an enchilada."

"Really? You never had a bean pie?"

"Really."

"They're like sweet potato pie, only better."

"I've never had a sweet potato pie."

"What's wrong with you, White man? Have you ever had pumpkin pie?"

"Sure."

"Sweet potato pie is like pumpkin pie, only not as slimy."

"Hmm. I'll have to try a piece next week. Is it good with grape soda?" I'm trying to be cute.

"No, fool. You don't drink grape soda with bean pie."

"No?"

"No. You drink Coke. We sell that too." She's beaming, radiant. "I'll give you a piece and a can if you pay me back next week."

"Deal."

The pie is firm and delicious. Far better than any pumpkin pie I've ever had. And it's not bad with Coke. I eat it and we chat about family and the foods our families eat. My first piece of bean pie, on interest free credit from the Nation of Islam, extended to me even though I haven't been all that smart with my money. Even though I haven't signed up to pray or admitted defeat or even sat through a sermon. I even called the book cheap propaganda. Even though I'm a heretic. Even though I'm a White devil. Coretha doesn't ask why I'm out of money. She doesn't want to fix me. She doesn't even want me to believe what she believes—in fact, she has a keen interest in keeping me from believing what she believes. Still she smiled and offered me a piece of pie. That feels pretty good. Almost like I belong. Almost like I'm not weak or in trouble with my money. Almost like things will be okay and I can keep going. After a while I thank her and head back to work.

This morning I put my beans in water to soak before I left for work, and on the ride home I think about them. The skins will be floating on the top, as will some of the beans. I've always suspected floating beans are bad, but I've never known, so I've always just left them. I'll have to ask Coretha about that next time I see her. The water will be cold, and the condo will be empty. Clean, but empty. Clean, and new, and white with vertical blinds and a gas fireplace on a light switch, with a 7-11 through the garage and across the alley, but empty and I'll be alone. I get to my stop and am half way past the Burger King when the smell of the grill catches me. The light inside is yellow and warm. There are thick sliced tomatoes inside, on thick buns that soak up the burger grease. And mayonnaise and fries with ketchup. It's just a combo meal. Anyone can afford a combo meal. It's under four dollars. I can afford a combo meal. But if I buy one, I'll be left with nothing but my beans and rice for four and a half days. The beans and rice won't get me through. I'll have to eat nothing for at least one full day. I guess that's no big deal; I've fasted as many as 24 days before. But I've never missed a meal I didn't want to miss. It would be a foolish choice to buy the burger. Better to make the beans and rice and use the four dollars on other cheap food. But anyone can afford a combo meal. I should be able to afford a combo meal. I'm sick of being at the end of my cash rope. Screw it; I'm going to buy the combo meal.

It is so nice and warm inside the restaurant, but I can't soak it up. I can't let myself enjoy this indulgence because I know it is foolish. It is a poor decision. I order the Whopper Combo meal with a regular Pepsi and its extra calories of sustenance, and I take a seat in the corner, not even removing my coat. I eat and feel like one of the people I see riding the bus for warmth, hunched over my food, stealing my absurd measure of temporary validation, hiding from the world that could so easily use the obvious "yeah, but" on me and ruin my moment of escape. And the moment is over in an instant. I leave the tray on the trash can and head back out into the cold to walk the rest of the way home, nothing but coins to my name.

As I reach the front walk of my condo, a woman from seminary named Jenny, an acquaintance at best, is heading back to her car from my front door. When she sees me she scurries back to the door and retrieves an envelope and meets me with it.

"Hi." She says. "My husband and I were praying about you last night and we want you to have this. It's not much, but the Lord put you on our hearts and we just felt like we were supposed to tell you to hang in there. It's fifty dollars." She gives me a quick hug.

I'm stunned. "Would you like to come in?"

"No, I can't. I'm late for class already. Maybe we can have you over for dinner sometime soon though?"

"Yeah." I say, totally disoriented. "Thank you. And thank you for the money, too. It really means a lot to me."

I watch her drive away and then go inside.

29.

I'll Be Home for Christmas. I guess.

Christmas. I'm in Zionsville. The descent into Indianapolis was turbulent, but I made the most of it by talking to the man in the seat next to me about wind sheer and winter lightning to scare him. He'd been drinking too much and talking too much for most of the flight, and it was cheap revenge. I hate when people talk to me on flights, even more than I hate the stinky grape bubble gum I usually chew loudly and blow to annoy my neighbors enough that they don't talk to me. I forgot the gum this time, so I was left with only storytelling revenge.

That's pretty much the attitude I have about being home in general, and I don't like the person I'm being. There will be new sweaters and themed holiday jewelry on my brother and his fiancé. She'll end up in some silly pissing match with my other brother's girlfriend, who is pretty much her exact opposite, except that they're both very competitive and want to be the favorite. For my part, I'll be grandma's date whenever there is seating to figure out, and that will be the joke. That one stings, because I always thought I'd be married by now, and it's sure looking like I'll be third, if I end up married at all.

Mom will have made Norwegian potato tortillas called *lefsa*, representing her side of the family, and German fruit *kuchen* for my dad's. Both will be served with country sausage shipped frozen from the Red Owl in Wishek, North Dakota where dad spent his childhood. There will be consumption on top of consumption, and suburban genuflecting in front of the Christmas tree and again later at the midnight church service that will open with a hired orchestra and end with oil lamps and "Silent Night." Everyone will be dressed in their finest, and the holiday will strain hard to create moments that feel like finding a handful of Zuzu's petals. Hey, whatever keeps you from jumping off the bridge, George Bailey.

I'm being a dick, I know. My parents throw up their hands and laugh when they see my shaved head and beard. They're very concerned about me, say I don't look well, ask if I've thought about taking a multivitamin. My brothers joke about how I sold my computer and blew through my savings, joke about my being a Jesus freak.

I guess I am one, too. At least to people watching. In Denver I've gotten rid of pretty much everything I own. I sleep on the floor on a sleeping bag. I gave away nearly all of my clothes, books, and music. I have two pairs of pants, two pairs of shorts, a sweatshirt, five t-shirts, two flannels, and two short-sleeved shirts I wear over the t-shirts in the summer. Plus underwear, socks, a coat, Tevas, Birkenstocks, tennis shoes, and the boots David and Danielle bought me. That's pretty much all I have to my name. I do my laundry in the bathtub, and recently I've been told I don't do it very well, which creates a keen paranoia in me about being the stinky fat guy. In the bedroom at my parents' house there is also a suit left over from Chicago, and a matching pair of dress shoes. I pray and I read and I talk about God, and I am very aware of how Zionsville is not awake, how it's wallowing in its wealth and refuses to look at the world beyond it. I am exceedingly tiring to my parents in this regard, and so I tend to spend a lot of time quietly disgusted and fuming about the gluttony here, even as I keep finding myself taking a second helping of whatever's on the table or the television. Jesus freak, and a dick. I wish the two didn't come up as a pair so much of the time.

It's just that there is so much more. There are so many taboos here, questions that will upset the applecart and maybe bring some reassessment of life, and nobody cares. Just a bunch of frogs in a pot, the temperature on their souls rising, and the damage is already happening. And it's so damned easy for me to slip right back into it, which terrifies me. I thought I was fine when I was in Chicago, and before that too. I thought I knew how life was supposed to unfold and what it was about and what the right balances were between job and family and church and golf and vacations and retirement and yes, maybe a mission trip or two and maybe a starving kid on the refrigerator. Leather seats feel good. New stereos sound good. Nice clothes too, and nice cars. Cute candles and knickknacks and thoughtful gifts and comforting books. Coffee after an elegant dinner. A scotch after a hard day at work. Burgers on the backyard grill. Bootstraps and tough love and trickle-down theories and all boats floating on a rising tide and loyalty to the contemporary interpretations of traditional values and the American Dream. I get it—I spent most of my life a spoiled recipient of the comforts of such a world. College didn't cost me a dime—other than what I earned during the summer to buy beer. It's a Sirens' song, a world of lotus eaters. I want it, but it's all bullshit.

The world just isn't the way Zionsville wants it to be, and while I'd never advocate ruining what the wealthy have earned by taking it from them to give to the poor who have not earned it, there is a whole world full of volitional sacrifice and generosity that holds the promise of both sides sleeping well at night. And I don't think a soul in Zionsville gives a tinker's damn about the fact that life, not just the portfolio, could be far better and far more satisfying than this, shuttled as it is like some veiled Chinese princess down wide streets of professionally serviced lawns in dark-windowed SUVs and minivans. I'm a Jesus freak because I want something better, where there is a tension about living in front of people, recognizing that how I live and what I consume does impact the people around me by modeling the wrong things on one hand, or causing them to stumble in their envy or resentment on the other. I'm a Jesus freak because I'm willing to encourage people to take a sober look at their lives and ask if they're really happy. Really. And that's the worst thing you can do in Zionsville.

Here's the other thing I realize: in my urban world in Denver I'm rewarded for bashing my hometown and the paradigm from which I come. And I'm a people pleaser when it comes down to it, willing to let some people be displeased with me so long as the people I've prioritized think I'm pretty cool. I think that's true for most people, and it's not fair for me to be all that harsh towards people from Zionsville because what they're doing is choosing to play by the social rules of the people they've prioritized. I find it horribly sad that I come from a place with so much, and so little peripheral vision. In the past several months I've learned that urban people don't much care for suburban people, and suburban people feel it. So they say, "Fine, we'll just wrap up the installation of this gatehouse at the entrance to our community, and agree to disagree." And the distance and incomplete lives of both sides return to their regularly scheduled programming.

I just want to be able to look at my whole life, and my place in the world, and feel good about it. And it seems like something I'd expect everyone to want to be able to do, with no areas that they have to avoid. That's not wrong, is it?

30.

Can One-and-a-Half Tango?

Lisa arrived in Indianapolis yesterday, and will fly home New Year's Eve. I didn't really want her to come. I've been distancing myself from her for months now, but the more I pull away, the more she scratches and pulls. On the phone a couple of weeks ago she said that she didn't think I was ready to commit. I could have chosen better words for my reply than, "No shit." She cried and said maybe she shouldn't come. I said I was sorry and that she should still visit, though we both knew I didn't mean to include that with my apology. She's here because she's taking her shot.

She's charming and outgoing and has been around the world. She prays and she cares and she feels a real tension about having a corporate job when there are so many needs in the world. She knows how to cook and my mom thinks she's the bee's knees. My dad likes her, too. My brothers watch us curiously, smirking. Grandma likes her because Lisa always talks like she's trying to be heard over the sound of the subway. I guess she's okay. It's just that she's so damned eager. I feel as though at any moment she may spit on her thumb and wipe something from my face like a mother who's dressed her 5-year-old up for church.

I'm trying, though. She's so sure that I'm the one for her, even though this is the first time we've actually met, and even though I've been telling her I think she's mistaken for almost a year now, that it's hard not to wonder if maybe she sees something I don't see yet. So I'm trying. Last night we watched a movie in the basement, on the giant screen TV with the eight speakers around the room. We ended up making out. Lisa speaks Italian and considers herself quite a lover. And she is good at the whole seduction thing—I had no intention of kissing her, but she took an inch at a time, asking if she could put her head on my lap, if I would play with her hair, kissing my arm, moving my hand to her collarbone, until she had me. Just like I used to do with Betsy, actually. I hate how many similarities there are; it makes me sick to think Betsy felt this way about me and was just "trying" because I seemed so sure about her.

Lisa's in the shower, and Dad calls me into his office to ask how things are going.

"Nah, she's not..." I stumble.

"Not what?"

"I don't know. Just not it."

"Because she's older?"

"Not really."

"Because she's not as good looking as Betsy?"

"No."

"What, then?"

"I just don't feel it."

"How so?"

"She's just so, I don't know, on top of me. She's so sure and so nurturing. I already have a mother."

"What's wrong with having a woman who will take care of you?"

"Nothing. But I want to be the one who wants it."

"She sure seems like a good one. She's grown up, knows who she is, fits in here," he takes a sip of his fourth coffee of the morning, "and she sure is crazy for you."

"Yeah, well, maybe I'm making a mistake." I say, wanting to end the sales pitch.

"You know what you want?" He asks, annoyed at my attempt to shut down his friendly discussion.

"Apparently not. Tell me."

"You want a woman who will treat you like shit, and you're not willing to settle for better."

"Good, Dad. More compromise. Is that the secret to a happy marriage?"

He knows he has me reengaged. "You know, for as much as you want to believe otherwise, all of life is a compromise. It's all choices and balances, trades between get to and have to."

"I know you think it's all about some long noble suffering, but it doesn't have to be that way. We serve a perfect God with a plan and a perfect love for each of us. We can do better than some crapshoot. We can do better than making do with what floats our way, or is handed to us by earthly masters."

He shakes his head at me. "This is one of those things you're going to have to learn on your own, but I'll say it again anyway. Life will not come to you. It will let you miss it entirely—it doesn't care. If you want something from it, life is set up on a system of rewards and consequences, and you have to be willing to face some consequences to earn your rewards, or you will face consequences for the rewards you steal by doing nothing."

"Don't shake your head at me like you have it all figured out." I shoot. "You don't. You sit here in this big house and drive your Mercedes around as you dole out your alms and your version of wisdom, and meanwhile people all around the world are starving. People 10 miles from here don't have power or food or clothing or even a place to live, but you're telling me about rewards and consequences.

I want to know, are your choices earning you rewards, or are you currently earning consequences for doing nothing?"

"I think that's a good question, a good reminder. But it highlights a big difference between us, don't you think?"

"What do you mean?"

"It's a tension I have to live in, and one that you're afforded the easy opportunity to throw rocks at." He takes a victorious sip of coffee and leans back in his leather chair, behind his custom-built desk, beside his custom-built gun cabinet. "I don't know that you have anything to say about the subject until you've earned the rewards to steward."

"Not in your world, that's true."

"But maybe in the world of entitlement and political correctness? Where Democrats play Robin Hood and where discipline is called repression?"

"Yeah, in that world, where a man isn't measured by the bulge in his back pocket so much as by the bulge in the front."

"Balls?"

"Balls."

He laughs. "With such great balls, it's surprising you're afraid of Lisa."

"I'm not afraid of Lisa. I'm afraid of giving up on my faith. I'd rather be alone than in a marriage where either of us settled, or where either of us was forced into a life we didn't want."

"Do you think that's what happened with Mom and me?"

"I didn't say that."

"No, come on, I'd like to hear your insights on this."

"Okay. I think you both settled. Not in the fact of choosing each other, but in the way you often choose each other. I think you bully and belittle her, and that somewhere she failed you or proved to you that she was afraid to trust you, so you stopped risking with her. And once that happened, it was easy for you to disappear into your career and it was easy for you to force moves on the family that none of the rest of us wanted. And the more you threw into the pot, the more impossible it became for you to do anything but insist that you were doing the right thing, even if no one else understood."

"That part sounds like someone else I know."

"Where do you think I got it? I don't know very many things, and you have to know that your voice is forever echoing in my head, as plumb line or accuser, depending on the moment, but I do know that I have chosen the better way, even if I have no idea where it's headed. And I absolutely know I won't ever sit back in my rocking chair when I'm old and wish that I'd put in more time in a cubicle or doing a job that I hated. Or making coerced choices dictated by that job and my own pride."

"You'll choose the better way, because you're listening to God."

"That is my prayer."

"Hmm." He nods to himself, raising his eyebrows and looking at his desk absently. It's his version of Colombo, and a posture that's really only kicked in since he started listening to a lot of the theological teacher R.C. Sproul.

"What?"

"So why is Lisa here?"

"I don't know. To find out, I guess."

"Are you sure she's not the one for you?"

"It would take some pretty darn clear communication from God for me to think she was."

"So sometimes you don't know quite what the perfect plan looks like, even up close."

"I think there are times when God doesn't say exactly what He's thinking."

"Why?"

"Because I'm either not listening, or else because He leaves room for the choice to go either way."

"So, how do you know the difference between compromise, in the sense that you reject God's plan, and an instance where He's leaving room for you to make the choice? Ultimately, can you know the difference, really?"

"Meaning because when I'm letting my desires override His voice, it will feel like He's letting silence be His answer, and silence means the choice is up to me?"

"Yeah."

"I don't think your question leaves room for me to say anything other than that there can be no way to tell the difference."

"Wow. So how do you know when someone else is shutting God out, if you can't even tell when you are?"

"There are some things that are very clear, some things that the Bible lists specifically regarding faith that is pleasing to God. In those areas it doesn't matter if you've found a way to drown him out because He's already spoken clearly."

"Like feeding the poor by hand."

"I hate when you say it that way, but I know that's why you do."

"That's what it is, isn't it? It doesn't count unless you're standing right there making sure they get their fill?"

"I think it's important to be impacted by the people you impact. I think that's called relationship. Otherwise it's just drive-by Christianity, one-sided and unempowering."

"But the poor are still fed. Sometimes more effectively so."

"You don't support arm's length ministry because it's more efficient. You support it because it's more convenient to you."

"What is my obligation? To feed the poor, or to be their buddy?"

"It is to treat them as though they are Jesus. If you knew Jesus was down at Wheeler Mission, you wouldn't just phone it in."

"Can you think of a time when Jesus needed the help of other people? Maybe a time when he was hungry or thirsty or needed a bit of information?" He asks.

"Sure. The woman at the well drew water for him. Martha cooked him dinner. The farmer left wheat in the field for the poor to glean. He had to ask who touched his robe, and there were times when he asked the apostles who people said he was."

"Good. So there are times when even Jesus looked to other people for help, and was impacted by their help. If Jesus is down at Wheeler Mission and asks a question of me—something about how to meet a need or how to get a job or something like that—of course it would be okay to tell him, right?"

"Sure."

"Not in my experience, and not to hear you talk most of the time. I've been to places like Wheeler, and all we're told is how we're not there to 'fix' the people. We're there to serve soup or whatever, but we're not supposed to offer them any real help, because real help creates too much of an unlevel playing field. We're supposed to hold back the best we can offer so we can offer the help they've been trained to seek out. And they've been trained by ministry people who mostly just keep the problem going. That's bad stewardship, and it's dictated by people who are stuck in ruts of bad ministry habits. If Jesus needs my help, I'm going to give him my help, including truths he's hiding from—if he's a homeless person with an obvious blind spot. That's how I'd treat someone like Jesus, but in your world that's called paternalism and disempowering."

"There are important subtleties in how help should be offered, or it robs people building from zero of what dignity they have mustered."

"Come on. You don't really believe that, do you?"

"Yes, I do."

"There is nothing subtle about sin that kills people. If you're burying yourself in a bottle, you need someone who will tell you the truth, not offer you comfort as you destroy yourself. If you're into prostitution, you need some practical help to change your life. And the sorts of practical help that actually make a difference are worth treating with respect. Stewardship goes beyond the gift—it goes into how the relationship the gift establishes is managed. It is not wrong for the stronger person in the relationship to attach strings to the gifts they offer, so long as the strings work to the good of the person being helped."

"Oh man. This is why you need to come downtown."

"This is why I refuse to."

And there we sit. I don't know how many times we've had conversations just like this, trading blows from caricatured positions, watching the tension escalate, wanting so much to find agreement and to be on the same team, but inevitably choosing the big dick contest instead. But for all of our disagreements, we have yet to let anger show. Scorn, sure. Contempt, absolutely. But I'm from a family of nice guys, where the one who gets angry first loses. If neither of us spoke for a day, neither of us would get up and walk away from this moment, because neither of us will lose. Instead, we will find some smaller point where we can share enough passive common ground to end on a happy note when Mom calls us to lunch.

End of the same old story there.

31.

Tuna Helper And Jesus

Everywhere I turn I see people wanting to be leaders. There's the usual collection of Christian leadership jokers with their herds of humming zombies, and if a person loved the wisdom of women's basketball coaches and retired executives, there are Christian leadership conferences to attend nearly every weekend. It would be like following the Grateful Dead, and about as useful. Though to be fair, Deadheads aren't claiming to lead a brave new world, which gives them much greater credibility and probably makes them the better source for guidance. Celebrities talk about using their celebrity to influence culture. In some churches the key is to be the "vision-caster" or the cultish personality around which the congregation can grow like coral upon a scuttled ship. In other churches, it's apostle-this and prophet-that, and suddenly the television preachers all decided to call themselves Bishop-whatever and started wearing these nutty pinstriped Nehru jackets with epaulets and aiguillettes looping their shoulders to indicate some vaguely military leadership post. Something about fashion and authority, they say, but I think the military touch has more to do with downplaying the hair helmets. Everywhere, everywhere, it's all chiefs and no Indians. Everyone's got a megaphone and they're all yelling "stroke," but nobody's at the oars. And at long last, after so much yelling and jockeying for insight, I don't know how many people really have a sense of what we're supposed to be doing with the lives we've been given anyway. I don't know where we're all being led, or to what end.

Of course, who'd want to row when there is so much glory in yelling? Who would want to simply live and labor and be present in an ordinary day, when the future doesn't hurt and the weather is so nice there? Who'd want to be stuck doing work when there are so many lunches to share and navels ready to be gazed upon? Not me.

That's pretty much what brought things to an end at Agape Christian Church. Pastor Woolfolk had no problem with my attending a different church on Sundays, so long as I was on time during the week. But I had people to meet, and a non-schedule to which I had grown quite attached. I was running out of enthusiasm for the job and for the tensions there, and I wasn't being a very good employee anymore. I'd learned too much. I had too much figured out. I was ready to become part of the solution, and I had ideas I wanted to try. I had relationships I wanted to spend time enjoying. I wanted to be a tremendous man of God. And it made me a poor fit for the simple work the church needed me to do. We decided together that I would move on, but if we hadn't decided it together, Pastor Woolfolk would have decided it for me. I knew it was coming, and I'd already found something else.

I'd read a book by Henri Nouwen, the Harvard professor who left his job to work and live with the developmentally disabled people of the L'Arch community in Canada, and I wanted to try that. Actually, I think I wanted to be able to have a similar story to his, where I was this super genius who was able to talk about how much he'd learned from the people who functioned so far beneath him. I knew I could make it sound good, and the choice sounded noble. Besides, the work wouldn't be hard; just make my way through the apartment complex to the four units rented by seven men with varying sorts of developmental issues to wake them, get them fed, send some off to work, entertain the others, make sure they get their medications, cook lunch for some and dinner for nearly all, and hang out with them. And sleep in the second bedroom turned office and staff smoking den in one of the apartments. I'd actually be paid for my sleeping time. And the job was only Sunday through Tuesday evening. Perfect. I told Pastor Woolfolk I understood his reasons and agreed that the fit wasn't working as it had, and wished him well. I grabbed a grape soda from the Nation of Islam store, where Coretha had the day off but wouldn't have cared about my goodbye anyway, and headed home, glad to be done with the light rail and that bus route and on to new and more erudite things.

Apparently the term "developmentally disabled" has fallen out of fashion. Today they're called "developmentally delayed." But to tell the truth, I think that's a silly name because I sure don't see any of them catching up. I thought I was going to enter a world where I would be this kindly fellow working with people who were naively friendly and honest and happy, with crisp edges regarding the things they could or could not do on their own. Wrong.

I want to be a leader, a difference-maker, and I'm chaffing that my arrival hasn't completely changed their lives. They lie and complain, a lot. And it feels lousy when Tim, the 40-year-old autistic guy I've spent hours with for weeks, freaks out if I happen to touch him. It's insulting—he should be playing by my rules of courtesy. And there are no clear boundaries regarding what the guys are able to do, nor is there necessarily any progress. One day things go well, and the next the skill is lost.

William cleans bathrooms at a hotel near the old airport, and it means the world to him, but sometimes he drinks too much of the free Pepsi at the bar and I get a call about how he's had diarrhea in his pants and I need to drop everything and go take care of that. He feels awful, but he doesn't really get the whole cause and effect thing, and the people who work at the hotel are pretty much the sort of people who would encourage an overweight 36-year-old with Down's Syndrome to drink caffeine until he crapped himself. William' roommate is Jimmy, who has Down's and is in his 50s. We think he's also developing Alzheimer's. Sometimes he gets so frustrated that I'll hear him upstairs from the office throwing things and yelling in his room. He has a hard time gauging how high to shave his sideburns, and how evenly, so right now he has none, and on the left side there is an extra channel cut in his hair about an inch higher than the top of his temple. When I take him out in public I wonder if people think I'm the cruel bastard who would cut a retarded man's hair that way. Both William and Jimmy have weight problems, and neither of them understands why they're on diets, and both of them will steal food and eat until they get sick if they can. Roommates Sam and Henry—I call them Sam Love and Henry Love—watch *Dukes of Hazzard* three times a day and know the lyrics to the theme song by heart. They both wear their cowboy hats whenever the show is on. Most of the time they're both great, but sometimes Sam will go into this strange compulsive mode and use his baseball card collection to build a card house one story high from the front door all the way through the apartment to the back, and when he does this Henry will sometimes end up trapped in his room because he doesn't want Sam to yell at him for messing up the cards. In the middle of the night Henry will call over to the office, crying because he can't get to the bathroom and doesn't know what to do. Autistic Tim's roommate, Nick, is in his 60s, mutters nonsensically, and his osteoporosis has forced him to use a walker. Tim and Nick have a nameless cat to which I'm very allergic, so I pretty much only spend as much time at their place as is required to prepare their food or make sure they've taken their pills and brushed their teeth. And finally there is Hungarian Vince, whose second-biggest disability is that he doesn't quite look retarded. His dark, googly staring eyes, thick glasses, lopsided moustache and often twisted pants mostly just make him look creepy. People often greet him as though they expect a normal response from a merely unfortunate victim of a lousy pick in the cosmetic lottery. And sometimes his first sentence is lucid and clear enough that people don't see there are only 54 IQ horsepower working under the hood. By Vince's second sentence, most people understand. The dynamic has been painful in Vince's life because unlike the other guys in the program, Vince has seen the expression on the face of every person who has ever suddenly recognized that he is not like them. Once a week I take Vince downtown to court-ordered counseling for developmentally delayed sex offenders. In Vince's case there was a woman at the bus stop who spun around to see his loopy grin when she felt the hand on her ass. Think Harpo Marx with dark hair and too much cheap cologne.

I'm sitting at Vince's dining room table as we're trying, again, to make Tuna Helper. We chose Tuna Helper because he likes the taste and because there is nothing that will hurt him if it's undercooked. The words of the recipe on the box confuse him, so whenever we buy the stuff, I take a black marker and mark out everything but the pictures. Then together we find the measuring cups and the different ingredients. I've permanent markered the cups so he will know how far to fill them. I've marked the kitchen timer and the stove dial. We've made Tuna Helper together once a week for two months now. He has still never been able to do it without my intervention, but I'm determined that he will have this one victory.

Which reminds me about the whole leaders everywhere thing. The rewards in this job are just about nil. If, after months of working at it, Vince makes his own Tuna Helper, it's his victory. Sure, I will have played a part in teaching him, but I have to admit that teaching one retarded Hungarian to make Tuna Helper one time (I don't even begin to believe this will become a lasting skill) is not exactly what I was hoping to read about on my tombstone. I want my efforts, and my life's work, and my life, to pile up higher than that, to be seen from further away than that. To be worth approaching and examining. I want to be a chief, not just an Indian. And the pain of not getting that, the pain of having a job and life description that bears the prefix of "I'm just a...," chafes a bit. Thank goodness I'm arrogant jerk enough to turn that pain into a nice dose of elitism so I can throw stones rather than deal with living a humble life. I can look at those visionary leaders, and those people whose words bring applause, and those pastors dressed like Austin Powers on parade, and I can say that all of their work is a reflection of their own need and greed because it all brings them a reward for their leadership. Mine brings me $6.25/hr plus half of the worst Tuna Helper in the world. I must be noble, right? Hey, that nobility is probably impressive and worth following...just like I followed Nouwen.

Vince ends up needing my help with the Tuna Helper—I let him put in one extra cup of water, but when he's about to put in a second extra I know my dinner will be ruined and I step in. We're still left with Tuna Helper stew, but we eat it. With frozen corn and store brand cola.

"Good job on this, Vince." I tell him as we slurp.

"Thanks." He says, looking up and staring.

And then he keeps staring.

"What?" I ask. The whole staff has been working with him to break the Hypnoto routine.

He smiles a goofy grin, the kind a person makes when they're waiting for the punchline they know is coming. With Vince it just looks like that.

"Hey." He says.

"Yes Vince."

"With God." I've been taking him to church with me for several weeks now.

"Yes?"

"What does God do at night when everybody's sleeping?"

Vince can't make sense of the picture drawings on a box of Tuna Helper; he's not going to get the whole Copernican thing. What did Denver Seminary teach me about this question in the Integrated Theology class?

"Well, Vince, at night God holds your heart, like this," I lay one hand palm up, and rest my other hand over it like I'm holding his heart, "and he squeezes it, like this. And each time he squeezes it, he says, 'I love you Vince.'"

He stares at me, grinning like he's waiting for the punchline.

"Huh." He says. And then he goes back to his Tuna Helper.

Shit, that was such a good answer, too. It's like pearls to swine around here. I'm a bright guy with some seasoned understanding about God and matters of great import. I could be out changing the world. I could be doing public relations for Promise Keepers and Habitat for Humanity. I could speak to a wide audience about life's seminal issues. Could I at least get a follow-up question? The rest of the important leaders at least get a follow-up question. Or an email telling them how well they did. Or at least a pat on the back or a "pastor your words changed my life" or something. I get "huh" from Hungarian Vince. Great.

✳✳✳

Speaking of seminal issues, a brief word about Flora, the staff person with the overnight shift before mine. *Como se dice* "hot" *en español?* She's 29 with shiny black hair and a body that makes me ache the way a big steak makes me want to take a bite. She's a total smart ass, and we joke rough. She smokes in a way that reminds me of the way the cashiers used to smoke in the break room at the grocery store back home when I was in high school—sort of redneck and with a chip on their shoulders. She's married, but she doesn't seem that sure about the basis for her marriage. It sounds like they fight a lot, and mostly get along when they go out drinking. She grew up going to church and frequently asks questions about God and faith, but also loves to make fun of my prudishness, all of which comes from her poking at stereotypes she accuses me of representing. She knows I'm attracted to her, and mercilessly toys with that fact. Company policy is that we're supposed to wash the sheets on the bed in the office at the end of our shift, but she usually doesn't. I think she knows that I can smell her on the pillow and that it torments me. When I'm feeling clean and strong I wash the sheets during the hours our shifts overlap, to make a point. Other times I leave them and smell her in the moonlight, imaging her coming, naked and taut, from the bathroom into the bed with me. Her husband is a high dollar salesman with a dark complexion and cold heart. I picture how she would gladly trade for a soft, poor, blonde guy with a giant heart and a pent-up need for love. Nothing will or would ever happen between us, but I can't stop myself from playing the game. At least not for long.

And I think about how much of my life is really just a clumsy acting out of some nutball fantasy that makes sense only in the middle of the night. Like the time when Danielle's friend came into town and I volunteered to pick her up at the airport because I'd met her before and had developed this huge crush on her. I greeted her with a card and two very lovely gifts: a Bugs Bunny Pez dispenser and a 1950s style cow and moon salt and pepper shaker set I'd ordered special from Ruby Montana's Pinto Pony in Seattle, along with my Elvis sunglasses. David and Danielle still bring that weekend up with tearful laughter about once a month. Apparently the girl didn't appreciate the quirky charm of my efforts. In my room at my condo is a green candle into the bottom of which I carved the face of a girl I once had a crush on. It was going pretty well, too, until the nose, which happened to be where the base of the wick was, broke, leaving Sara looking like an Eskimo. It's bad enough starting off working from the nice guy angle because the pure physical attractiveness thing just isn't there, but adding the extra warping pressure of this Christian subculture thing, and all of my own zealousness to be pure (a zeal, I confess, that is much more active in the moments when temptation or opportunity are not present), and I'm quickly becoming a tragic loss. The other day Henry Love was walking around his apartment naked and I noticed that he has a huge penis. I thought that was a real waste; most of this population is infertile, so what was he going to need it for? The thought that immediately came into my head was if he thought the same thing about my brain.

***

It was a long night. I pulled the unwashed pillowcase from beneath my head and threw it across the room, trying to keep thoughts of Flora at bay. I began to pray, and soon I was past my temptation and well into the prayer. I've been wanting to be used, to be a holy man, to see the face of God. And as I lay there, I felt like I was laying in blackness the way a stage is black, and a white spotlight began to creep towards me. It was God, and I knew that when the light touched me, I would be truly in his presence, and I would be known completely. The light was gentle but pure and crisp, friendly and inviting, there in part because I had invited it, drawing closer. It slid up the side of the bed. It rounded the corner to the surface of the bed. And when it was maybe two inches from my arm, I panicked. I stopped praying and I wanted desperately to get out of that moment. I was terrified. I opened my eyes with a start and lay there, trembling. And then I began to cry, for my junk, yes, but mostly because after all of this time, when the reality of Him is upon me, I'm still absolutely scared to death of God.

I don't know what time I finally drifted off.

The morning sun fills the room. I get up and throw the sheets in the washing machine, slip into the clothes I wore yesterday, and open the bedroom door to go check in with the guys in their apartments. Vince is eating cereal in front of the television, repeating a commercial slogan he saw during the Broncos game yesterday.

"Fosters. Australian for beer." He's really trying to get the accent. He shakes his head at how it sounds and takes another oversized scoop of flakes.

"Good morning, Vince." I say, walking past and opening the front door.

"Hey." He says.

I turn around.

He puts his spoon down in the bowl, and uses that hand to pat his chest.

"Been listening to my heart." He grins like he's waiting for the punchline.

I stop. I stare. I don't know what to say. I stammer something about that being great. I feel happy and shamed and confused about what to make of his comment and its ultimate meaning. Hungarian Vince is the first person I ever introduced to Jesus, my Lord whom I love and fear and who uses me in spite of myself.

32.

Mugging the Tooth Fairy

Moments when God crawls up the side of my bed in the form of a spotlight are rare. Instances where I encounter some evidence of my positive impact on the world happen about as frequently. Most of the time I help Vince do his shopping and then steal his Pizza Rolls. Or I'll hang out with Sam Love and Henry Love watching television in their apartment longer than they'd prefer, hiding, journaling in tiny print on unlined pages, browsing their kitchen now and then. Well, more like now and now.

I don't know if there is anything more disgusting and virulent to the souls of other people than authority, especially authority self-conceived as love, living out its addictions at the expense of others. In my case, I don't want to be bothered to get up and steal my own food, so I ask one of the guys to bring it to me. Or I don't have the energy or desire to pack everyone into the car and head out for an adventure somewhere. Somewhere like the mountains or parks I sometimes get roped into hauling everyone to when one of the other staff people insists it would be a good idea.

I said it casually, but it hits me in waves now that I've put it out there: I steal food from retarded people who are depending upon my honor and my professed dedication to their wellbeing. I am teaching them that this is how love treats them. I am teaching them that nothing is their own, and that I may intrude upon their privacy whenever my ever-growing stomach experiences the urge. And William and Jimmy, the two men on diets, don't see me other than when I stop in for mandatory rounds for medications or that sort of thing; they don't have anything I want badly enough to climb the flight of stairs to their empty-cupboarded apartment.

Most of the time I ignore it by keeping all of the rationalizing "yeah buts" swirling around. Yeah but:

I'm nicer to them than any of the other staff.

I take Vince to church with me, and sometimes others.

I am only making six dollars an hour doing this job, and I have no car, and I count on the grocery coupons that come as perks with my employment, where the men in the program actually have a surplus of both funds and food.

I am the guy who puts medicine in their ears.

I am the guy who once rested his hand in a cooling puddle of semen one of the Love's had left on a blanket.

I am the guy who will take the whole crew out to the gourmet burger place.

I am the guy who took Sam and Henry Love to the country line-dancing bar, even though they were dressed like cowboy clowns (or so I thought until we walked into the place and I saw everyone else there). I bought them beer and we played pool. At one point Henry shot the cue ball off of the table and it rolled across the room and under the next table. Sam went after it, but rather than going around the neighboring table, he crawled under it. The hot shot young man in the western shirt and Stetson with the date in tight acid washed jeans with acid washed bear claw bangs was horribly offended, and began to ridicule Sam. I'm the large man who walked over to the young man and said, "You two are dressed the same way. He's retarded. What's your excuse?" We returned to our game and I had fun eyeballing the young man the rest of the evening, joyfully aware that his being humiliated after mocking a retarded man wouldn't bode well for his chances of seeing his date's acid-washed undergarments.

I'm the guy who's here because he read Henri Nouwen, damnit.

Not that I'm actively aware of the trade I'm forcing. Not that I consciously think about how I charge my greedy, thieving behavior as an uninvited guest against my gentleness with the challenges of retarded men. It's more that I keep myself unaware of my own monstrosity by keeping a tally list of cute anecdotes or moments of praise from the guys. I think about how William loves to sit on the floor beside my easy chair in Vince's family room and stroke my arm saying I'm his friend. I think about William, who is barely verbal, singing "bright, bright sun-shiny day" along with the radio in the back seat on the way back to work after coming home to wipe the diarrhea from his body. I think about Vince lying in bed listening to his heart. I think about how God really does love Vince, and how he loves me too, but I know better than to pay attention to my pulse and think about God's love in such immediate ways. I prefer a bit of distance. I'm much more likely to stop and notice the sunset on a Sunday evening and whisper some prayer like, "you never take a day off, do you?"

I think I'm something of a hero in my Bible study because of the work I do and the way I live. I'm broke, and every Tuesday evening someone from the study picks me up from work to drive me to whichever apartment we've chosen for the evening's study and flirtation. I regale the group, in casual, matter of fact terms carefully chosen for maximum self-aggrandizement, with stories of life with the loving, demanding, challenging, least of these who fall all too often to the care of people of far less godly character than what is evidenced in me. I scoop praise from the group like a world-class melonballer, dragging my words and my eyes and my heart tweaks across each of them to extract my reward. My stolen, too quickly, too greedily consumed reward. Stolen from my friends just as it is stolen in equally ignominious ways from the men who trust me in other areas.

I do the same thing over meals with people who want to meet me because some shared friend thought we'd like each other. I have become a master at the dance of godly caveat, of feigned vulnerability carefully Teflon coated and shined up. Sometimes I work to make someone I've just met cry at the stories I spin— that's a favorite response of mine. Sometimes I talk about the challenges and how God is showing me something—"again," I say so as not to be ranked as only learning this lesson for the first time and thus be found wanting. Deep down, but only way deep down, I know that I'm cashing in on these moments because I don't really believe God loves me, or that His love for me is enough. I want the politely declined reward to be insistently thrust upon me—now in my humble posture, and later in Heaven because I didn't quite cash it in fully here. As though I could fool God and man and myself and double up on the prize I did very little to earn in the first place. As a child I once pulled the coins from the glass of water the Tooth Fairy had filled without removing the tooth, and was thus rewarded two nights in a row. When I got away with that, I didn't know which was worse, the doubt I developed regarding the reality of a Tooth Fairy who could be so easily tricked, or the justice I was certain to eventually experience if indeed she did exist. Little has changed, I'm afraid.

And if the abusive choices I make to favor my addictions over the retarded men, my friends, and my friends' friends weren't enough, I turn the screws that much further with my family. They love me, and my mother in particular has determined to be my champion in all things. No matter what I say or do, she will find something to praise, and she will almost always offer her praise in the form of a comparison to her own value. She's an easy mark, and it kills me to think what I take from her every time I get the chance. Not only do I milk every good deed for all the praise I can get; not only do I trumpet every clever insight of my own or someone else's to my credit with my mother; not only do I use her protective fear to elicit additional care and concern, I turn every bit of what I'm doing into a fine-pointed weapon to pierce and condemn her for not doing likewise. She offers me praise by lowering herself, and I slam my heavy boot on her back and demand she drop further yet. So immense is my hunger, so desperate my greed, so small my faith, so complete my preference for my addiction over the love and truth that is everywhere around me. I would suck my mother dry if her willingness to allow it didn't come so easily, and then so quickly leave me disgusted and ashamed. And bored, with the concomitant temerity to insist that praise from her does not matter because her job description requires her to say such things. What a monster. In the end a stolen reward is nothing but a foolishly rushed upon condemnation, and I am full up.

Still I have the audacity to pray, to call myself a believer, to cite the Bible and to claim that I am some sort of a positive presence in the lives around me. I believe what God says about me and my value. I know what I experience in prayer. I know that He is near, that He even lives within me, but there is such a disconnect. I simply cannot keep the realities of my behaviors, the extorted expenses of my addictions, in front of me at the same time as I speak of how I am fearfully and wonderfully made. I know that in the same night I can experience the failure of lurid fantasies concerning a married woman, and also the immediate reality of a God whose love for me is greater than my ability to remain still and experience it. It is an exquisite torture, the evidence of heaven and of hell mingled and foaming as ravenous fighting dogs within me. And I can't tell for sure which fighting dog I'm rooting for, and I couldn't even begin to muster the courage to shoot the other.

✵✵✵

Meanwhile, life with Vince and the gang continues. The Tuesday afternoon sun has warmed the steamy grass beside the steps to Vince's apartment, and we lay on it together, waiting for Skinny Robert to arrive to take me to Bible study. Vince is wearing grey slacks a size too big for him, cinched tight and lopsided under a very long belt. The tail of his purple silk dress shirt hangs out in back. His thick glasses look like the smudged observation window at the children's aquarium. He doesn't know the injustices I perpetuate in his world. He doesn't want me to go. He will miss me until I return next Sunday, and he will be sad when Robert arrives, but he will be proud to spot Robert first and to ask Robert how it's hanging.

Vince speaks Hungarian fluently, or at least as well as his elementary level English. He loses his thought mid-stream pretty often, but for the most part he can carry on a conversation. When he calls his father, who lives about ten minutes away, they always speak Hungarian.

"Hey Vince," I say. "Can you teach me some Hungarian?"

"I don't know."

"You speak it, right?"

"Yeah."

"Maybe you can teach me how to say something in Hungarian."

"I don't know."

"Okay, well, how do you say 'give me some money' in Hungarian?"

He stares blankly at me, waiting for the punchline. He is suddenly being tested, and he is uneasy.

"Try it this way. How would you say 'give me some money' to your dad?"

He furrows his brow and lunges towards me, yelling in a rough voice, "Give me some money!" Then, fearful that he's broken one of the rules of appropriate social behavior, he quickly rolls back to where he was lying and says, "Only joking."

"No, Vince. You know how when you talk to your dad you speak in a different language, the one I don't understand?"

"Yeah."

"That's Hungarian, right?"

"Yeah."

"If you were speaking in that language, how would you say 'give me some money'?"

His face shows that he is confused and is starting to feel as though he is failing me. He hates when he feels stupid. A bit of panic is creeping into his face. I should shift away from this line of questioning, but come on, how hard is it to offer a simple phrase, after all? I push on, selfishly.

I make the hand gesture where I rub my thumb and forefinger together. I ask, "How do you say this in Hungarian?"

"*Adja meg az egyes penz!*" He says. Or something like that.

"Great job, Vince!" I exclaim. "*Aja mage es eggs pans?*"

He nods. Then a look comes over his face like the punchline is going to be bad. Then he begins to reach into his pocket to give me his money.

"No, Vince—I was just trying to say it like you did."

He stares at me, the look returning to happy punchline, but still not making complete sense.

"I don't want your money, Vince. You keep it, okay?"

"Okay."

I lie back down, breaking eye contact with him to let the moment cool. And suddenly I know what I will talk about at Bible study. We are, each of us, split into two worlds: the spiritual world where we pray and feel something of the eternal beauty of our creation; and the physical world where we are wet turds. I am capable of some kindness, but I am also capable of tremendous failures. Still, I have been created as an eternal being for whom God was pleased to die to be reconciled. I can pray and can experience something of the ecstatic, something of the eternal and ethereal. And I know somehow that truth could be translated into the physical reality of my daily, corporeal world. But somewhere this obvious thing, this obvious translation, has been lost to me. Call it the retardation of the Fall, perhaps. It's obvious when I'm praying that I'm supposed to take what I encounter there and apply it to my everyday world. And in my everyday world it's obvious that there is a greater truth that transcends what I experience and that promises the hope of redemption. But for the life of me I cannot make the leap. And I feel as though I'm failing—God, myself, the world, whatever. And a bit of panic begins to set in. I make clumsy, lunging attempts at a translation, in the way I live, how I serve, how I think of or relate to God or the world, and then I see that they are clumsy, or wrong, or even punishable, and I recoil. I live on the grassy hill in the sun with a God I'd like to understand, whom I'd love to please and with whom I would love to converse and experience the world, whose company I miss when I don't feel him near me, and it is torture that I cannot quite comprehend what it all means, or what he's after.

Jesus is the hand gesture. Jesus makes sense to the physical side of me and to the spiritual. Vince can say Jesus' name in English or Hungarian, but only if you point to the crucifix and ask who hangs upon it—Vince will fail if you start in one language and ask for the translation. I cannot start with prayer and translate the Truth to the world. I cannot start with the world and extrapolate sublime Truth. I must always fall back to the person of Jesus, without all of the language on one side of the divide or the other, and so long as I do that—work from the independent reality of Jesus instead of the lexicon of either of my languages—I turn out to be less retarded than I thought.

And God will applaud my success. Even if then I don't understand that all he was trying to get me to see is that he loves me and wants me completely, and instead I try to empty my pockets before him.

And in Bible study people will think I am insightful and am developing this great relationship with the people I'm serving. And later I will find an even richer way of talking about all of this with friends of friends. And then I will call home and I will make my mother feel as though she is nothing compared to me, and I will hang up feeling the cold comfort of a sacrificial compliment whose value I'm too big an asshole to appreciate. And then I will pray and God will start again at trying to help me see the hand gesture and what that gesture must ultimately, even if fleetingly, mean about my life.

33.

Faith Sails Unraveling

"Wow, you really got sunburned today." The dock master says to me as he ferries Skinny Robert and me from Robert's sailboat to shore. The lake is encircled by mountains and is one of my favorite places.

"That's nothing," Robert says, "he's really swollen—he's usually my size."

I start to smile, but my face is too tight and burning. I know better than to punch him, either—he'd just slap me and leave me howling. The dock master laughs politely and drops us at the beach.

It's been a great day, just the two of us out on the *Zuzu's Petals*, whipping up and down the lake with its Rocky Mountain shores. I spent most of the afternoon sitting on the bow, my feet dangling to the tops of the waves, enjoying the Bob Marley Robert was playing back in the stern. There is room for two to sleep comfortably below deck, which is our plan for after dinner and an aloe vera hunt in town.

In the car Robert asks, "Hey, tell me about your trip home. How was your brother's bachelor party?"

"Partial." I say. "I went to the bar and played pool with them, but when they decided they wanted to go to the strip club, I refused. Dad agreed to take me home and told my brothers 'there are some things a father doesn't need to see.' But he didn't get my back, and I know he would have gone with them if I hadn't insisted on not going. He definitely left me looking like the stick in the mud."

"What did your brothers say?"

"They were pretty offended. And to tell the truth, it was a hard decision. I went in thinking it was a horrible thing to do the weekend you're supposed to pledge your life to someone, but I felt like a real prude not going and forcing them to choose like I did. I'd hoped that telling them about why I thought it was a bad idea would convince them. I had even hoped that later they'd thank me for helping them avoid the choice."

"Did they understand your reasoning?"

"I don't know. I told them, but obviously they went anyway, and they see it as a simple matter of tradition."

"Boys will be boys."

"Yeah." I say.

"It's hard to think of a more poisonous lie than that in a man's world, isn't it? It's permission to be a child forever, and nothing that people describe with 'boys will be boys' is ever good for the boys."

"I guess that's right. For me the hardest part was that in not going along, I felt like I betrayed my brothers and wasn't going along with being a guy. It felt like I was either supposed to go or be seen as neutered."

Robert laughs. "Well, there is something to be said for the surgery. And it's not like it would impact your dating life any."

"Cute. That reminds me; how's Nurse Bubbles?"

"Crissy is fine. I guess. She's deciding between me and the old boyfriend. I'm the local love interest I guess, but things aren't looking good for the future."

"Maybe we should call the vet together." I say. "Get a group rate."

"Neithers will be neithers." Robert says.

"Do you ever wonder if maybe you've been given the gift of singleness?" I ask.

"Some gift. Like the gift of one-leggedness."

"Could it be that we don't have to be excited about every gift we receive right when we receive it? I don't want it, either, but sometimes I wonder if that might be what God has in mind."

"I don't think so." Robert says. "There are times when marriage seems far away, especially after the way things ended the first time. But there's something about having gotten married once, about having entered the covenant once, that feels like God intends marriage for me again."

We find a strip mall with a pharmacy that sells sunburn lotion, and a pizza joint where we can watch the Avalanche play. We've made it our mission to inject the phrase, "he bites my Jagr" into hockey parlance, and we look for opportunities to use the phrase during the game. Once, at a Broncos game, we ended up a few rows behind Avalanche forward Mike Ricci, who we always refer to as "Yard Sale" because whenever he falls down all of his gear scatters all over the ice. We used the exclamation in a few different ways, and at one point we got a laugh out of him. At the pizza place a few men turn and grin at our clever slam of one of the game's superstars. "He's not a dedicated athlete, you know. He has his own brand of peanut butter. Who could manage two kingdoms like that? He's not serious about the sport!" God and hockey, and aloe vera...what else does a person need?

By the time we return to the lake the dock master has left for the evening. We swim out to the boat. Nobody else is around. We change into our spare clothes and break out the cigars. Robert has never smoked one before.

"No, like this." I say.

He coughs. He spits. He tries again a couple of times, but when it burns out he doesn't relight it.

"David and Danielle are pregnant." I say.

"Really? Cool for them."

"Yeah. It is."

I smoke some more. Minutes pass, the moon glazing the night as the breeze brushes the rigging against the mast and turns the boat gently around its bow-end mooring.

"You know, Robert, in the past month the only human affection I've had has been a couple of hugs from Danielle."

"Been there."

"They say that babies who aren't held become sociopaths and serial killers."

"And Starbucks baristas." He helps.

"I feel like bad things are happening to me, like I'm starving from lack of contact."

"Keep talking like this and you'll sleep up here." He says.

"I feel like my dreams are dying."

"What do you mean?"

"I used to dream about the details of my future. A thousand different romantic ways to propose. A million gentle things I wanted to whisper to my wife. I pictured a toe-headed daughter riding her pink bike with glittering tassels past me yelling, 'Look Daddy.' I dreamed of teaching my son to make an omelet, and making a complete mess. I saw myself surrounded by noise and color and action and needs and crying and being the dad who could shoulder it all, who could make it all better. And who would be a wizard on the backyard barbeque. I dreamed of catching my wife looking at me lovingly, and of her simply kissing me and returning to whatever she was doing when I asked why she was staring at me."

"Mmm." Robert agrees.

"I remember my dad's 30th birthday. I was six, and my brothers were four and two. My dad was married when he was 23 and was finished having children by the time he was 28. I'm 25 now, and I'm way behind schedule. And I don't see any prospects. I feel like I'm freezing to death, like the way people lose their fingers and toes first, and then the cold creeps nearer and nearer to their cores, and eventually they're found stripped naked with some grotesque grimace on their face when after all of that freezing they suddenly feel hot and go running out into the snow. I already feel the fingertip dreams like my little girl and her bike with tassels, or even the little girl herself, freezing and breaking off, lost forever."

I puff on my cigar. A few seconds pass.

"Who said you're supposed to be on the same schedule as your dad?" Robert asks. "And can you imagine what your world would be like if you had married Betsy?"

"I know the bullet dodged me there, and I know I'm grieving the loss of a life plan I never picked up on purpose. I know it's just what I assumed somewhere along the line without ever thinking about it. But that doesn't make any difference; it still feels the way it feels."

"I understand. I feel a big chunk of that every time I take Daniel back to his mother at the end of a weekend at my place. It wasn't supposed to be like this."

"So why is it, Robert?"

"The Fall, I guess. Sin and death spilled everywhere."

"I know that answer too. Does it make sense to you?"

"No." He admits. "I can tell it's true, but in terms of comfort it feels more like a wet blanket than a warm embrace."

"Stupid Adam." I say.

"Stupid Eve." He adds.

"Dumbass."

"Bitch."

"I'd have done the same thing."

"We all would have."

"Hey, relight your cigar."

"Nah. It's not my thing." And he throws it into the water. We fall to silence and I wonder how bad it is to call Adam a dumbass.

"I'm so sunburned I can feel the heat coming off of my body."

"You smell like my grandma. The aloe vera, not the cigar. She says cigars don't go as well with her vodka as a pipe." His grandmother, in a tiny Nebraska town, could not be less a drinker or smoker.

"If you keep talking about how I smell like your grandma, you can be the one to sleep up here." I say.

A minute passes, the end of my cigar glows orange, and I practice blowing smoke rings.

"Why do you do it, then?" Robert asks.

"Do what?"

"Put so much energy into your walk?"

"For the fame and fortune." I say.

"No, really. Why?"

"Hmm. I guess because I don't know what else to do. I don't know how I'd stop. I have so much bet into the pot that I can't fold my hand now. I need God to have something he wants me to do, some role to play. And I do believe that the whole God thing turns out to be real."

"But that doesn't mean you have to build your whole world around doing the stuff." Robert says.

"No, but I want as big a piece of Him as I can get. I want to be as defined by Him as I can be."

"Sometimes it just seems like you overpay. Sometimes it seems like you choose to overpay." He says.

"You're right. I do." I don't know what else to say. "Did I tell you about my cousin calling the other night?"

"No."

"I was asleep, on the floor and feeling all holy about it—though it really is a great prayer reminder that helps me remember what I want to be about—and my cousin called, drunk."

"Oh boy."

"He was doing the rounds. I've had nights like that myself, when I called people I hadn't spoken with in years and then slurred weird things into the phone until they could finally get me to hang up. He'd already talked to both of my brothers. The younger one told him he should call me and gave him my number."

"Nice."

"He told me what a Jesus freak, what a freak in general, they'd said I was."

"I could have called you and told you that without the long distance charges." Robert jabs.

"I've spent so much energy with my brothers and my family, and I hate that I'm the joke."

"Nobody's family understands them."

"You're right. Of course you're right. I'm just feeling melancholy. And your question about why I do this is a good one. Maybe it's partly to keep distance from people."

"Like Loma?" He asks.

"Yeah, maybe especially her. I could sure go for a hug from her."

"It would be squishy."

"She's such a bite in the ass. But I feel like after my experiences with Betsy and Lisa what I need is someone at least as strong as I am."

"She is that. Too bad she's your opposite."

"She would keep me tied to reality, that's for sure."

"Do you think she'd be more interested if you had a better job and a more solid sense of what you were doing with your life?"

"I don't know. Robyn married Jon even though she's totally grounded in the world and her career, and he's just teaching at the street school."

"So what about Loma?"

"I don't know what she wants, other than to push people away. I suppose some stability couldn't hurt, but you'd think being a designer and working with so many artists she'd be more comfortable with my..."

"Quirkiness?"

"Not the most masculine word, but yeah, my quirkiness." I say.

"I think she knows she can get what you have to offer for free. You keep coming when everyone else throws up their hands and walks away."

"I don't know how many times the word 'boundaries' has come up when I talk to people about her."

"Speaking of which, it's time for me to get to sleep. This talk about Loma has me thinking about Nurse Bubbles, as she'll be happy to learn you call her, and we'll end up spending the whole night whining to each other if we don't stop now. You still won't have any boundaries tomorrow, and we can talk about it then."

"Cool. I'm going to sit up here for a while."

"Sleep well. I'll most likely kill you in the morning." He quotes from a favorite movie and then disappears into the cabin.

I work my way back up to the bow and hang my feet over the edge like I did this afternoon. I know I'm a mess. I know that I'm completely cliché, completely tied up with my own junk, and that I have only the faintest of credibility with how I'm spending my life. Conversations like tonight's drive it home all too clearly. I don't make sense. I've known people like me before, and all I wanted to do was choke them. I sound like a weirdo just wandering through some tour of God, checked out and clumsy and crippled by the normal stuff of life everyone else seems to be able to manage just fine. Loma is my new Rachel, my new receptacle of best effort and safely unrequited love. Nothing will ever happen with her, though I will continue to bash myself into her just to feel the pain in the extremities that I know are freezing and dropping to the ground in the form of frostbitten black dreams. It's melodramatic and silly, I know, but it is what it is.

The bigger dilemma is that I don't know why I'm doing all of this with God. I talk about my motivation being to know as clearly as possible in this life that from which I have been separated. I want to know as much of God as I can, because I'm living for the moment of my death. I dream of that moment, of the moment I first see Jesus, and I want it to feel like I've been only barely removed from him, and all I have to do is lean forward into an embrace. An embrace. How sweet that sounds to me tonight. And his, no less. I want to know exactly how to respond, because I want to have spent my life in his company. I don't want to be uncertain about whether to bow or hide or weep or run or leap into his arms or what. I want to press into the ever-shrinking gap between us, to savor the distance, to feel it, to yearn against it, and then one day to melt through it and into his arms in the moment of my last breath. I think it's a beautiful goal. The rub is that it's hard to engage with life itself when life is pretty much only an object lesson or a testing ground or a barrier that I'm ultimately interested in eliminating.

The moon rests on the water's horizon, and a path of white reflected lunar light pours itself to me. For a long time I quietly sing and pray. I think about the time when I felt like Jesus and I were hanging out for the day, and how when I stopped to get gas I told him, "You know how much money I have in my pocket—you decide when to stop the gas pump." The pump stopped at exactly $11. I reached into my pocket and found a ten and a one-dollar bill. I laughed and said, "Okay, you know how much change is in there too. I'll top this off, and you stop it when I get to the last penny." I didn't have any other form of payment on me. I began to top the tank off. Eighty-two cents later the Jeep would take no more. I fished around in my pocket and found exactly eighty-two cents. It was a delightful moment, a moment when this Jesus with whom I'd been spending the day played a game with me and I knew he was right there. That's the Jesus, and those are the moments, that delight me and make me long for the embrace that will come when the veil between this place and the next is removed. This is the Jesus who inspires me to be weird, even if I am clumsy and even if I tend to over-pay. Even if people like Loma find me too confusing to be desirable as a result. I thank Jesus that I know him.

And then I suddenly feel a tiny invitation in my gut to step out onto the water. I know that if I step out, it will hold, just like it did for Peter. I sit trans-fixed, the moment pregnant with the magic of what if. The feeling urges me to move, pleads with me to simply step out onto the water. I feel my muscles beg-ging to slide off the edge of the boat. And then I think about how Peter began to sink, and I think about something else, and then I think about something else, and then the moment is gone, and I find myself sucked back into my brain once again. I don't move.

What did I have to lose? There was no prospect of shame if I had stepped onto the water and fallen in. It would not have surprised Robert if I had tried. And there was an incredible experience to gain if it had worked. What if the wa-ter had held? What if? What would I do with that fact? How much would that upset my understanding of the world, and how wondrously so? But once again I'm shown that I simply do not believe the way I say I believe.

Why is it so much easier to venture out away from a career and into minis-try and poverty than it is to simply risk getting wet? Am I that tied to my control and my brain? Is this all just a game, something where I am willing to trust what I can argue, but not what I can only feel and act upon? Have I changed that much since I felt the huge leap of moving out here just because I had a hunch? Am I worried that God won't come through? Am I working to protect my fragile faith, worried that if the water doesn't hold I won't step out later with other things?

Maybe. Probably. Yes.

When I was at Teen Challenge mom's friend Melinda had cancer, and I prayed and told my mom I thought God wanted to heal the cancer, but wanted it to be something that we all contributed to. Not a surprising strategy given the "tremendous man of God" setting and personal place I was in at the time. I told her I thought we should pray and do different sorts of fasts for her. Mom gave up Diet Coke, and others gave up different things, and every time they wanted the things from which they were fasting, they would pray for Melinda. An entire community grew around her.

Once when I was home I went to her house to meet her. Mom had told her a great deal about me. She was desperate. As we sat by the sunny window of her Victorian living room, she asked me what I thought she should do. She was overwhelmed with fear and sadness.

I told her to sing.

I felt like an idiot, a little idiot child with no decorum regarding the gravity of her situation for saying it, but I told her she should sing. I told her there was still much to celebrate, no matter what happened, and that she should sing. Tears came to her lashless eyes and rolled down her sallow cheeks. She asked me if I knew she was from a family of musicians, and that her mother had sung with the Metropolitan Opera. It was the perfect answer, and it melted her. I had her sign my journal, as I have had each of the retarded men do since, to pray for her. I still believed that she would be healed, and not just in some "it brought the family together and she died in peace" sort of way. I still believed that her sickness would be removed and that she would show up at church or the movies.

But she died about six weeks after I told her to sing. And that was the last time I've ever believed that a miracle has been promised to me, and it was the last time I ever let someone else see that I had even so much as a hunch that something special could happen. I felt like I had abused my mother and her friends, and Melinda too for that matter. I'd been wrong, and I'd been wrong while claiming to speak for God. I was ashamed of my voice. I was ashamed of his behavior. I'd believed him, and they'd believed me, and we'd all been duped. I didn't have a place for that. I was already well aware that I was living this quixotic life, this forever chasing after the next grand endeavor, and I knew that the dragons usually turned out to be windmills in my own world, and that was okay because in my own world I was after the adventure and the prospect that one day, just one day, the dragon would be real and I would know my identity as a gallant charging knight. But I had no sense of the caveat about my tendency to trust illusions when I told my mother to believe that her friend would not die of an emaciating cancer. I had no place for that, and my childlike faith, the romantic faith that believed, was made to feel like a fool. So I put it neatly away, folded respectfully but tucked away with the other relics of childhood and childish dreams, like the batman cap or the magic flying blanket.

I knew that something had broken in me when Melinda died, but I still assumed that when I was alone, sitting for an hour on the bow of a friend's boat in the moonlight, and I felt as though Jesus were inviting me out onto the water, I would trust enough to risk it. I was wrong.

34.

Aidan

Today is the day Danielle will have her first child. Two nights ago I joined them for a dinner of spicy Chinese food because someone had told her that spicy food sometimes induces labor. I arrived at the hospital in shorts and an untucked light blue shirt, Tevas on my feet and a cooler on my shoulder. In it were green grapes, shrimp, cheese and crackers, drinks and other assorted party snacks.

Danielle's parents were in the room with the happy couple when I arrived, and together we enjoyed the sun and the sound of the mother/child heartbeat monitors. Quiet music was playing, most notably Rich Mullin's "Let Mercy Lead," a song sung to a child named Aidan, which is what David and Danielle have decided to name their son. David is nearly twitching with excitement, and Danielle has felt great ever since the spinal block. We keep replaying the Aidan song, and David says he wants it to be playing when his son arrives. Danielle's mother, Sue, glows in the striped sunlight pouring through the window blinds. Randy, Danielle's father, says Sue looks ready to be a grandma, rolling back and forth in the blonde wooden rocking chair. The expectant grandmother nearly explodes with joy at the thought. Danielle says not to eat all of the food; she wants some later.

And then it is time for Randy and Sue and me to leave the room for the delivery. We stand in the hallway outside the room, and we listen to the activity inside. We joke about whatever comes to mind. The sounds inside the room escalate, and then we hear the cry of a baby. I congratulate Randy, and he congratulates me on becoming an honorary uncle. Randy hugs Sue, and then he notices that she is looking out of the corner of her eye as though she is listening carefully to what's happening inside the room.

"What?" Randy asks.

"He only cried one time." Sue answers.

We all pause, straining our ears. It's the first time the possibility of things not going perfectly seems to have occurred to Randy. I know it's the first time I've considered it.

Inside we hear Danielle.

"What? What's wrong?"

There is motion inside the room. The door flies open and a nurse runs down the hallway.

"What's going on?" Danielle has not given in to her fear, but it's clearly building within her.

We hear David speaking to her in low tones.

Sue's hand rises to her mouth, and her eyes go red and wet. Aidan has still not made another sound.

The three of us step across the hallway to look back through the open doorway without blocking it. There is a curtain drawn between us and Danielle. Sue pushes into Randy's chest.

We hear something about the NIC-U, and we hear the locks being flipped on the wheels of a cart, and then the cart with Aidan under its plastic bubble passes through the door and by us. David is following closely, pushing the curtain aside. Danielle is covered in sheets and baby blue hospital grown. Her eyes are locked on David, who turns back to her and stops. A fierce promise transpires in their gaze, and David runs to catch up with the nurses and his newborn son. Danielle sees her mother. Time stops. A nurse closes the door.

David is gone a very long time. When the doctors wrap up with Danielle, Sue goes into the room. I stay with Randy in the waiting area. We pace and wander around some from time to time, drinking decaf. At one point two nurses heading from the NIC-U see us, but not until one of them says, "But it sure doesn't look good." Her face freezes, both Randy and I are transfixed, and then she decides to pretend that she wasn't talking about Aidan as she and her co-worker pass us.

I promised to call back to Zionsville and tell family friends how things went. I try my mother, but she's not home. David's mother and her husband are in Maine, and I wouldn't dare be the one to call them anyway. I try the church but get voicemail. I dial a friend of David's mother, and she answers. I hadn't realized just how unprepared I was to say anything yet. As soon as the thought about my words comes to me, I collapse into tears in the small phone nook.

"Something's wrong." I say.

"Oh my God." Betty Sue gasps. "How wrong?"

"It doesn't —"

"What?"

"He only cried once. He's alive, but we don't know what's happening."

"Oh, no. Oh, Danielle."

I'm a wreck.

"What do you know?" Betty Sue's voice pushes through my trembling groans.

"Nothing." I choke out. "I heard a nurse say it didn't look good. He's not going to make it." I don't know this, but the horror of it tackles me and I say it.

"Oh God. I'll start calling people and we'll start praying. Has anyone called Don and Sue in Maine?"

"I don't know. I think they were getting a flight today anyway, but I don't know if they've been told anything yet."

Hours later David and Danielle are alone in her room, and friends and family gather in hushed tremor in the waiting area. The diagnosis is hypo-plastic left heart syndrome. There is something wrong with how the blood is pumping and how much oxygen is getting to the blood. When Danielle is wheeled to the NIC-U, or when David is with Aidan, the machine providing him oxygen doesn't have to work as hard. When the physicians touch him, Aidan's body needs 20 percent more help from the machines. Comfort? Terror? Why does this happen? We're told that surgery is going to be likely.

A day passes.

And a second. And still we wait together, stunned, wanting to hope, holding back grief, not wanting to lose faith, not wanting to jinx the process.

On the third day Aidan is wheeled into the operating room, still having shown no improvement. Still having never made a second sound. The operation will involve snaking an instrument through an artery in his thigh all the way to his heart. There is an imbalance of pressures in his heart. There will be massive amounts of anti-coagulant used to keep his blood from clotting too quickly, but the same drug will also make the surgery extremely dangerous. We wonder how much difference the altitude pressure will make. David and Danielle come and go. Friends from seminary wait with the parents. A thousand understood theological answers, and nothing to say about what is happening. We pray. We pray a lot. We hear Danielle's response to the news that the surgery did not go well, and that Aidan died on the table. Fierce embraces are exchanged. We weep and weep for what seems like hours. I hug Danielle and find myself apologizing for the stubble that has grown during the three days of vigil. Through horrible tears we find ourselves laughing. There is simply too much to feel it all. David and Danielle go to be with Aidan. He was cut open during the surgery, and when he did not survive, there was little reason to close the incisions well. With all of the anti-coagulant in his body, the blood soaks through towel after towel. David holds his son until his shirt is drenched with infant blood.

Aidan is cremated. I go with David to pick up the ashes. It is my first time holding the boy. Now the hard part begins for David and Danielle, and to an extent so much less that it barely counts in comparison, for all of us.

35.

Why God Made Moms

Mom came out for the funeral, where Aidan's song was played. Some older people questioned the choice to have a funeral for a baby who died after only three days of life. Other people said things like how at least the grieving process wouldn't be as hard because David and Danielle never really knew Aidan. Other people seemed to keep track and have strong opinions about how much time was appropriate to dedicate to mourning. It was horror on top of horror for Danielle, who has had to not only grieve the loss of her child, but has also had to fight for a sense of permission to do so. She's had to face the obnoxious question: Are you still a mother after your child dies?

The answer is most certainly to the affirmative.

But I don't know much beyond that.

Every mother knows grief. Regret, fear, failures, changes in motherly roles. All of it is a very particular grief truly known only by mothers, and it is experienced in miscarriages, funerals for children, and even in the celebration of a continuing and decent enough relationship with children who have long since outgrown their mothers' laps. And not unlike Danielle, it seems most mothers are challenged regarding the value of their desires to be mothers, challenged for the practicality of their love itself, and eventually challenged to find something else do drop neatly into the space left achingly void in their hearts when the child moves along—the space that is only truly matched by the individual children who create those spaces in her heart in the first place.

My mother is trying to figure out what's next for her. My dad will be retiring soon, early, and he knows what's next for him. A growing passion for Romania has mystified us all, but he has already repeatedly visited a tiny village to work with an orphanage and church there. Mom is feeling the pressure to find her own next thing. We assume grandchildren will be coming at some point, but she feels like she's supposed to have a ministry or job passion, something she does outside of the home. In the past she has talked about children's books.

As we discuss our respective aches to be used, to have a mission in life, it strikes me that we're cut from the same cloth. Maybe we're not the only ones. Both my mother and I are desperate to point to something outside of ourselves to demonstrate our worth and our utility. Strangely, somewhere we've come to believe those are the same thing. But they are not. There is a great difference between being worthless and useless, and there is a great difference between the things that make us useful and the true measure of our worth. One is what we do, and the other is what we are. One is developed and grown, and the other is full and unchanging from the moment of our conception.

But it's hard to build an economy on worth. It's hard to move a society forward, what with our dedication to Darwin's rules of merit-based dating and all, with inherent personal value. Grades don't measure intrinsic importance.

And it does come down to importance, because in measuring importance we find some way of measuring our relative position to our need for the God we're all desperate not to need. We're certainly here to do work, and utility is an important thing, and there are absolutely a great many valid and critical reasons why we build such potent structures of reward and punishment around utility and counter-productivity. The trap is that for all of our obsessions regarding our status on the scales of utility, none of it means squat about what we're really worth.

Everyone knows this. I know this, and my mom knows it too. God loves me. Good. I know. It's good news, warm and fuzzy and sweet sounding. But it's totally useless information because it sure as hell isn't going to help me get the job if I put it on my resume. The phone company won't take my intrinsic value in lieu of payment for my delinquent bill. No wonder it's so hard to pay attention to. No wonder I can hear about God loving me, and still have this incredible need to go prove that his love has been rewarded, and his mercy preserved for someone else. No wonder I can conceive of being useful enough to be worth something more than was already worth grieving from the first moment of my existence. No wonder I don't know wonder.

God grins about the ironic coolness of Truth. What could be more useful than the useless truth about my worth? What could be more helpful to me as I live in a fallen world than to finally get that I am loved beyond the reasons to love me, and that I am worth more than the love I earn? What could be more practical knowledge than to know, in a way that means I know it as though it is absolute fact, that however my other endeavors may go, however many dragons turn out to be windmills and however many times the water doesn't hold beneath my feet and however many times the people for whom I pray still die, that however any of these things go, there is nothing to be gained or lost regarding my ultimate position in the universe? What could be more practical wisdom in the world than the wisdom that would free people to live and love for the sake of loving and living, not because they were looking for a reflection of themselves by which they could measure their own cosmic height? What could be better, more practical and helpful knowledge to the world than for us to know that we were all born already tall enough for this ride?

And as soon as I think it, I lose it again. As soon as it becomes clear, it slips from me. I think that's because as soon as I think it, as soon as it becomes clear, I want to translate it into action, and as soon as I do that I hit the wall of translation that my soul, and creation, is flatly unable to overcome.

That's what mothers are for. My mother loves me and has been willing to launch tears on my behalf since she first learned that I existed. So what? What do I do with that? Nothing. What could I do with that? It's already complete, full and whole and in need of nothing from well before I could even begin to respond. And for as long as a mother is a mother, from the first moment to every visit full of discussions about the meaning of life and our fragile grasp on our ideas of what we will do with our days here, there exists a love that has no concern for our utility, because there is so much to revel in regarding what we're worth.

My mother would fight as fiercely for my life, and would grieve my death, as beautifully and majestically as Danielle has with Aidan, with plenty of passion and plenty of tears for a myriad other evidences of love as well. And my knowledge of that fact is not useless knowledge. It reorders the world and it thrusts me to the top of the value chart—not in a way that competes with other people, but in a way that sure as hell tells me where I stand as compared to my job or the stupid phone bill.

I'm glad my mom has been here with me this week. I tell her so as we walk to the gate at the airport.

She cries at good-byes. I've always sort of thought that was silly; I'd be seeing her again soon, so what was the big deal? Finally, finally, I believe I'm beginning to get it.

My mother's claim to the emotions far exceeds my own, but I think I understand how they work, and the excitement mingles with sadness when I think how long it will be before I can truly know them with my own child.

I think there are certain people, like a mother's son, who infuse one's world with a wonderful sense of "just right." My mom loves Christmas Eve because everyone is home. All of the chicks are in the nest. I believe she finds a great deal of purpose and satisfaction in her love for us, in her role as mother. When we're home, everything is "just right."

Just right is a good way to feel. In good-byes, my mom has to let go of just right. She has to feel it drain from her and she has to brace for how not just right things will be after the good-bye.

Motherhood, from the first introduction, is a steady tearing away from just right. Mothers pour themselves into their children, almost unilaterally, knowing the whole time that the good-bye is coming no matter what they do. And yet, for some reason, they continue to pour. It is a love that overflows, splashing and careless because of its excess. It is a love that tries not to demand, just to be allowed to exist and to matter. It is a love that sacrifices and empathizes and wants always more for the beloved. It is in the quiet sharing of the love, in the moments when the child, having no idea how to respond, simply closes his eyes and rests to the sound of a lullaby that the mother knows just right.

And then comes the good-bye. The moment of powerlessness, of not quite rejection, but a silent desperation to love more, to pour and have back the moment of the lullaby. It is a wave of fear and sorrow that for a moment challenges the value of the bond. It watches the beloved until he can no longer be seen around the corner. It watches the airplane until the speck disappears in the clouds. It weeps for itself as it cries joy in the beauty of its existence and devotion to the beloved.

As I watched my mother board her plane, I briefly tasted that good-bye, that seeping nausea at the loss of just right. I had no idea how to respond. It scared me and hooked me at the same time. But, oh, how I long for its return. How beautiful to have someone for whom my love was so strong. How gripping was my desire to love, and how completely was I willing to risk. How thankful I will be to know it not only as a son, but as a father.

As I walk along the concourse windows, watching my mother's plane push out and taxi away, I can't help feeling overwhelmed by the joy of it all—by the bittersweet mixture of loving and being loved this way, by the glimpse into what it is like to be my mother, or any mother, and I ask God if he knows the feeling.

He assures me he is quite familiar with it.

36.

Sandy

Not all mothers are the same, I'm sorry to say. The first time I went looking for the Prodigal Coffee House, a place that's open in the evenings to provide a safe haven for runaway teenagers, I knew I was near the correct intersection, but I didn't see the coffee house. I did see a corner restaurant called Mother's, though. Certainly that would be a good place to find a friendly face and ask directions. Surely anyplace called Mother's would know about runaway teens, right?

Mother was a gay man who looked like Captain Kangaroo in a white home-decorated sweatshirt with a giant bejeweled brooch hanging like a drunken parrot from his breast. I asked if he knew about a place nearby that catered to runaway teenagers. His response still gives me chills.

"Honey, if there were runaway teenagers around here, I'd know about it."

I told him I must have been given bad information, and beat a hasty retreat.

***

Mother's, it turns out, is about 200 feet from the Prodigal Coffee House, where tonight maybe 40 teens microwave popcorn inside and smoke cigarettes on the front steps, and seem to have somehow continued to live without having been seen by the predator across the street.

That could be a divine thing, or it could be a simple reflection of the invisibility granted to, and coveted by, teenagers who don't want to be known, and certainly don't want to be discovered by worried parents or worrisome authorities. Most of them are known by multiple pseudonyms. Pooh Bear, Pee-Wee, Cubby, Reggie (with hard Gs like in "regular," so only people who know the boy as he's living today will address or ask for him correctly). The names usually reflect memories from a not so distant, and generally not so pleasant, childhood. Names of fictitious characters or heroes of different sorts. Names both claimed and given. Most of the kids have at least two such monikers, and they change them every so often. I assume it has something to do with making themselves as difficult to track down as possible, but I'm sure there's also a good deal of truth behind the idea that they go by a revolving list of nicknames because they don't really know who they are yet, and they absolutely don't want to be saddled forever with the choices they have to make living the way they do. An alter ego comes with a fresh credit history, and when the things a person does under one name become too great to cope with any longer, the entire persona can be dropped and a new name adopted. Maybe the disconnect is why celebrities and killers refer to themselves in the third person. Our old names and sense of self can't handle the whole truths about us.

When I come here, I generally make my way to the chair under the stairs, under the window across from the sofa. I don't like to initiate conversation, mostly because I have no idea what I would have to say to the kids. I'm of a runaway temperament myself, and I don't know what advice I'd be able to share that is so important that I should approach them. I tend to camp out and let people wander past me, and listen to them or tell them about myself as they choose. I'm the outsider—they have an entire culture of their own, and the staff and regular volunteers know much more about what to say to them.

Usually the place is loud and the sofa across from my chair gets a good deal of use. Tonight I sat down before I noticed that there was someone sleeping on the couch. Pooh Bear, a nurturing but emotionally stunted young lady who would be a sophomore in high school if she was not living the all-night life of the Goth crowd, is being especially protective of the girl on the couch. She's full of drama and urgency in her attempts to maintain quiet and as little motion as possible back in this portion of the room. She nods that I'm okay; I'm just sitting here, my chin in my hand and my elbow on the arm of the broken recliner, watching.

The girl on the couch looks like she could be from Zionsville. She's fourteen, maybe fifteen, with straight, well-conditioned sandy blonde hair, jeans, white and pink tennis shoes, and a grey Michigan sweatshirt with blue letters. She's lying on her side, semi-fetal, with her top arm crossed in front of her stomach and ending in a fist that wraps around the folded cuff of her oversized sleeve. Her other hand curls up to a light touch on the bottom of her chin. She's wearing an Irish engagement ring with the heart pointing out; does that mean she has someone or not? I don't remember. The skin of her face is free of blemishes, and she is remarkably pretty in an Ivory Girl sort of way. Like I'd picture my daughter being, I guess. Her gnawed-upon thumbnail shows the remains of a mother of pearl polish job that's due for a touch-up.

I've never seen her before. And she doesn't look the part of a runaway. She must be new. So beautiful and so sweet, and so young. She shouldn't be here. None of them should be here, but I'm used to the others. I wave Pooh Bear over to me.

"Who is this?" I ask.

"I call her Sandy 'cause of her hair." She says. "Clever, huh?"

"Yeah. What's her deal?"

"She ran away last night. From Salt Lake City. She got in a bad fight with her dad and he locked her in her room, but she got out. She used all her money to get here on the bus."

"Why here? Did she know someone? Did she know you?"

"I never seen her before today. I think she just wanted to get away and start someplace new."

"Is she sick? Why is she sleeping?" I ask.

"I gave her something. She's had a hard day."

"I bet. She probably didn't sleep much on the bus either."

"No. It was harder than that. Want some gum?" She offers me some Big Red.

"Thanks." I say, taking a piece. "Why was her day hard?"

"She, uh. I don't know."

"What?"

"She did a guy for $20."

"Oh man." I say.

"Yeah. It was her first time. But don't tell anyone, okay?"

"Yeah. Thanks PB."

"Hey, try to keep people quiet back here, okay? I gotta grab a smoke." And she's across the room to the front porch.

Sandy. Fourteen. At home yesterday. A virgin this morning. A prostitute before dinner. Asleep on who knows what right now. I can't even imagine what tomorrow will bring. I sit and watch her, and soon there are tears rolling down my cheeks. Thank God, at the very least, for this place and the people who will be here for whatever's next.

This all could have been avoided. Today. I spent this afternoon watching movies and playing computer games at Skinny Robert's apartment while he was working in the apartment complex rental office. Sandy was going through hell. If I'd known I would have helped. If I'd known I would have given her whatever she needed. A rage passes through me, and I experience a deep desire to find and kill the man she met this afternoon. What kind of person would do what he did? I can't even bear to ask, with her sleeping right there.

How horrible could things have been at home that this was preferable? Her clothes are clean, her shoes new and name brand. She wasn't poor. There are no bruises on her face. She doesn't seem to have been beaten. Pooh Bear said it was Sandy's first time. It must not have been incest she was running from. Well, if the story is true.

It's a silly question. There is no way she knew what she was getting into. It's not like people can really plan to run away, and even if they do plan for it, they can't actually know what they'll encounter. I don't think they, or any of us, choose between the frying pan and the fire—we only choose to flee what feels like the frying pan. It's not a matter of upgrade; it's only a matter of escape. And as soon as the choice is made, a promise is made to accept the consequences for the choice. And the consequences are as much a portion of the revenge as leaving is. It's like shooting yourself in the foot to leave bloodstains on someone else's carpet; it's not a rational choice, but there is an incredible pull to make such choices, especially when you're young and feeling powerless. You make the choice, and then suffer for it. Lamentably, there is no shortage of people willing to facilitate the suffering.

For twenty damned dollars.

Sandy. The new name of a life suddenly on the trajectory of ruin. The new receptacle of lies, poisons and strangers' demons. I say that I wish I'd known, that I would have done something. But what? What would I have done, and for how long, and for how many? By the time the Sandys in the world have run away from home, the best that places like Prodigal Coffee House can do is temper the desperate choices forced by desperate situations. By the time kids walk through these doors, their worlds are already on fire.

Moths aflame and burning in flashing streaks straight to an inglorious impact with the cold hard ground, each of these kids. There is only a lightning moment in which to catch a burning moth before it is too late, and even then fire burns moth wings so quickly that the damage can never be completely remedied. Sandy can never have back the parts of her that were burned away this afternoon, no matter what comes tomorrow. The fire is everywhere, and the moths shoot all around this place, all around this world. The only mercy in the arrangement is that the ground comes quickly, because the pain is too great and the fire too dangerous for busy people to know what to do for the moths. For fourteen year old children. For fourteen year old children there is simply too little to be done? At fourteen it's already too late? Can that be?

The rage I feel is justice. But it is also the knee-jerk reaction of someone who is staggeringly offended to be bothered by the sudden and flaming needs of strangers who feel as though they should be the responsibility of someone else. Their parents. Their teachers. Their clergy. Their friends and their friends' families. There should be a program for these kids. I don't want flaming moths getting so close to my hair, to my face, to my eyes. This is not supposed to be my problem. I have plenty of my own to worry about—this should not fall to me. This is not my problem!

Shit. This is my problem.

And it is the chosen problem of the staff here. Well-educated, beautiful (the staff is all women), absolutely capable of pursuing a host of other options if only they'd been able to ignore the burning moths. They're not workers. They're not preachers. They're not teachers. They're mothers—mother-ers—patching healing where they can, misting the air to fight the flames without washing the moths to the ground, praying and crying and being strong and enduring when everyone else gives up. And coming back day after day, tragedy after tragedy, rape after rape, disappearance and murder after disappearance and murder, failed attempted and eviction following hope and effort, and followed again with hope and effort. These kids shouldn't have to be the problem of the Prodigal staff, but they are. Thank God.

And Sandy—I want to wake her up to find out what her real name is—is also my problem. But she was my sister before she was my problem, and somehow I am part of the flame that has now touched her. I don't live in Salt Lake City, and I've never met her, but I am part of the problem that has forced her out of her rightful name because I am part of a world that has forged a deep and abiding addiction to convenience and complacency, that will admit to seeing problems, but will ask someone else to address them. It will ask someone else to bring the pizza rolls so it can continue to watch television. It will ignore children dying on the street so it can get to the movies on time.

I am part of the world that has forgotten the power and ability of community. For the shaping of perspectives; for the weight of accountability it can bring to lives and groups. Today the world cares little for its ability to be a living safety net that can catch little girls when their fathers seem to be greater monsters to them than what they will surely encounter in the leering looks of men willing to buy a young girl's virginity. And it's no better for young homeless boys; just ask that Mother across the street, honey.

I feel, deep down, my responsibility for the suffering of this young girl curled up across from me, but I don't really understand a thing about how to be part of something else. I don't get how community can do the things I know it can do. I don't know. But there must be something that can be done—there is so much wrong that there must be something.

Frankly, the weight of Sandy's reality is greater than my ability to even think about solutions and strategies and moral incumbencies. I'm having a translation issue that's not letting me escape this reality into the comfortable distance of my brain. Sandy won't go there with me, at least not while she's still right in front of me. But I know I'm going to have to make some changes. I'm going to have to learn something about fighting fires in community. For another hour I sit, crying, drying up, crying again, telling Pooh Bear and the others that I'm okay. Pooh Bear hugs me and tells me it'll be okay.

Will it? Will it ever be okay?

As for lovely Sandy, the fourteen year old homeless prostitute with a pink and yellow bedroom standing empty in Salt Lake City, she's still asleep on the sofa when I leave for the evening, with Pooh Bear standing guard, two charred moths orange and glowing in the light of a fire against which they don't have a chance on their own.

37.

Why God Invented Dads

I've been working with the retarded guys for over a year now. I earn $1000 per month, and give $100 to Jon as support for his job at the street school where he teaches Bible and Math to kids who have lost their invitation to public schools for one reason or another. And the rest? I don't know where it goes, but it's gone as soon as it's mine. Rent, my share of the utilities, food, an occasional movie, a book here and there, and credit card payments. Lots and lots of dollars to the credit card companies, who have stopped raising my limit. I have been picking and choosing which bills to pay for months, and I'm going backwards.

When I was in Chicago I couldn't find ways to spend all I made, and I know that I haven't reined myself in enough during my time here. Of course, I only earned $5,000 the first year I was here and about $10,000 the second, which isn't much. It's May 26. In a little over two months I'll be 26. I should not be at the end of my financial rope, but I am. I could go and get a real job, but I don't want that. I pick up extra shifts here and there, and I sand and stain the decks of mountain homes with David when it's warm, which helps some, but I don't see a way to keep the job I have.

I'm going to have to ask my dad for a loan. I don't know if he'll do it, either. The last time I borrowed money from him I paid him back so irregularly that it was a lousy experience for both of us. Of course I was in high school then, but the memory still lingers, and I expect he'll feel as though he's learned his lesson. Besides, I could go and get a job job any time, right? I was the big shot advertising guy; there must be people lined up to hire a guy like me. He won't actually point those things out, but I feel like that's part of the unspoken dynamic between us. He answers on the third ring.

"Nyellow."

"Hey Dad."

"Howdy."

"Whatcha doing?" I ask.

"Just about to bring the chicken in from the grill."

"Oh. Well, I don't want to take a lot of your time."

"You're welcome to my time." I hear the screen door to the back deck open and close as he carries the wireless phone with him. "What's up?"

"Well, I've kind of run out of money."

Silence. I hurry forward.

"I'm just making so little that I can't gain ground on old debt. I've got my budget under control, but I'm not even able to pay the minimums on my credit cards anymore."

"Uh-huh." The lid on the grill slams down. I don't hear him pass back through the screen door. He must be standing outside where Mom won't hear the conversation. Not a good sign.

"So what I was hoping is that we could find some sort of loan plan."

"I don't know. Last time wasn't good."

"Dad, that was eight years ago. I'm not the same person anymore."

"You know, part of good stewardship is proactive—you have an obligation to earn enough to get by. I don't think I'd be doing you any favors if I helped you delay learning that." He says.

"I know you think what I'm doing is foolish –"

"I've never said that. This has nothing to do with what you're doing –"

"God pays what God pays, Dad."

"That's not exactly the sort of argument that's going to help you in this conversation."

"I don't want to have to argue for your help. Believe me, I don't like this any more than you do, and I'd go anyplace else for help if it meant I could avoid asking you, but I'm out of options." My voice breaks a little. I hate that. Spoiled brat.

"How much do you need?" He asks.

"Nine thousand. That's the total of my debt. I'd be willing to pay you interest and I'd be happy to have my paychecks sent you and to have you send me an allowance so you'd be completely in control of the repayments."

He laughs. "You want to know how interested I am in doing your budget for you and having you come to me every time you want a few extra dollars from your paycheck?"

"So you're saying no."

"I need to think about it. If you need an answer now, it would be no, but let me talk to Mom and I'll have to get back to you."

"Okay." I say.

"Okay." He says.

"Have a good dinner."

"You too."

I'm trembling with rage and fear and frustration and self-loathing as I hang up the phone.

"Argh!" I yell. At my dad, at God, at myself, at the world I've chosen to trust with this whole path of life, at my own foolish choices, at my vulnerability and weakness. Just flat stupid weakness. I wouldn't want to invest in it either.

But that's what it feels like I'm asking for: an investment. I know that it's his money and that I'm a bad credit risk because I have no idea what I'm building, but isn't there something else worth the money? Isn't there something about what I'm doing that has real value, some value that isn't monetary? I feel like I'm on an important path, and that at some point support for me will have some value, even if the reward doesn't come directly back to the person investing the money. Am I not some sort of conduit to what the Kingdom of Heaven is doing in the world? I feel like the rules of the worldly economy don't apply to me in the same way. And even if they do, isn't this time in my life worth something, for all I'm learning? I'm scratching at it, but I can't tell if I'm scratching at something real or if I'm just scratching to try to claw my way out of feeling like a screw-up who's just had to look at how much he's screwed up and is trying to negotiate a loophole.

The phone rings. That was quick.

"Hello?"

"Hi. My name's Jeff Johnsen. I run Mile High Ministries and was told by Pastor Tony at Agape Christian Church that I should meet you."

"Oh? Cool."

"Tony said he thought you might be a good candidate for a position we're trying to fill downtown. Do you have a minute?"

Uh, ye-ah. "Sure."

"The place is called Bud's Warehouse. Have you heard of it?"

"I don't think so."

"It's sort of like a non-profit Home Depot. We take in donated building materials and then sell them at very affordable prices mostly to folks downtown."

"Okay."

"Bud's employees are mostly people coming out of prison or off of welfare. We provide a place that teaches them basic skills and then helps them find positions elsewhere."

"Sounds cool."

"We think it is. But we've had a hard time getting it rolling. It's been in existence for about two years, and we've had a few real successes with people, but the business itself has struggled. We just lost the executive director, and we're looking for someone who can come in and turn the business around."

"Wow."

"There's a strong board of business people, so there will be plenty of support on that end, but we need someone with passion and energy who can bring in donations and manage employees in a loving way."

"Sounds good. How many employees are there, and how big a place are we talking about? And just how much difficulty is the business having?"

"There are currently three employees, though we've had as many as twelve. The place is at 26th and Larimer, right on the edge of the Five Points area. Oh, of course, you'd know the area—it's only a few blocks from Agape."

"Sure."

"It's a 15,000 square foot warehouse with an office, conference area, and plenty of space to grow."

"What about the difficulties getting the business rolling?"

"Like I said, there's a strong board, and we initially raised $150,000 to get things rolling. But there have been quite a few bumps along the way during the past two years."

"Uh huh."

"And this is where we're looking for someone who can really come in and grab the reins. This afternoon the checking account balance is at about $13,000."

"Okay."

"And the business is losing roughly $8,000 per month."

"Geez."

"We're committed to making the business work. We wouldn't bring someone new in and only give them a month to make a turnaround."

"So what kind of turnaround time is the board committed to?"

"Well, there is no set timeframe. While the board is solid, not everyone agrees that the best option is to continue."

"No pressure there." I quip.

Jeff laughs. "I know it's a lot to consider all at once. But the business model has proven itself in places like Phoenix and Baltimore, so we know it can work."

"Man, to turn an $8,000 a month shortfall around." I say.

"There's more. If Bud's works, we have quite a few other things we'd like to do. The vision is for Bud's to be so successful that it can shoulder the load for other ministry-focused businesses as they get off the ground."

"So the vision isn't just to turn Bud's around."

"Exactly. We're looking for someone who can turn Bud's into a big fat cash cow."

I laugh at the audacity of the plan.

"I know, it's a long way from where we are today. But the cash cow part brings up another important attribute we're looking for in the new executive director. He or she will have to be willing to work doubly hard, and make Bud's work doubly hard, because there will be more than just the weight of one donation-dependent business to manage. There will be hard choices, and times when it seems like the profits that could pull Bud's a step ahead will be diverted into other endeavors over which you'll—or whoever—will have no control. The person we're looking for will have to be a quick study of people, able to produce on the business front, navigate and manage a board, and be a team player who will submit personal gratification to the needs of the larger effort."

"It sure sounds exciting." I say.

"Would you be interested in getting together for breakfast sometime the first part of next week to talk about it?" He offers.

"I'd like that."

"How about the Butcher Block? It's just down the street from Bud's, and I love greasy spoons."

"So do I."

"Say Monday at 8:30?"

"Great. See you then. And thanks for calling."

"I'm looking forward to it. Bye."

"Bye."

***

Here's a question that doesn't come up every day. What do you wear to create a first impression in a meeting at a smoke-filled greasy spoon with someone who is looking for an impactful business person to run a ministry in the ghetto? Dress up and you look out of step with your environment. Dress down and you may look too ministry-focused to be seen as able to rake in the dough. Normally the answer would be to follow the lead you'd seen set by the person you were going to meet, but I'd never seen Jeff before. I nearly called Pastor Tony to ask, but I knew I'd never hear the end of that. After all of my consternation about it, I forgot to take any clothing with me to work with the retarded guys on Sunday. I ended up scurrying the guys to their respective destinations Monday morning, then I grabbed the pager in hopes that I wouldn't have to leave our breakfast and burned a streak across town to the Butcher Block in the jeans, sweatshirt and boots I'd worn to church the day before. Jeff was already seated at one of the booths when I arrived. He looks like a skinnier version of the actor Owen Wilson, with green eyes, a beard and a curly-ended strawberry-blonde mullet. After a quick greeting he apologized for being dressed up in his khakis and golf shirt, but said he had a meeting in Lakewood immediately following ours and that he had to dress the part. That's when I knew for sure that I liked the guy.

Breakfast with Mile High Jeff was without question the most incredible meal of my life. Not only did the giant smothered breakfast burrito and Mountain Dew only cost $2, but every topic we covered felt like a pure Vulcan Mind Meld. He'd read everything I'd read, and seemed able to quote about half of it from memory. In most instances the next book he'd turned to was different from the one I'd picked, so we compared notes on where our thinking had gone.

I told him about my previous couple of years, about my family, and about my experience with Sandy at Prodigal Coffee House, which turns out to also be a Mile High Ministries endeavor. He told me about Mile High, about his history, about Christian economic development, about community, and absolutely set my brain on fire.

Two days later, yesterday, Wednesday, I met the Bud's Board. I'm not sure I have all of the doubters pegged, but I know for sure who the scrappers are. The chairman is a general contractor named Bruce; loud, strong, with blonde hair like you only see on Vikings or little kids, and a face that I'm sure turns bright red when he yells. The next scrapper is also named Bruce and is also a general contractor, though I got the impression that his business has moved to a larger or more commercial scale. Red moustache, white Volvo, tweed earth toned clothing. Dresses like he has daughters, and has a quiet enough disposition to give me that impression too. The third scrapper was Chris, a vice president at a brokerage firm. I don't remember which one, but it was one of the big ones. Eddie Haskell from Leave it to Beaver. High energy, but a nervous sort of energy like I've seen in brokers and real estate agents before. He seemed like he was probably the life of the party as he cut his teeth in the fast times, hard-partying financial industry of the 1980s. He reminded me of people I'd known in Advertising. I liked him, but knew that his type is either the greatest ally a person can have, or the one most likely to deliver the bullet to the back that you never see coming. Given his participation on the board, I assumed he was more the good kind.

There were a couple of people whom I immediately identified as doubters ready to close the business. Susan, the only woman on the board, looks and dresses like the accountant she is. Where Eddie Haskell Chris was full of ideas to support a young new hire, Susan wanted someone with a time-tested track record in business, education, ministry, accounting, fundraising, and probably a dozen other areas. Viking Bruce disagreed.

"We're looking for someone young, aggressive, and willing to muscle this place to success. We don't need theories and programs; we need balls!" He said.

And Susan shut up, pissed. He knew it and clearly didn't care. I thought of my dad.

Bill the Banker, a retired branch president and the only Black guy on the board, also seemed to be one of the people who was more in favor of pulling the plug on the place. To be fair, the numbers obviously work in his favor far more than they point to a viable business. It also seems that Bill is handling a micro-lending program that falls under the same Mile High Ministries umbrella, and my impression is that Bud's Warehouse money is somehow tied to his lending program's operating funds. As Bill began to explain some of that for background purposes, Viking Bruce urged everyone to stay on task. Eddie Haskell Chris and Tweed Bruce echoed the thought.

There were a few other people also in attendance, but I didn't really get reads on them. One works making outdoor signs, and is apparently in the process of creating some for the warehouse. One runs some other urban ministry and has a cleaning company or something like that to make ends meet. There was one Latino board member, a pastor who arrived late and whose particular interest in working with youth seemed not to match what I understood about the job. I don't think I answered his questions very well.

After about an hour of group interview, I was asked to step outside and explore the warehouse while they talked. When they called me back in, they offered me the job.

"Now, as to salary." Bill the Banker began. "You'll learn from the books that your predecessor's salary was $48,000 per year, but you're less experienced and the business is no longer in the same place financially. We're only able to offer you $24,000."

"Plus a bonus structure we'll have to figure out together." Viking Bruce added.

Bill the Banker scrunched his face quizzically, and responded to the chairman, "We never talked about that."

"Come on," Eddie Haskell Chris said, "you can't expect someone to take on this much work for so little money. And if—when—the business turns, a bonus is completely reasonable."

The Bruces agreed, and emphasized the point that the bonus would only be paid out of profit.

Andy, the ministry leader with the cleaning company, and the black Member's Only jacket, pointed out, "Though profits are supposed to be turned over to other ministries, so the problem is that then we're looking at choosing between paying a bonus here or impacting lives elsewhere."

Jeff jumped in. "We can figure this stuff out over the next couple of weeks, if you're interested in the job."

I nodded vigorously. "I'd like to see what we can come up with regarding the bonus, but I want the job and don't want to get too hung up on the money until we figure out a way to turn this place around."

Viking Bruce smiled and exchanged a look with Chris.

"There is something else." I say to Jeff. "I noticed when you showed me around that there is a shower in the bathroom off the office, and a second room connected to the office. Plus there is the break area with the refrigerator and microwave. Might it work for me to live here?"

"Now that's what I'm talking about!" Viking Bruce came out of his chair. "Just get it done! Buy in and pick it up! Hell yes you can live here!"

"I don't know." Bill the Banker said. "I don't know if that's legal. And just a month ago that they ripped the security grate right off the wall to break in. It's probably a liability risk. And not safe."

"Ah, he'll be fine." Viking Bruce dismissed Bill. "There's no law against living here, and it's not like anyone's going to ding a non-profit for letting its director live in his office. And nobody's going to mess with someone his size."

Susan turned to me. "Are you bullet-proof, by any chance?"

"So far." I said, not really sure of my meaning. People laughed.

"Good deal. I assume you need to give two weeks' notice?" Viking Bruce asked.

And that was that.

***

So it looks like I pretty much doubled my salary yesterday. Today is sunny. The birds are singing and for the first time in a long time I'm feeling like I can see a little distance down the path in front of me, and it looks like someplace I want to go. I've spent the day reviewing my budget as best as I can remember it, doing laundry and even ironing clothes. But one of the details I hadn't really thought about before is that I don't have a car. I'm going to need a car to get to meetings with board members, donors, and with what I'm told is a fairly large and constant number of people in the suburbs who want to learn more about Bud's Warehouse and about urban ministry in general. I can't afford one. I don't see how I'll be able to for a while yet, either. There's no way I'd be approved for a car loan with my outstanding debt and a brand new job. I haven't heard from my dad, and it looks like I'm going to have to take a pretty big late fee hit before my first Bud's Warehouse check comes in, and that's not going to be good for the credit rating. I've wanted to call home to tell my folks about the job, but want to make sure everything is official first, including the bonus thing.

I hear the mailman make his delivery outside. In it is a large, fairly thick manila envelope with my parents' address in the corner. Dad has sent Suze Orman books before, about money management and that sort of thing. Sue has sent articles about William Wilberforce and his enduring battle to end slavery, with notes about how I should return to advertising. Items that come from Zionsville usually serve mostly to ridicule me and leave me reeling for days. I stare at the envelope without opening it for a moment, assuming from the feel of the contents that my father came across a Fortune magazine article whose title he will have circled in the table of contents, and that he will have added a yellow sticky note saying something like, "this is the reason you're going to have to learn this lesson on your own." Jerk. He doesn't understand that I don't want to be just like him. He doesn't understand that I've seen something he doesn't see. I think of throwing the envelope into the garbage without even opening it—I don't need that kind of crap from him right now. Screw it, in a couple of days I'll be able to

172

call home and tell them about the new job. I open the envelope with the intention of finding some line in the article that I can turn back on him later to highlight the shallowness of his world.

Into my hand slide 20 or 30 heavy gauge pieces of paper, bordered with scrollwork and fancy lettering. There is a note typed on my father's letterhead.

"Enclosed please find stock certificates that today traded for $9,270. This is not a loan. Take this gift and start again. I love you. Dad."

He signed the last word.

38.

The Cost of Ascending Ministry

"But why?" Henry Love doesn't know why I'd leave. He's 22 and has only been living in the program for a year. He's never had a staff person leave.

"Bye bye." Sam Love preempts, angrily. He's five or six years older than his roommate, and has seen a great many staff people leave. They both feel the upsetting of their apple cart deeply. Henry is trying to find a place for it. Sam knows not to bother.

"I'm really going to miss you both." I say. "But we can still go to movies sometimes." I mean it, but I wonder how true this will turn out to be.

"But why you go?" Henry asks again.

"I have another job, Henry Love." I say his name with extra vigor, wanting to connect with the funny game. "I won't be able to work here anymore."

"Don't call, don't call us that." Sam Love—Sam—says. "Don't call him Henry Love and don't call me Sam Love. That's not our name."

"Stop it!" Henry yells at Sam. "Stop talking like that to him!"

"It's okay Henry." I say. "It's just a funny name to remind us that we're friends. We'll still be friends, even if Sam doesn't want me to use that name anymore."

"No we won't." Sam argues. "We won't be friends anymore."

"Stop it, Sam!" Henry slaps Sam.

"No hitting." Sam replies, and then takes a few steps away and begins practicing his air guitar and singing the "Dukes of Hazzard" theme song.

Henry laughs at Sam the Entertainer. They are perfect roommates. So good for each other.

"Henry, can we still go to movies together after I start working somewhere else?" I ask.

"Yes!" He emphasizes that of course we can and that the question is silly. "I miss you."

"I'll miss you too, Henry." I say, rising from the kitchen table, the diet Coke I took from their refrigerator in hand. I turn to the front door of their apartment.

"You can leave the soda here." Sam says.

I stop. I've done nothing but consume from the excesses of these gentle men.

"You're right, Sam. I will leave it here." I place the can on the entertainment center. "Better?"

"That's not where it goes." Sam says, still playing air guitar.

Nailed to the wall by Sam Love. He can't go with me through my convoluted rationalizations, arguments, and far-flung theories and constructs, but he can recognize truth far better than I'll ever be able to.

I carry the diet Coke to the sink, pour it out, and drop the can in the recycling bag. "Sorry Sam."

"That's better." He says.

"See ya Turkey." Henry says, smiling so big I can see his molars.

"See ya Ham." I say back, and close the door behind me.

I descend the three flights of stairs to the parking lot and am on the sidewalk heading for Vince's apartment when I hear Sam yelling from his balcony.

"See ya Turkey!"

"Turkey!" Henry echoes.

"Turkey Love!" Sam yells.

I turn and they're both pressed against the rail, waving as though I may not be able to see them. I swear Heaven says farewell in such ways. I wave back like I'm trying to be seen by an airplane. Someone of normal IQ is parking their car beside me, and I couldn't care less.

"See ya Turkey Lips!" I scream back at them.

For a moment I am every father who ever left a crying child in a window as he headed off to work for the day, and was greeted eagerly upon his return in the evening. I have stolen a trusting heart, caused it pain for the connection, and have been forgiven. And I know what I have done. Could it have been avoided? Should it be avoided? Is what I feel I have to do with my life more important than the small scratches my passing leaves on the worlds of the people who care for me? Is the trade for the pain countered well enough by the good I have brought? I don't know. I don't know. I have done so much wrong. I have said I was doing the best I could when in truth I was only doing the best I was willing to do. I know better. I could defend myself against other people, but I cannot defend myself against my own doubts. But I am willing to accept the waving and laughter of two retarded men as the summary word on the matter, at least for now.

Vince, on the other hand. Vince, and his heart. The heart he listens to. The heart that tells him he is loved. The heart that risked with me. The heart that knew the companionship and the joy of feeling normal with me. The heart that trusted me far more than a man of greater mental acuity would have. Vince. I broke his heart. He did not get angry. He did not plead. He did not ask questions. He did not cry. He just looked at me as though he was waiting for the punchline. He listened and nodded and went quietly to his room and laid down on his bed.

GALL

There is something profoundly wrong about the way I see the world, and about the way I make my choices. I don't care what sort of "that's just the way it is" bullshit rules the world, it's not right to inflict wounds for the sake of progress.

39.

Benevolent White Moses

On a wintry Wednesday evening about a year and a half ago, I had to leave the church service because the tears were coming on and I didn't want to make a scene. I ended up in the parking lot, absolutely bawling. I wanted to be used. I was past the whole deal about wanting God to take my life or have me die and go to Heaven, but I very much wanted to be used in some useful and meaningful manner. I was also convinced that the manner of my utilization should be somehow in line with the skills and abilities God had given me. But I felt like my life was being rejected, or at the very least that it was taking too long. I ended up standing in the snow, and angrily saying, "Well, I'm not letting go. I don't care how long you shake me and ignore me, I'm not letting go." In my mind I had pictures of those little dogs people drag around the kitchen floor on home video shows. I was going to be one of those. I could control my determination to lock my jaws. Still I sobbed within my grief and self-righteous desires for what felt like 20 minutes or so, until I was finally distracted by the huge amounts of snot with which my nose was blowing bubbles. Even my most sublime moments end in interruption by the mundane, and the mundane is almost never flattering.

Bud's Warehouse, burning and rapidly sinking ship that it is, with rats swimming away from the flaming wreckage and looking in scornful disbelief over their shoulders at me as I swim towards it, may well turn out to be the place where my prayers will be answered.

Of course I have just about zero credibility with my new employees. We aren't exactly part of the same demographic. There are currently three employees: Juan, Marcos, and Hector. All of them grew up in rough worlds. Juan, now in his early 20s, was an Olympic hopeful in boxing, who lost his opportunity when he fell into a street fight and got sideways with the law. Marcos is in his late 40s, with a black and grey ponytail, a patch over one eye, and scars from where acid was spilled on him in a fight when he was in prison. He usually wears a black leather motorcycle vest and boots. He also has a black t-shirt with an American flag on it, beneath which is written "try burning this one, asshole." He can't read, but he's the only one who speaks Spanish, which helps in roughly half of our sales. Hector is about three months out of prison and is definitely the meanest and toughest of the three, though I have no idea who would win fights between them.

The warehouse is in an area controlled by an L.A. street gang called the Crips. Their color is blue. A couple of days ago Hector was standing on the sidewalk outside the warehouse waiting for his ride home. In a red sweatshirt. A car full of Crips passed on the one-way street, whipped fiercely around, and came to a screeching halt on the sidewalk about two feet from Hector. A young Black man leapt from the passenger side and leveled a shotgun at Hector.

"Don't you know where you are, boy?" The kid with the gun demanded.

Hector didn't even move the sole of his shoe from the wall against which we was leaning. He didn't even take the cigarette from his mouth. He started his response with the sound of air brakes. "Tss. Fuck off, Stupid. I don't play that little boy gang-banger shit."

The young man with the shotgun yelled threats at Hector and climbed back into the car, which pealed out backwards, spun around, and screamed away in the direction it had originally been heading.

Juan and Marcos and I had been standing about 50 feet away, in the open garage door on the same street. They had both been ready to fight. I'd pulled my cell phone from my pocket and flipped it open to be ready to call 911 from a good hiding place. After the car sped away they went and shook wrists with Hector, exclaiming what a tough guy he was. I went to my office and signed us up for an alarm system with silent alarm buttons that can be worn looped over a person's belt.

But that's cool, our differences. I may end up learning from them how to deal with immediate threats, and they may end up learning from me how to live in a way that brings a person into fewer such conflicts. And we'll all learn something about life and God and the things we have in common and how they're more powerful and more important than the things that make us different.

If there is one thing that I've always felt, it's the sense of being different. Usually not better, just different. Life in Denver has been the same feeling, but even more potently so. When a person does ministry, it is exactly their differences that enable them to do the ministry, though it is our universal similarities in respect to struggle that bind us together enough to bother with one another. The trick is what to make of those differences, and what an honest assessment of those differences means in terms of obligation to action.

I've been thinking a lot about Moses, a Jew who grows up living as a sort of royal stepchild to the Pharaoh. But he identifies with his people, who are slaves in Egypt. As an educated, affluent member of the ruling class in America, I've grown up living much like an Egyptian in that it is my people who hold the higher position in this culture. It is a race thing to a great extent, but mostly it's a class thing, and I'm from the upper class. I'm also the eldest of three sons, and there were a great many times I was left to watch over my brothers. During those times, or to lesser degrees at school every day, their well-being was in my hands.

Pick on me, and who knows how things will go. But pick on my brothers and I'm coming after you.

It's easy with brothers, but it's harder to know what a person's duty is to people your parents don't teach you to see as your responsibility. Moses knew he had a connection to the Jewish slaves, but I don't imagine there were a whole lot of father and son discussions in the royal den about compassion and empowerment of the poor. At least I assume there weren't; there were none in my house growing up. It's not surprising to me that it took Moses until he was an adult to make his stand; there is a great potential cost to identifying with the people upon whose backs one's own world has been built.

But there came a day when Moses saw an Egyptian beating a Jewish slave, and on that day Moses knew the Jew was his brother. And his brother was being beaten by someone who for whatever reason was not Moses' brother. That's the day everything changed, and Moses had no idea it was about to happen.

Today, especially in the cultures of boundaries and bootstraps and therapeutic preoccupations run rampant in ministry circles, people talk about a cute and quaint love for the underdog, but this is not a real love. If I were Moses, and my brother was being beaten in front of me, in today's Christian world I would be expected—under threat of malicious whisper delivered behind my back in the form of prayer request—to go and shield the slave, to embrace him without removing him from the situation, and to take the blows on my back if I was really feeling like a hero martyr. From that posture of shared submission, of identification with the beating, I would be expected to ask what my brother had done to receive these blows. I would recognize the authority of the man with the club and I would submit to his authority as I sought to dissuade him from his course of action. He's the one with the club, after all, and I've been taught that the man with the club, in whatever form the club may appear and deliver its abuse, is usually in the right. Not Moses. Moses sees an Egyptian beating his brother, and he kills the fucker, dead, and stuffs him in the sand.

Many of the people I serve at Bud's Warehouse have made mistakes, and the world is undoubtedly built upon rewards and consequences, and there is a right and just debt to be paid for the mistakes we make. But here's the rub: abuse is never justice. And the people who live with, or are raised by, people who are not in the ruling class are at a two-fold disadvantage. The first is that they don't make the rules about what is a mistake. I don't mean moral things; I mean the consequences of trusting people and systems who lie and laugh behind their *caveat emptor* slogans, who withhold credit, concern, and compassion for people whose worlds teach an entirely different sort of common sense. The system, which exists in spite of what an incendiary phrase "the system" has become, has been and will always be built and maintained by people with something to preserve and something to gain, to the exclusion and loss of people who are unable to fight back in the same ways. The rules, and the understandings that work to measure mistake from wisdom, are the property and purview of the people who create the rules and have the power to enforce them. The second disadvantage experienced by the people I'm here to serve is exactly what the Jewish slave experienced, which is an inability to achieve justice without the aid of a guide or a liberator. This dynamic makes the wait for justice interminably long, and the waiting is a warping experience that leads to despair far more often than it leads to deliverance. And what's more, there is a tremendous cost in admitting that someone else must help if the person being beaten is ever going to be liberated. When a person admits such a thing, they immediately fall to the mercy of their deliverer. Most of the time the person or organization that shows up offering deliverance services one day is the same person or organization that will press charges or steal your money the next. If a person is not in the ruling class, if they don't know the rules of the game, it's nearly impossible for them to be anything but casualties of the game. And that's abuse, not justice.

My job, and the task of Bud's Warehouse, is to bring knowledge of the system and the resources of the ruling class to bear for the sake of people who will know little but abuse in their lives otherwise. My job is not to be a living shield for the men in my employ, or the people who comprise my neighborhood and customer base. My job is not to find out what they've done and negotiate for fewer blows from the Egyptian overlord. My job is to knock the fucker out, and it's entirely possible that the differences between my brothers and me will forever be so great that they don't see what has been done for them. And that's fine, because in the end this isn't even about them, any more than Moses' response was about the experience of the individual Jewish slave being abused. The response is about doing what is right with the position and ability granted to Moses, or to me, or to the Bud's board, by Providence.

This, as I said before, feels like it could be an incredible answer to my prayer to be used, and I've moved past the point in my experience where being the White stranger shamed me into shaving my head; I wear my hair in a crisp left-handed part and in the past four months we've made this business go forward to the tune of donation receipts closing in on $100,000. I'm a yuppie tooling around Denver in a white Saturn sedan, clubbing Egyptians and buying justice for three men who've never known it before.

40.

Uh, About that Moses Thing...

Our hero, which he must be if this never-ending self-obsession spilling page after page serves as any indication, is lifting a trick from the runaways at Prodigal Coffee House, and is currently looking for a new name. He has run from frying pan to fire. His new job has shown him how low he's willing to go, and for how little. He has determined, while the search for a new name continues, to refer to himself in the third person. The third person hero, the literary critics call it. Could there ever be a first person hero who was in any way believable?

Before this chapter ends the reader should expect efforts at self-aggrandizement even from this hidden vantage point. Our hero is that sort of hero, all PR and bullshit. If you see this man, do not buy a car from him, even if he tells you about the silicon in the radiator and offers you a great price. You must assume there is a catch. There is always a catch. Everything follows a pattern.

True to the law of patterns, our hero, as all heroes worth their salt, has a secret lair that reflects his true nature. While Superman has his icy Fortress of Solitude, and Batman hangs out in his cave, our unnamed hero lives in a filthy room adjacent to the filthy office in a filthy warehouse in a filthy part of town. The carpets make people motion sick until they realize the motion is actually a complex pattern of industrious migratory ants. The cockroaches are kept in check by the black widow spiders in the corners. That smell is the sewers of this industrial neighborhood backing up into our hero's shower. The snoring sound is either our hero, or one of the men who sleep immediately outside of his grate-clad window on the covered loading dock. Our hero spends his nights fearing those men, and any other noise he hears in the giant gray building.

Rare would be the evenings when we would not find our hero, and his little white car, locked within the warehouse. This, he would explain, was the result of his having no good, quick, or safe way to enter through the large garage doors without leaving himself, his car, or the warehouse unduly vulnerable to the malevolence of the area's ubiquitous and xenomisiacal interlopers. He would be likely to explain it thusly, mostly because he would feel too weak simply admitting that he was afraid being a slow White guy with possessions in an area populated by economically desperate minorities. Faith and fear race up opposing sides of the same mountain, and whichever one gets to the top first wins the ability to stop the other in its tracks.

Dress and act like a White Moses, run scared like a White Moses.

Ah, but the daytime. Our hero lives for the daytime, when the smog-shrouded moon's Kryptonic trance lifts, the doors of his lair roll open wide, and his powers return. He is the king of breakfast meetings, and lunch meetings, and even multiples of each. And what makes him the king is his ability to spin every moment and each fear, each sacrifice and every hopeful success, into fundraising, vision-casting anecdote. Wool to gold. Men in ties shake their heads about our hero's lifestyle, and donations are never, ever more than a day or two away, if the men in ties escape the meal without writing a check on the spot.

"Do you know what a mule driver is?" He asks the chubby suburbanite who recently sold a flourishing business and is now looking for clues about moving from "success to significance."

"Only if you're talking about the hike down into the Grand Canyon." The chubby suburbanite strains the words through a too-large bite of his first two-dollar breakfast burrito, which he will not order with coffee next time.

"When a drug dealer is transporting drugs from one place to another, it's common practice to hire someone else to drive the vehicle. For longer distances, there will be multiple drivers, each driving a leg."

"So the drivers meet someplace and hand over the car to the next guy?"

"Yeah."

"How does the first driver get home?" Chubby is all about systems.

"I don't know. It doesn't matter." Our hero replies. "What does matter is that Marcos is a mule driver on the weekends a couple of times a month."

"Marcos is the one with the ponytail and the eye patch, right?"

"Right."

"Wow."

"Yeah. So here's the dilemma. Obviously that sort of work isn't what we're looking to have our employees do."

"Right."

"But we know that it's exactly what they'd do—or at least he'd do—if he was no longer a Bud's employee."

"Okay."

"So, what's the solution? How should Bud's respond now that he's told me about it with the assumption that I won't use it against him?"

"Did you tell him you'd keep it a secret?" The chubby businessman asks, wincing at the taste of his coffee after a mouthful of salsa.

"No, but that's not really the point."

"I guess not. So you have to find some way to make him choose against it."

"Right."

"And you can't coerce the choice."

"Right. I can't give him an ultimatum or I'll lose the invitation to engage with his world."

"It's sort of like having a teenager." The businessman says.

"Maybe. More like having a teenager who's already run away and is willing to meet you for lunch and a little advice and allowance once a week, but who refuses to be owned by the allowance. And he's not a teenager; he's a man with gray hair who has made plenty of adult choices and has experienced more things in his life than I have, and is far more street savvy than most people."

"That would be different."

"But you know things won't end well for Marcos if he keeps taking these risks. He's at the bottom of the food chain. He doesn't even have a driver's license, and he can't read, and he's poor enough that he doesn't have a whole lot of walk-away money saved up. Plus he's already very much a part of a culture that works that way."

"Wow."

"Yeah, wow. That's why what we're doing is so important in the lives of the men who work at Bud's. It goes far beyond teaching them to show up to work or how to drive a forklift or run a cash register. What we're really doing is introducing these men to a whole different way of interacting with the world, and showing them a whole part of society that works from an entirely different paradigm than they do."

The chubby businessman who has been looking for something significant to do with his time and money, looking for a return on his success, is thinking now. "Yeah."

"In his world the biggest studs are the people at the top of the food chain, which means people who have made great money as their own bosses, answering to nobody."

The chubby businessman laughs. "Entrepreneurs answer to more people than anybody else."

"That may be, but that's sure not how Marcos or the other guys see it. They assume that you've taken big chances, have made smart choices, and have kicked butt along the way. Their world works more like a wolf pack, where the dominant wolf is the one to follow. They'd see you as a dominant wolf. Power sells. Power earns you the right to speak into their worlds. And you can do it in ways that I cannot. I'm their boss, not their hero or their role model. The best I can do is to make them feel like they're part of something that's succeeding and to introduce them to people who represent a world they'd choose over the one they already know."

"Is that all?" He asks facetiously, "That's a lot. That's a big deal."

Our hero knows that reflected affirmation is the green light for the big ask. The chubby businessman is sold on turning his success into significance at Bud's

Warehouse, where his success is applauded and his opportunity to make a difference clearly marked. He doesn't know it yet, but his bank account has already dropped $10,000, and more will come during the next year.

"It is. It's a life-changing deal not only for the individuals who encounter a better option here, but also for their families and their communities who will see the aggressive risk-takers like Marcos turn their lives around instead of getting caught and thrown in prison. My job is to be the bridge between driven men who have achieved something in their lives, and driven men with something to prove. Men who only need a mentor to absolutely revolutionize their worlds."

The chubby businessman is nodding. Our hero watches the squint of his eyes to gauge how much to ask. The chubby man doesn't look away. He squints a little tighter. No need to go for the cash in this meeting—a little tour will bring him into the fold. And it really is about recruitment, not money. The primary benefit of getting the donation is that it keeps the connection active and the prospects of additional collaboration strong. Though the secondary benefit is that if one person gives and our hero returns to the board with the good news, other people are more likely to buy in further. Nothing generates success like success.

"You say you're wanting to reorient your world from success to significance. I can help you do that, and I can help you make sense of it in ways that right now are only vague hunches. And where I can't help you, I have a team of maybe two dozen men who have either been where you are, or are themselves right where you are, and they will make this whole reorientation real and concrete for you, so it doesn't slip from you as the distractions of your ordinary life come and weaken your grip on this moment of clarity in your career."

The businessman knows he's being closed, but the power is still his, and he's ready for the bottom line. Our hero finishes his Mountain Dew and looks for the waitress. He always does this to break the tension. It allows him to come back to the situational table he's set, but to return to it sitting on the same side as the person with whom our hero is seeking to establish an action-based relationship.

"Donna." He calls, and lifts his cup at the waitress, who smiles and agrees to bring him a refill. He turns back to the businessman. "Did I tell you she's a descendant of Martin Luther's?"

"No."

"Yeah. I was reading 'Bondage of the Will' in here one morning and she told me. But she had no idea who Luther was. All she knew was that her grandmother had told her they were related. She was pretty impressed to learn what an important man he was. Ever since then when I walk in here she arrives at the table with a Mountain Dew before I even sit down."

The businessman watches Donna filling a scratched red cup with the yellow soda at the fountain. Our hero continues.

"What I'm hoping to find for Marcos is someone who can impress him, spend some time with him, and introduce him to a world that makes better sense than being a mule driver."

The businessman nods.

"I picture you riding along with him as he picks up donations one day. Just spend the time together and see what happens. I'd encourage you to listen to the details of his life outside of Bud's and see where you can offer practical advice or help, and then make your way in as the alpha wolf would protect a subordinate. Don't think of it as a paternalistic thing—he's not a kid—but do stay clear in your mind that what he'll respond to is power, especially power wisely applied. If you find something, let your action be flashier than you would do in Littleton. Flash is power in his world."

"I can do that." The businessman says, in a matter of fact tone similar to the way he would say, "I could afford that" if our hero had asked him about a hypothetical ability to purchase a building or an expensive vehicle. Our hero knows there is no reason to make the businessman feel like a novice in the land of significance when there exists the option to work from the businessman's comfort in the land of success.

"But make sure you dress in clothes you'd be willing to throw away when the day is done." Our hero says, laughing. "The Bud's van is missing a back window from where the homeless guys broke in so they could sleep in it, and it's also doubled as a toilet more than once."

"Really?" The businessman asks.

"Oh, yeah. You'll love it. It'll probably bring back memories from when you were getting your business off the ground. There are holes rusted through the floor, and the brakes barely work. Hell, the whole engine only keeps running because Marcos won't let it die. A couple of weeks ago he climbed into the driver's seat and got stuck by a needle someone had left behind."

"Did he get tested for HIV?" The businessman asks, alarmed.

"Yeah, it came back negative. But I don't know if it would show up right away anyway. Do you?"

"No."

Two days later, our hero introduced Marcos to the chubby businessman who recently sold his company and has been looking for a way to make the transition from success to significance. They spent the day driving around the metro area picking up donated building materials. The following Tuesday a nearly new box truck was delivered to the loading dock, driven by a smiling, rather chubby man who has since helped Marcos secure his driver's license, insurance, and weekend work that doesn't involve mule driving. And our hero has gained yet another anecdote to sell the vision of Bud's Warehouse. Ministry, it would seem, is all about selling.

41.

Echoes From Insatiable Canyons

"Is that supposed to impress me?"

Meet Loma. All of my friends, I mean all of them, have come to the hard-fast conclusion that she is a recalcitrant bitch without peer. My journal is full of more crap praising her than a sane person could handle even knowing about.

"I don't know. I think it's pretty cool. And it's not like I'm doing it for you. I have better things to do than pursue the impossible goal of impressing the great and terrible Loma, keeper of the cool and mortal threat to any so foolish as to actually enter her lair in the name of love or kindness."

Meet me with Loma. Flustered, caught, bitter and wholly devoted to hyperbole.

"'An hour of sleep's enough if a man's a fighter'? You're really doing this?" She asks.

"I've gotten down to only sleeping four."

"So what time do you get up?"

"3:21."

"3:21?"

"Yeah."

"Why the twenty-one? Why not 3:30?"

"Because my radio will play for nine minutes before the alarm sounds, so I have that time to wake up and still be up on time."

"On time? Are you on crack? Nobody's up at 3:30 in the morning."

"Fine. That way I have nine minutes to gain consciousness before the alarm goes off. Better?"

"So then what do you do?"

"I pray and read the Bible and drink tea, and journal, and then go to work."

"You have a four hour quiet time?"

"Yes."

"Every day?"

"For the past few weeks anyway."

"And you think this is supposed to impress me."

"Again, you soul-crushing nightmare, this is not about impressing you."

"Soul-crushing nightmare? Aren't you so highbrow."

"I don't know why I told you."

"Because you thought it would impress me. You think everything you do will impress me. Living in the ghetto. Moving down here to this cute apartment with the church across the street and the yellow bedroom and the periwinkle bathroom and the pea green living room with this stupidly expensive antique furniture. Your reading, your praying, your calling, your successes at work, your stories about the ghetto boys at Bud's, your loyalty, your poetry. It's all about impressing me."

"Shut up."

"It is."

"Shut up."

"You know who you remind me of?"

"I bet it's a cartoon character."

"You know what, it is. You remind me of the guy who sells comic books on *The Simpsons*. You think that if you can master the history of the Superman series and if you can ridicule people who don't give a shit about Superman for not knowing shit about Superman, you will be impressive. Meanwhile, you're just getting fatter and fatter, less and less relevant, and more and more obnoxious in your silly little niche of a world."

"Gee, thanks. How's your fucking dinner?"

"Impressive."

"And how about the nineteen-year-old you've been stalking at the swing dancing place?"

"Shut up."

"Bedded him down yet, Mrs. Robinson?"

"Not cool."

"Cool? Well, I guess I wouldn't know cool, not owning any snazzy vintage clothing or making an obsession out of pretending to live in an entirely different era like you cool people do. Sorry—my mistake. And you say I'm the one from the comic book convention."

She stares icily at me. Root beer eyes, wild black curls heaped up above ears studded with diamond twinkle, a loose hoop bracelet on her right arm, sliding into a tight navy blue three-quarter sleeved shirt that hugs her large breasts gently but firmly, as I've dreamed of doing. I don't know why we return to these moments so frequently or so suddenly. We were laughing two minutes ago. But we get here so regularly that it doesn't even feel like fighting anymore.

"How can you say that you care for me or that your quiet times are worth anything when you can be so mean to me?" Loma asks.

I feel my body and my voice shift to nice guy mode, burying the hatchet. The irresistible chance to profess my patient love. My kryptonite. "When I offer something to you, or when I pray for you, I keep thinking it will matter to you, even if it takes a while for you to believe it."

"I don't want anything from you."

"I think you do. I think that's why you're here."

"Okay, I know you make good Thai food."

"Loma, I'm your last friend. You've said so yourself. I've spent the night standing in your window in case the stalker came back, so you could sleep. I've been there after every disappointment with each guy you've thought you've liked. I pray for you and I spend all sorts of time with you. I am the only person you haven't been able to drive away. I think you're confused and sad and that my sticking with you matters to you a whole lot."

"No, it matters to you a whole lot. My role could be played by anyone. You just need someone to pin down and fix your attention on. I happen to be it. You work hard to come up with the things you do, and you offer yourself, all of yourself, so cheaply that it's hard not to take some of what you're offering. I'll admit I do that. And I do care about you, too, but don't keep insisting that this is all about me. This is about you. I'm your mirror, the passive responder that tells you and the people you tell about me what a great guy you are, what a martyr for love. The more I work against you, the less what I say matters because you just find some way of making me seem like a little kid who doesn't understand myself or what you're offering well enough to see what a great deal I'm passing up. And you love that because it means I become a little bit less real and a little bit more just a reflection of you. But you know what real is? Real is that I couldn't fit on the pedestal you keep trying to put me on even if I wanted to, and the more you say you're there for me 'anyway,' the more your so-called love makes me feel like I'm failing against a standard I never signed up for and have no intention of ever caring about." She cracks, and the tears begin to flow.

My heart leaps in satisfaction at being the one, the insider, she cries in front of. My heart wants to console her. I notice she's a little chilly in that tight shirt, too.

She sniffles. "I know I've driven my friends away, and I don't know what's going on with me, but I think it's happening at least in part because the image of me that you keep chasing me around with makes me want to run away. I don't want to have to break down and cave in and be 'loved' back into some model of a person you think I should be. And even if I did like the model you're selling so hard, I don't think I'd ever be any more real to you anyway. I'd always just be your mirror, the person changed by your love whose real life was traded in to show the world how important you are. But it won't work. You can't have me. And I wasn't going to tell you this, but so long as we're here now anyway, I did end up bringing Mano home with me. The huge danger you've been warning me about for months."

She locks my eyes with furious venom and watches her words hit me. "I'm not a virgin anymore. And yes it was stupid and yes I'm just one of the women he sleeps with and yes you and my parents and God would all be very disappointed with me, but I don't live in the world my parents think is still out there, and I'm almost thirty and God's not exactly delivering a husband to my door, and your damned scolding looks and words of wisdom and forever taking crap from me have felt like you've been claiming me and my sexuality and my virginity as your own, like someday I was bound to cave in and marry you and you were just trying to preserve me as well as you could so you could have me as fresh as possible to yourself later. Now you can't. And don't even start crying—I see your wet eyes—I am real, not some puppet for you to control. I'm not your mirror. I'm not just some reflection of you. I'm not your damned Superman comic book."

She's a bitch. But something is cracking inside of me as she speaks. Something dark and terrifying is pushing through the surface of the soil.

Suddenly I'm flashing back to a moment at work last week. I'm still flat broke, and that morning I'd received a card from my grandmother back in Zionsville. In it were words of encouragement, and a $100 bill. Maybe an hour later a woman, who looked much like Loma might after she's given birth to a few kids, made her way into the warehouse from the driving snow. She was wearing black tights, cheap open-toed shoes with clear plastic straps criss-crossing the top of her foot, and a light jacket. In the stroller was a baby, a girl of maybe six months. Trailing on her coattails were two boys, probably three- and five-years-old. Their noses were red and running and they hid behind their mother. The woman was trying not to cry, but it was clear that the cold and something else were driving her to the edge. She told me that they'd been living with her father, but that he'd kicked them out of his house that morning. She'd just cleaned the office of a man down the street for ten dollars, and asked if I would be willing to pay her to do the same. I looked at the kids, and at her feet. I wanted to help her, but I was not about to pay her ten dollars to clean my office while her kids sat and watched, and then send them all back out into the snow. I refused, but pulled the $100 bill from my pocket and handed it to her, telling her to go and get a hotel room, to get herself and her kids out of the snow, to get warm and take the day to figure out what she would do next. She cried profusely. I told her to pay me back when she could, that she knew where to find me and that I'd be around. Then she took her kids and headed back out into the snow.

Every night since then I've dreamed of that woman. Usually I'm running after them through the snow, slipping on the ice, unable to catch them. I want to do more. She told me her name was Maria, but I want to know her last name. I want to know where her father lives. I want to know which hotel they're going to use. I want to know that the kids will be warm. I want her not to cry. I want her to know she's not alone. I want to help her get out of whatever cycle has brought her to such a state. I race after them, feeling as though I've failed and am desperate to make things right.

Last night I dreamed that I was raping her in a dead end alley, her kids watching and the brick walls running in blood under dark clouds. We were already in the act, and the only violence was the recognition of the situation in which we were engaged. There was a look in her eyes, and with every one of my motions, the look showed that something she knew was being confirmed. It enraged me, and I thrusted harder and harder, and each time was a moment of fierce self-destructive victory for her, as though she knew it would go this way all along. She did not fight, and I was horrified that this was all happening in front of her kids and she didn't seem to be bothered. On the contrary, the cries of her children seemed to prove to her that she was successfully teaching her children a hard lesson about people like me. The terror and the rage of the nightmare was too awful for me, and I made myself wake up.

What is that thing women know, that victory in violation? Is it a fear confirmed, horror chosen as satisfaction over the skeptical voice that calls fear foolishness? Is it the same thing Loma proved with the asshole from the swing bar? How do I know it enough to build a dream around it? Is it true of men, of power, of women, of vulnerability, of fear, of humanity, of God? What is it? I don't know. All I know is that there are too many people living like Maria in the world, too many Lomas with their Manos, too many truths in their protective counterattacks, and way too much rage within people like me who feel this hellish ambivalence about serving, saving, or raping weakness in its pathetic apathy. After Moses fights to save one Jew, the others ask who the hell he thinks he is.

Who the hell am I?

42.

What Christians in the Mexican Mafia Already Know

"I know exactly how you feel." Jeff Johnsen says. "And I don't have any good answers to share."

"So you see how creepy this stuff can be?" I ask.

"Yeah. I think anyone who does ministry for very long hits the same wall."

"I feel like I'm manipulating donors, and betraying the people I'm supposed to be helping."

"It's a lousy feeling to feel like you're pursuing something so pure, so right and perfect, only to realize that even in the best kitchen some eggs get broken."

"But I don't see any way around it." I say. Suddenly I remember what Tony told me about Pastor Woolfolk. "I can only be as honest as the moment is."

"I'll tell you a story. It won't make the confusion go away, but it may help you see it better."

I push my napkin under the plate with my smothered burrito on it, showing Jeff I'm ready to listen.

"I met a man a few years ago who is a big deal in the Mexican mafia. I was with a small group of urban ministry leaders in Mexico City, and our host told us he wanted us to meet this guy. There were maybe seven of us who went together to this man's office—more like a small palace—above a downtown nightclub. There were armed guards everywhere, and it was about the most intimidating place I've ever been."

"I bet."

"Well, it turns out this man had become a Christian a year before we visited him. He'd grown up in a Catholic culture, but he never knew Jesus. He had an amazing conversion story, but that's not important here. What is important was that this guy suddenly had this dilemma. What to do with his job? It's not like the Mexican mafia plays nice, or does a whole lot of philanthropic work. Of course we were all biting our tongues because there was no way we could see how he could possibly stay in his job."

"So how did he justify it?" I ask.

"He couldn't, of course. But he was really over a barrel. First off, he thought that he would be allowed to live if he tried to get out, but he wasn't sure. That wasn't the hard part for him, though. The hard part was that he knew if he quit, someone else would step right into his position. And that person wouldn't have the same internal conflicts about what he was doing. Getting out not only wouldn't solve the problem, it would probably make it worse."

"But that wouldn't be his responsibility."

"Wouldn't it?" Jeff asks.

"So what did the guy do?"

"I don't know what happened later, but at the time the best he'd been able to conclude was that he was going to stay in his place to influence as much change as he could—to create a "kinder, gentler Mexican mafia"—and then when he could do no more, he would get out."

"That sounds like total bullshit." I say.

"I thought so too, at the time. But on the flight home what struck me is that in many ways I'm doing exactly the same thing. I think that's what our host wanted us to have to struggle with."

"But it's not like you're having people killed."

"No," Jeff says. "But the Mexican mafia makes no claim to being a gate-keeper between this life and communion with God in the next."

"Neither do we." I say.

"Not explicitly, but you know as well as I do that some of the people who come around looking to help or donate are really looking to buy indulgences. They want you to tell them some stories, to tell them how much good their gift is going to do. They're looking for ways to be right with God, and to the extent that we let them see us as a way to do that, we play the role of intermediary between them and God. We may be friendly, and the gates may not be locked, but we're gatekeepers just the same."

"So what's the solution?" I ask.

"I don't think there is one. If I quit on Mile High, or if you quit on Bud's, someone else will step into the same place, and that person may not struggle with managing the power they have over people in a loving manner. If I shut Mile High down, or if you decide we should pull the plug on Bud's, another ministry will be planted in the same place, with the same dilemma. I think the best we can do is what the Mexican mafia boss is doing—take it where we can take it, live in the fire of the dilemma, and mitigate the damage as best we can, admitting that the system is flawed." Jeff says.

"You have so many years invested in Mile High now. If you'd known all of this when you were first starting, would you have still started it?"

"All I cared about doing was serving inner city people as though they were Jesus. I just wanted to love them and care for them. Is the system perfect? No.

Has the organization benefited people? Yes. But it doesn't do any good to ask if I'd do it all again. I don't know. What I do know is that a lot of good has come from being here. I pray that more good has come than bad, but it's a prayer because I'm not always sure which there's been more of. But no matter what, the good hasn't come for free."

"How's that for truth?" I mutter.

"Not soft, is it?" He asks.

"Not soft." I say.

43.

Where You Put Your Dick

"What do you mean you feel like it's a done deal?" Viking Bruce, chairman of my board, and purchaser of this morning's breakfast, wants to know.

"Just that it's been a great year, and I feel like I can see how Bud's will make it, and that makes me start to feel bored."

"Bored? Geez, there's a long way to go before Bud's is in the clear, even if what you've been talking about works out."

"It will work out."

"And when it does, if it does, that's when the rewards start kicking in for you. You're actually saying you'd consider leaving, after all of this effort, before you get to see the place fly?"

"I'm saying that I think there are planners, architects, builders, and managers. The planner is the one who says, 'we should do something here.' The architect says, 'it should be this.' The builder takes the idea and makes it real. And then the manager keeps it running. The people who are heroes are almost always the builders, or even the managers. But I'm more of a planner or an architect, and I've been working from weaker abilities doing some of the building, and I know I won't like being a manager, and I don't think I'll be good at it either. I've been okay during this time when there is room for chaos because we've been going so hard at everything else, like the fundraising and relationship building, but it feels like Bud's is about to grow past my sweet spot."

"I don't know what to say."

"I'm not saying it's right now, Bruce. And I know it's different for you—you're a builder. Frankly, the whole sensation makes me feel like I'm being incredibly disloyal."

"Do you think maybe you are?" He asks.

"I don't think it's disloyal to admit that I'm thinking and feeling this prospect coming towards us, no. But I don't know, maybe I am being disloyal in a larger sense." I take a bite of my seafood eggs benedict without a thought to irony. "I keep thinking about this time when I was five or six and there was a girl from down the street, a tomboy named Amanda, and one day when we were climbing trees I told her I didn't believe she was a girl. You're grinning—you know where this goes?"

"You show me yours and I'll show you mine."

"Exactly. Except that after she showed me hers, but before she pulled her pants back up and I could still get away, I ran home."

A look comes over Bruce's face. Disgust. Distain. Horrible news about me. It was wrong of me to even begin to talk about this feeling. It was going to be an illustration—I had no clue I'd have to defend something I did 20 years ago.

"It certainly wasn't a high moment in the history of my masculinity," I confess. Now I'm stuck in the story and have to keep going. "And I can't help wondering if that's sort of what I'm looking at here. Bud's is in a place where it's—where you—are counting on me, and I'm saying I'm not sure that the vision of the business, or the way we do a lot of things, is what I want to be tied to long-term. Especially if I stick around until the business gets rolling and can be handed to someone else, and my departure doesn't hurt much."

"There are some board members who are only still involved with Bud's because of you. If you leave, it will hurt." Bruce says. "To me it comes down to a character issue."

I'm the guy who left everything to move to Denver, who has done cool things for God, who has brought Bud's forward from the abyss, who prays and studies four hours every day. Character? Character? From a rich guy? Character?

"Do you think there is ever a point where a person can leave a job, then?" I ask. I can't tell if this is foolish hyperbole, or valid defensiveness. But I do know I suddenly feel like the kid in the equation, misunderstood and judged for talking about something that's still in process.

"I think the Bud's board has their dicks out on the table, and you have to ask yourself whether or not you're man enough to commit." He's turning a little red.

"Look, Bruce, I'm not giving notice or saying anything at all certain anyway. I'm just telling you what I've been starting to notice about my feelings and thoughts, and I'm telling you about it because I'm trying to make sense of it."

"I know. I know what you're feeling. I think about folding my business all the time, about how much easier it was being a one-man show. I hate having to carry this cell phone with me all the time. What I'm telling you is that sometimes you simply have to make the choice to whip it out, to commit and stick with it."

"Even if it's the wrong thing?" I ask.

"Sometimes the important thing isn't what you're committing to so much as it is simply making the commitment."

I raise my eyebrows. "That sure seems like a great way to bring about tragedies."

I recognize the look. I've seen it on my dad, and on my boss in Chicago, and on the fundraiser at Teen Challenge when I asked questions about the Hitler sermon. It goes beyond a difference in age or experience—it's the look of own worldview not getting what the fuck the other worldview is talking about. Bruce continues. "It's the only way I know of to create stability or a warrior class. Think of the pride that's required to always think you will get it right, and that you know better than the rest of the people standing with you."

"It takes a lot of effort to live on purpose, and free," I say. "And what you call pride I guess I'd call responsibility."

"So what are you committed to? What would you pull your dick out for?"

"That's what I'm saying. I feel torn because I don't know that I have ever really done that, and it seems like I'm supposed to. I've been let down and hurt by the things I've committed to before, like my old girlfriend or advertising or people at church, but when I think about them I feel like I wasn't as invested as I should have been." I say, not at all sure why I'm confessing to this guy. "I wonder if my pain came in part because even though I thought I was, I wasn't committed enough to go all the way through the storm with them. I feel like I should commit to Bud's no matter what, but I know that Bud's isn't 'it' for me, and I can't make myself commit in spite of that. But what freaks me out most is that I may be doing the same thing with God—telling Him I'm committed, but preparing myself to run away."

Bruce shrugs a little as he nods. "There's no way you can really be committed to God if you can't commit to the life He's given you. It's part of the incarnation thing. You have to engage Jesus as a person, and you have to recognize that God is present in the real world. That means sunsets and tornados, but it also means situations, organizations, and especially people. He lives within you and within me, and there is an incarnate expression of God at work within Bud's, or my company. If you can only invest yourself in the God you have to close your eyes to pray to, your faith and the understanding of God in your world can only be partial."

"Even if it's the wrong thing." I say.

"If you think about it, there can be no wrong thing. Different things have different costs, but so long as you engage for the right reason—which is to engage because you know God is there—there is no wrong commitment. There is the step of counting the cost, and if it's more than you're ready to man up to, that's one thing. But to be afraid to commit because it may hurt you or let you down later is just silly, and it is a prison that will keep you from experiencing God in real life."

"Wow. That's a lot to think about."

"Thinking is your worst enemy."

"Thinking is bad?"

"No, thinking as much as you do is bad for you. It paralyzes you and keeps you from living or enjoying God in life. It makes you responsible for too much.

If you just say, 'God, I'm going to bite down on this because I want to experience you in it, will you please meet me there?' you create a contract with him that He'll honor. He'll protect you, and it's up to him how much challenge to allow in it for you. That's what it means for him to be your Lord—not this crap you focus on about being right or mimicking the behaviors of dead saints. You're still trying to earn it. God's much more Nike than that. Just do it!"

I don't know. I can't tell if he's right. I want to be man enough to impress him. I want to prove that I'm willing to take the risk. But I can't. I don't see how to keep doing this stuff, forced into shortcuts and contributing to something I'm losing my taste for, and saying that I'm just trying to influence it as far as I can before I jump out. Something feels far too compromised about that, too sold out. I don't know how I'll ever know which is the right choice, or which is the wrong one.

44.

Meeting Demons

I'm dreaming. I'm in Jeff Johnsen's house, modified. There is a puddle of water at the bottom of the stairs, on the hardwood hallway that leads into the kitchen. I have no idea where it could have come from. For some reason that puddle is a barrier to avoid. Because of it I am led through the dining room to the other kitchen entrance. I feel something behind me, guiding me, benevolent. I am in somebody else's dream, being shown something. This is a spiritual thing. A thrill sweeps over me; this is the result of all of my extended prayer times—I'm breaking through!

In the kitchen there are two people. The lights are on, and the feeling between the two is akin to the informality that would exist in a break room between shifts. The two people are surprised to see me, and look behind me with expressions first of surprised betrayal, and then as though they will accept either the command or the dare. The first is a 15-year-old dressed like a skateboarder, with spiked bleached-blonde hair and a coral necklace. He stands beside a chessboard.

"Think you can beat me?" He asks. I know, I don't know how, not to answer; he is the spirit of pride. He has the look of someone by whom I would never be intellectually threatened, and that is the point—to challenge me and to raise my arrogance in response. But this is off-limits time, and the guide behind me is introducing me to my demons, who have been with me since I was eight years old.

I remember the day they arrived. I was home from school, sick with a fever, and I remember writhing in bed screaming as though I was having a panic attack. I'd felt pierced in a place I couldn't name. My mother came running to me in alarm. By the time she arrived at the door I was calming down. I told her I didn't know what had happened, and neither of us ever said another word about the incident, though for the next year or so I would occasionally think back to the moment and wonder if I had simply been pretending, trying to attract some weird attention.

The boy with the chessboard looks fifteen, but he is actually about my age. He, the spirit of pride, especially intellectual pride, has been the strongest malevolent player in my world.

The second person is the same age, but appears as a little girl, maybe 12-years-old, sitting in a high chair. Too old to be in a high chair. Beside her the refrigerator door stands open, and the racks are filled with corndogs. The detail and the clarity of what I am seeing is way beyond what I experience a normal dream. It is quite different from waking consciousness, though; there is a prioritizing of my perceptions that makes it feel somehow even more lucid than normal life, where it occurs to me we spend most of our energy simply selecting which things are worth our attention or fit into our thought matrix.

"I just diddled myself." She says, making the masturbatory reference to repulse me and confuse me. And to tempt me perversely. She is the same age as was my cousin when she was molested by our great uncle. When I was 11, my cousin and I spent two weeks visiting my grandmother in Arizona. The molestations happened over the course of the two weeks, and I was the only person she would tell until two days before our departure, when we told our grandmother. The uncle was Grandma's sister's husband, and her sister was one of Grandma's only friends. Nothing was ever said to my great aunt, and nothing was said to my cousin's parents for almost a year. By then my great uncle had died. My cousin has never known justice for what my great uncle did, and the perversion of both the act and the subsequent inaction in my family have echoed in the darker recesses of my psyche ever since. This is why dreams of rape in an alley are especially terrifying and vile to me. I promised my cousin I would not leave her alone with our uncle, but on two occasions—once to get him an aspirin from my grandmother's kitchen, and once to run into the gas station to buy us candy—he tricked me and I returned to her on the sofa or in the back between the bucket seats in tears. Ever since I've been terrified that I could ever be capable of such a thing as my uncle did. Perhaps more perverse than that, a part of me has always felt an odd sort of rejection that he didn't choose me.

The little girl in the high chair is intentionally crude, intentionally juxtaposing vulgarity with images of youth, and an obvious refrigerator full of Freudian phallic food reference. She is lust and lust's ever-present companion, gluttony. In this timeless moment I know not to acknowledge or bother being repulsed by her. I see how my repulsion would play directly into the hands of pride, who stands never far away, ready to attack from behind. My suspicion is that all demons are equally clear and easy to see as undesirable when they are encountered directly.

There is a door leading from the kitchen to the back yard, and I am led through it onto the wooden deck. There is a flood light at the corner of the house, and I can see the deck and the yard in high-contrast clarity. A fat old dog, the sort whose behavior is nearly impossible to predict, and whose fangs may fly without warning, wiggles its way to me, its tail wagging in an arthritic fever, head down, looking through its brow. I know not to offer my hand. It is rage. In my world this demon, and the behavior it inspires, have been kept locked outside, perceived as manageable, if impolite and prone to unpleasant odors. Of the three demons who arrived that day in third grade, it has had the least direct impact on my life, but I have dreamed of this one before. The last time it was a kitten who kept attacking me, scratching me. I threw it into the fireplace, where it began to burn. Out of trapped mercy I pulled it from the flames, and it began to attack again. My fear of, and enabling willingness to avoid rather than battle, my own anger riddles and torments me far more than do the often comforting and even useful temptations stemming from pride, lust or gluttony. I am the least familiar with the dog, with rage. I have found this to be a common thing in my stratum of the Christian culture, where passive-aggression, self-destruction, repression, and elitism are far more in vogue.

The dog goes into the kitchen where the other two demons remain. I run and padlock the door, against which the three begin to pound in an effort to escape.

I am led through a gate from the back yard to the front, where my car is parked in the street beneath a sky growing pink and orange from a sun rising like a glaring lie in the west. I run to it, and as I open the door, I see a man on the front porch. He turns from ringing the doorbell and moves towards me, carrying a brown paper lunch bag in front of him. Terror wraps about me.

The man looks like an 80-year-old Black man with graying hair. He is wearing a black vest, and at his biceps there are thin black armbands over his white long-sleeved shirt, like bankers wore in the Old West. Where the other three demons feel about 25-years-old, this one is ancient, like before the Earth had yet cooled ancient. He is backup, called in by the others. And where the other three certainly have wished me no good, their orientation has been focused on my distraction or my slow demise. They have been mostly content to hassle me and make me second-guess myself, to cause me to sabotage my dreams, order too much pizza, or miss womanly curves in the night. This one, though, this one is here to absolutely fuck me up. He oozes threat of death and utter destruction. I can feel his power tugging at the edges of my perceptions, and I know that if I went with the tug, I would see something in him that would terrify me beyond words. I know in that instant that part of me, some part that is unable to make enough sense of him to allow the perception through to my mind, is protecting me. I stand by the car door. He arrives and stops on the opposite side of the open door. He holds the brown paper bag, folded over neatly three times at the top, out to me.

"Boy," he says, with a gravelly Southern twang that rattles in desolation through millennia. "-"

My alarm goes off. It's 3:21.

45.

When Questions Outgrow Solutions

"So what about you and God?" Skinny Robert asks two weeks later, the moon rising behind him on our first chilly sailing foray of the season.

"I don't know what to think," I say. "I feel like maybe I've fallen in love with the voice, and lost something of my desire for the speaker."

"Because of the programmatic ministry stuff, or because of the prayer times?"

"Both, I guess. In different ways. The more I think about it, the more it seems like the history of man is the history of man putting anything he can find between himself and God. From the first fig leaf, to blame placed upon his wife, to the law, kings, priests, culture, doctrine, philosophies, ministries, family, career, addictions, doubt, science, denominationalism, political party loyalty. Anything. Because in the end the last thing we want is to be truly known by God. So long as we feel like there is a buffer, maybe we feel like there is some sort of excuse, something that can keep him from us."

"So you think that's what you were doing with the prayer times?"

"Maybe. Yeah, probably. I was pretty impressed with myself, and I think I was also using it as an excuse to not engage with my world in other areas. I think I was also doing the prayer time to be able to experience something cool, rather than to listen to a God who's more interested in leading me through a life in the real world." I say.

"So you've stopped praying?"

"No, but I've been sleeping a regular night's sleep, and am only spending more like an hour in prayer and study."

"That's still a ton." Robert says.

"I don't know. Maybe."

"What's the tone I hear?"

"I keep thinking that the whole dream could have just been God saying, 'would you get over yourself already?' Like I was pushing and obsessing and wanting to be some super guy when all he was looking for was some submission and steady obedience," I say.

"So what, he let you see a glimpse of something else, or he wanted to scare you back or something?"

"I can't tell. For as scared as I was, I was also pretty proud of myself for showing up on the evil radar, and that can't really be something to celebrate, can it?"

"Beats me."

"Something changed for me with the dream. I feel like I had my limbs pruned back, like the false parts of myself were knocked off, and what's come from that is this really cool peace that has to do with God being big and my being small."

"That sounds like a good thing. Isn't it?" Robert asks.

"That's what's messing with me. I feel like I've been pushed back into a better place with God and life, but what I'm afraid is that somewhere I agreed to back off so the big demon would leave me alone. It feels possible that I traded this really cool direct connection with God for a weaker attack from my enemy, even though it does feel right ever since. And then I start thinking about how one great way for God to snap me back into a better place with him would be to give me a glimpse at something that highlighted my need for him and my place before Him. But I can't tell if that's true, or a cop-out. And then I realize that I'm over-thinking everything again." I let my head flop back and I watch the water behind me while Robert responds.

"Can a person engage God directly, though? I mean, aren't even our words just containers for Him, and isn't every limitation also a buffer? Even our word-less minds couldn't even begin to really interact with him."

"I agree," I say, bringing my head back to face Robert. "That's part of what makes it impossible to speak of him in ways that do much good. Think about the beginning of the book of John, where Jesus is described as the Word. He is the point of translation, the summary, the Truth. And even he didn't use words nearly so much as he used life. That's where my thinking is heading."

"Where?"

"To life. That words aren't enough to interact with God, and neither are any of the other things, like ministry or prayer or church or any of that. But I wonder if a life, one lived in full acknowledgement of God, but without a direct orientation towards Him, where He passes through us and we see him projected into the world, rather than our looking away from the world back at the light, might not be the way it's supposed to be."

"That's what Kierkegaard said, isn't it?"

"What?"

"That when sin is rooted out the soul rests transparently in the power that established it."

"Cool." I say, remembering that passage from Sickness Unto Death, and how that was the moment that I decided Kierkegaard was full of crap because it seemed like if that were the case, then God is nothing more than some great light, or the backdrop to our living. I remember thinking that Keirkegaard seemed to be talking about a man carrying a mirror through the world, watching himself in it to see which background looked right for him, with God just being good lighting. And that didn't sound enough like the self-annihilation I'd come to demand in Lordship after reading Pascal. My freaking, knot-tying brain. I'm my own labyrinth. I start thinking about Icarus flying from the labyrinth, wondering about some metaphor for escaping my own thoughts. And then I remember there is some song about that, something about "But Mama, that's where the fun is..." What song was that? What a freak I am.

"I've never gotten exactly what that actually means." Robert says. "What does that look like?" I'm almost startled to hear Robert's voice.

"I don't know what Kierkegaard meant, but with what I'm talking about, it means what it means, I guess. It means that life is not just an object lesson, not just some puzzle we're supposed to stare at until we figure it out. It means that God is not coy. It means that pain has a place, a redeemed purpose in the world because it is part of the place where a holy God is active. That would be a big change from the sense that pain is either punishment or something from which to escape. What if it is actually something to embrace?"

"Consider it pure joy, my brothers, when you experience trials of many kinds." Robert quotes.

"Exactly."

"So what are we supposed to do with our lives, then?"

"I don't know, maybe it's enough to live as though life were for real, not just a metaphor or a trial run in which we are only killing time before the headliner of Heaven comes on stage. Imagine all of the evangelicals deciding that life was worth actually embracing, not just cramming into Jell-O moulds so they'd come out shaped like every other Promise Keeper with a ten percent tithe and a minivan to pull into their vinyl-clad house every night, while most of the world shivers in the dark, muttering confused curses of betrayal about Americans and the God they sold to the whole village. Imagine if being a Christian were about life, and not about mastering the formula for Christian living. And why, by the way, is there a difference between living and Christian living?"

"So how would your life look different if you bought this?" He asks.

"I wouldn't do professional ministry."

"Wow. Really? Why?"

"It's too compartmentalized for me. It's not right for us as a people to hire specialists to do the sorts of things I do at Bud's. Or to have to sell other believers on helping. It's not personal, and it's not real. It's sincere the way a politician or the greeter at Wal-Mart is sincere."

"So you'd say screw the people you're helping?"

"I would certainly have a different approach to people. I wouldn't interact with them as a representative of an organization, but as an individual, as myself. I would do it in a more matter of fact way, and one separated from my job description. I'd do it just as a part of my regular life, as part of what I'd choose to be as a follower of Jesus in the lives of people whose paths I crossed. I think that would be vastly more honest."

"Honest?"

"Yeah. Right now the fact is that I need the Bud's employees more than they need me—and that Bud's needs them more than they need Bud's."

"How?"

"Bud's needs to make money to pay my salary, and it needs to make money to stay in business. Its being in business meets an emotional need in the board to feel like they're doing something productive with their faith—something they can hide from God behind, and something they can point to when they tally up what sort of person they are. If Bud's didn't exist, and neither did other ministries or places where a person could contribute and get their 'good Christian' points, what do you think would happen?"

"I think the whole world would burn."

"I bet that's what most American Christians would say. But I don't think so—not if the Holy Spirit is real. I think the Spirit would continue to convict people and what would change would be that individuals would do things on their own. I think that's how a lot of ministries get started in the first place—one person feels a burden from God to address a situation, usually a specific situation, and pretty soon other people are drawn to it and it takes on a life of its own."

"And becomes a hiding place." Robert says.

"That's what I'm thinking right now." I say. "So right now the raw material in the ministry economy is need. The consumer is the affluent person who is willing to buy however many 'good Christian' points they feel it will take to cover them with God. I'm the merchant and sales person. In the end Marcos and the other guys are strip mines I pick at for the raw materials I can trade for donations and donor comfort, and we don't think much about how we are really tearing down the world by making everyone weaker."

"How are you doing that?"

"I make the donors weaker by giving them the cheap solution to their deep, God-based needs. If the appetite to impact the world originates with God, then I'm comfortable saying that it is a healthy desire. But I come along like a McDonalds or a Wal-Mart, selling shit that is either not healthy or else of a quality that will never do the job for long. I sell them an easy out, junk food, products with a one-week warranty that are cheaper to replace than repair."

"But what about the Bud's guys? How are you making them weaker?"

"By undermining their worlds. Take Juan, for example. The other day we got onto the subject of welfare. He grew up in the projects and the bulk of his family's income came from welfare. His dad is a great guy—a hard-working brick layer—but for various reasons they've usually worked it so they were on welfare and Juan's dad got paid in cash."

"Okay."

"Well, as we were talking about welfare, it became clear that I, and the people I represent, see it not only as a line between success and failure, we see welfare as a reflection of flawed character, the difference between a valuable member of society and a drain upon society. At best it's a safety net a person may need to fall to in times of great distress, much like we'd look at bankruptcy or rehab or something like that. Those things leave an indelible mark that forever remain a legitimate basis for evaluating a person. Sort of like how felons are let out of prison, but aren't allowed to vote anymore. But Juan's perspective was that it was free money and only a fool wouldn't take advantage of the chance to get it."

"Seriously?"

"Yeah. But here's the deal. If I get him to agree that it's a character issue, he has to come to some pretty harsh conclusions about his father and about nearly everyone he's ever known. Is it a noble goal to convince Juan to choose the congratulations offered by me or the board, with our consumption of his world for our own ends, over his loyalty and wholehearted acceptance of his family? It's laughable to think that he would ever do that; in his world, unlike mine and the one in which I was raised, people rate higher than principles. What he gets, that we don't, is that principles are not always the same thing as truth. And that truth, from the Trinity on down, does not exist outside of relationship."

"Whoa."

"And for whatever practical realities may be worth considering about welfare and generational change and all of that, we don't have enough of a relational context to truly be part of a cultural shift. We're buying and selling commodities of our own choosing and design, and ultimately we're not interested in what they want—we're only interested in what we want to sell them."

"Harsh."

"Only because we don't see it. We're completely blind to the fact that the people to whom we do ministry are little more than blank slates upon which we seek to write our own legacies. It's the way power has always hidden itself in the guise of love. What's worse is that we're trying to sell our own twisted take on God to these guys, too. And it's dangerous ground when rich men show up to introduce poor men to Jesus, whatever the books they sell to rich people may say about how the Sermon on the Mount was talking about being poor in spirit, not in gold."

"I'm with you on that."

"From what I've seen of Latino culture, my employees would never say the sorts of things about their fathers that I say about mine. They would never bash the places they come from the way I do. There is a respect, a work ethic, a deference and an appreciation both for the realities of life and for its contradictions that I simply don't share as an educated, affluent White boy in late twentieth century America. But I have the power, and I am the conduit to a very hungry consumer base, and part of what sells is the exportation of educated, affluent White Christianity. Ask anyone around the world. Ask the Starbucks manager in Tehran."

"Makes you wonder what you're really selling the guys."

"I use first Thessalonians 4:11 in my discussions with donors a lot. That's the passage about living quietly, minding your own affairs, and living by the work of your hands. I draw that part of the verse out to talk about a simple life, like the ones the Bud's guys can know if they have a simple, stable job with us. Then I come down hard on the second part, which says they should live in this quiet way so they will command the respect of outsiders and be dependent upon nobody. With donors I talk about how we're working to help Bud's guys become independent in a system where the cards are currently stacked against them. But that's not really true. If there is one thing we are injecting into the worlds of the men we serve, it's dependence. I'm selling them a vision of a world that they don't have, and that they cannot acquire without the help we're offering. And we say it's for free—that it's something we'll actually pay them for as we teach them—but the cost is that they must trade in their worlds and become dependent upon us."

"How?"

"Well, aside from asking people like Juan to reject his family in favor of our rules, I'm the one writing the paychecks. I've been granted the power. Under the rules of straightforward capitalism, I can do whatever is legal and will be tolerated by my employees. My proselytizing, for Jesus or the Republicans or for whatever other reason I carry this torch, it all fits perfectly into the laws of supply and demand. The ways in which I speak into the lives of the men at Bud's Warehouse are my prerogative, and if dealing with that while doing a day's work is not worth the six and a quarter an hour we offer, the men can go find another job and I'll talk about how we grew them until they outgrew the place and call it a success. There will always be more employees willing to take my branding iron for a time. Men will line up to have the board, the business, the donors who learn their secrets without their permission, and the rest of us write our names upon them as though they have become our artwork, our possession signed and displayed to our glory. If you ask me, that sounds an awful lot like dependence. In so many ways it's much worse than a simple job where wages are unreasonably low. We're buying our way into lives to shape them into the image of our own dysfunction. We're doing it in God's name, and we have polished it nicely, but in the end what we're really doing is going out of our way to put something between ourselves and God."

"I still don't see the alternative, though."

"That's only evidence of how screwed up the whole model has become. In a fallen world where everything else gravitates to the crappiest lowest common denominator, why would we ever think this area, which is so consistent across so many different sorts of ministries, is one place where not only have we gotten it right, but nearly everyone else has too?"

46.

Tearing

I feel myself beginning to rise from the depths of my slumber, but have not risen to the point of consciousness or time, when I feel it fall heavily upon me, crushing and suffocating like cold melted clay, forming to my back as I lay on my stomach. I am pre-verbal, pre-cognitive, but I know this is a creature attacking me.

I know, from some place that has never thought about it, that there is only one word that will deliver me from this. I struggle to even conceive the word, and once I fight through the strings of syrup in my brain, I drag it like a sledge from my brain to my mouth. It takes forever, and the whole time I am being crushed. I cannot breath, literally, and the weight is incredible. The word is taking forever, and I can't engage my muscles to move my mouth. I feel like there is no air within me, but finally I am able to push some last wheeze from my core, and it oozes through my throat and past my tongue, and over my dry lips.

"Gehz," slurs onto my pillow, and I feel a pencil-sized hole form in the ice under which I'm trapped, still being crushed and still unable to move. I breathe in a fraction of air and cram my soul down on the bellows again.

"Us." And the hole widens. I know this is going to work. I breathe again.

"Jes-us." I strain. I breathe.

"Jesus."

"Jesus save me, a sinner."

And the weight lifts straight up from me and is gone. I repeat the prayer and catch my breath for twenty or thirty seconds before I turn my head to see if there is anything visible in the room with me. Of course there is not.

Outside the day has dawned clear and the birds are singing. My room is drenched in yellow light, and I smell the bleach in the sheets I washed yesterday. It is a beautiful morning.

I rise and drop my Rich Mullins CD into the player, thrilled by my deliverance, but unwilling to dwell upon it further. I have a life to lead, and a Lord to follow, and no time for such distractions.

Today is a big day at Bud's. The board has continued to be split for over a year now, and the more conservative faction wants to divert needed money away from the Warehouse and into the micro-lending pool, forcing Bud's to downsize and relocate. They also want to revisit my compensation package, which has begun to grow as the business has shown some profit recently. The more aggressive ardent believers are willing to play meltdown over the issue, and this is the first board meeting where I haven't known exactly how things will go. If the conservative side wins, it could be enough to kill the business, and it would be a huge betrayal of support within the larger ministry umbrella. The route I've seen to Bud's continued success would be ruined, and in addition to the insult I'd feel from the lack of support and the shortsightedness of the choice, I'd be placed into the situation where my departure would certainly be a huge disappointment to the people who want to see the business succeed. If the conservative side wins, and I leave, the subsequent collapse of the business would be blamed explicitly on me. But if the conservative side wins, and I stay, I have absolutely no idea how I can do anything but ride the ship to the bottom of the sea.

If the aggressive side wins, there will be ramifications on the relational front, both within the Bud's board and within the board of our parent ministries, and at least one person, retired banker Bill, would quit his job with the ministry. I don't see how today will be good news, and for as much as I've thought and jockeyed and prayed about today, I have no idea how it came to this, or what real life things could have been done differently. This crossroads was set before I was hired.

I've already spoken with the provider of my back up plan, the president of a wholesale plumbing distributor with whom I've built a relationship, taking him from cold call to participation on an ad hoc advisory board. He's offered me a position handling his "troubled accounts" in case things don't go well. It's a secular job, but it could be okay. The accounts I would address total about $9 million worth of business, and are "troubled" because his business has grown so quickly that some longer-standing customers have felt like they've fallen through the cracks. My task would be to court them back through detailed attention and aggressive bids. The company president thinks I've done that well with Bud's, and he thinks I'd do it well for him.

I'm thinking about this as my white sedan floats through traffic up Broadway, smooth and rising northward like columns of bubbles in a champagne glass, the air-conditioning on for the first time this year. Traffic brakes briefly as a man in a tie cuts hurriedly across from the west side of the road to the east. He's running to another man, who is cradling and trying to resuscitate a homeless woman on the sidewalk. She is quite clearly dead. The soles of her feet are black from city soot, and her pink dress is hiked to just past her hip, her head on the cement. She is wearing no underwear, and there is blood trailing from there to the ground. She looks vaguely familiar. Traffic picks back up, and I move with it, eager to get to the board meeting.

The whole board is present, and tensions run high. Years of frustration

GALL

spurt out in unproductive ways. Fingers are pointed, blanket statements tossed about. The conservative side has prepared for this, and after more than a year of losing these encounters, the dye is already cast. They will win, and I will lose. It is not a surprise, and while it would usually be emotionally wrenching, I keep thinking about the woman on the side of the road.

It was Maria, the woman I gave the $100 so she could get herself and her kids out of the snow. And I drove right past. There was no good place to pull over. I'm wearing a white dress shirt and didn't want to sweat. I had a very important meeting to get to. She was already dead anyway. There was nothing I could have done. But none of that matters because in the moment I looked at her from within my bubble and she could have been the evening news. She wasn't even real to me.

But she was real. She was a human being laying dead on the sidewalk, just feet from me, and she may as well have been a dog for all I did in response. There was a time when her father bounced his baby girl on his knee. There was a day when she learned to jump rope. Another when she learned to ride a bike. Once she sold lemonade for five cents a glass. She didn't deserve to die alone, violently, at the hands of another or under the influence of some drug by which she will be defined in the coroner's report and medics' cold defensive humor.

Bad things had happened to her along the way, and each was a tragedy. Each was an assault on the little girl who didn't deserve to be scarred. Each was a crime. And no one came to her rescue. No one brought justice for the abuse. The family of man is as guilty for its ambivalence as my own family can ever be for the experience my cousin encountered at the aged hands of my dad's favorite uncle. Maria fell through the cracks because the rest of us live on false scaffolding that prevents us from seeing her, let alone reaching down to save her. Maria died, and I drove by. I had a very important ministry to go fight for. Maria died because I was more important than she was. And so were the ideas and principles and rescue program I serve. I was so busy with myself and my idols designed to efficiently do God's work that I could not be interrupted. None of us is willing to live in ways that leave us open to interruption. We want the protection of organizations. We want to "have people for that." Specialists at following Christ so we won't have to do it ourselves. Maria died, and somewhere someone will use her as evidence that we need more ministries to help people like Maria.

Bullshit. What we need is to be willing to stop the fucking car.

47.

Tatters

I left Bud's the next week, after it became clear that priorities other than my salary would have to be paid, and that my salary itself was going to push the budget beyond what it could bear. Banker Bill stepped in to run the place, as his salary, more than double my own, was already covered by the micro-lending program and the one loan it had made in three years. Viking Bruce said he didn't blame me; that he wouldn't expect his employees to show up if he didn't pay them. The conservative board members...actually, I don't know what they thought because I never spoke to any of them again. I assumed they felt betrayed and as though my departure proved things about my lack of commitment, faith and maturity. The Bud's employees didn't really seem to care. During my time at Bud's, we ran through about 20 employees. We called each of them successes in some way, but the fact is that the only two whom I'd even begin to think of as successes are Marcos and Juan; the others either quit from frustration or were fired for not measuring up. Eddie Haskell Chris helped Marcos buy a house. Juan left soon after I did, and I'm told he's a highly valued employee at a hotel downtown, which is no surprise because he was a rock at Bud's too.

It tore me up to see that the guys didn't really care that I was leaving, that it was such a matter of fact thing. I have to assume they felt the same abuses I discovered we were perpetuating upon them, and saw what an unimpressive person that made me, all sizzle and no steak.

I haven't ever spoken with Henry or Sam Love, or Hungarian Vince. I have no idea what has become of Cajun Ed the fecal masturbator at Teen Challenge, or of Insane Jarrod. I've had no contact with any of the people from Agape Christian Church or the Nation of Islam store in the year since I left Bud's. I have no idea what came of Sandy the teenaged runaway, and neither did anyone else at the Prodigal Coffee House when I asked about her. I see Jeff Johnsen from time to time, and I hear bits and pieces about how things are going for Mile High Ministries. His continued presence and enthusiasm for what he does haunts me, and I know that there is a piece I'm missing, but frankly I'm too worn out to search it out. Sometimes I wonder if the demons have something to do with it. Other times I thank God that I've lost my taste for that fight. Bud's has moved to a smaller building, owned by one of the board members, and continues on. It turns out that my departure caused the same sort of energy input as had greeted me, with people refusing to let it die. After a while under Banker Bill's leadership, it sounds like the board found an outstanding leader, and things are looking good for the business.

I spend time with Skinny Robert, and with Jon, and with David and Danielle and their new son, Cole. We all attend different churches, and none of us seem very happy about them. I had a girlfriend for three months, but she broke up with me when she decided I wasn't over Loma. I went from that discussion directly over to Loma's apartment, where we got into a fight. I went from there to the reggae bar and drove home less sober than I should have.

It's been a year. I wear a tie to work at the plumbing distributor's, and have become extremely familiar with the differences between urinal plumbing options. I've automated some of the processes the distributor uses in soliciting business and in measuring customer satisfaction. Most of the troubled accounts have found peace. I lost some weight on the Atkins diet, and then regained it. Everyone in the office knows I'm a Christian.

I am most certainly not a tremendous man of God. I never was. The world I came to Denver to build blows gently in ashes and tatters.

48.

Salvage

Home for another Christmas. Dad and I play a game of chess in his study. He asks about priorities. I tell him my first priority is God, my second is my family, my third is my life's work, and my fourth is my friends.

He asks how satisfied I am with my world as it meshes with my priorities.

I haven't been truly active in a church for two years, since Robert, Jon, Loma, two other people, and I left Church in the City for reasons I've pretty much forgotten now, and certainly don't care enough about to spell out.

I am not doing any ministry work, and it's still hard for me to say that just being a decent guy who points to God now and then is enough. So the God part isn't where I'd like it to be.

I live 1,000 miles from my family, who have all ended up staying in Zionsville. Both brothers married high school sweethearts whose families are also from town. I don't talk to my brothers except when I'm home for holidays. I'm not satisfied with the family part.

My life's work? I don't know what it is. It certainly is not selling shitpipe. I spend 50 hours a week at a job, not a career or a passion. I'm not content with the job item on my priority list.

Friends? Loma and I seem guaranteed to continue on the same path forever, unable to come together, but also radical spoilers to any sort of relational happiness with another. I want her, and she wants to be loved by someone else sort of the way she's loved by me. Skinny Robert has a fiancé he'll be marrying in August, which makes him pretty unavailable. Jon is a recluse with his wife and Doberman. David and I are still good, but it's not enough to build a world around. I'm in Pastor Tony's Bible study every Friday night, but they have a new baby and he's incredibly busy. The rest of the list of friends is weaker than this. There is nothing keeping me in Denver but habit and pride.

My dad makes the point that it may be worth thinking about moving home, where at least I will be around family.

Here's what I'm coming to understand. We all want to be loved, and we all want to be seen—and we all hate being made invisible by the agendas and social regulations of people and structures that don't see us for who we are. We want to express who we are, and to be loved through those definitions. I wanted to be loved as a radical follower of Jesus, a learned man devoted to doing good in the name of the Lord. But I was mocked. I don't know if I'm able to give up insisting which parts of me a person sees, and I don't think I'm willing to be loved for areas other than the areas I think represent my true self. I want to be loved and seen for the person I know myself to be, not for the person others have decided I am. I don't think a person can ever get that from their family, and I don't know if I'm ready to let go of the descriptions and definitions I've clung to so I'll know who I am and so I can tell people who I am and how to love me.

But I have no idea who the fuck I am anymore anyway. Will being loved by my family, who is unable and unwilling to see me as anything but what I've always been to them, make me quit trying to figure it out? Will I just get sucked back into some inferior way of life and of seeing myself?

✳✳✳

I also meet with Pastor Glenn at Zionsville Presbyterian. I tell him about where I've been and where I've arrived. He smiles, not mockingly, but knowingly, when I talked about church and ministry and identity and family and doubt and prayer and faith and my tattered dreams.

"You know what I think?" he asks.

I turn my palms up.

"I think there are two important questions a person processes through in life regarding God."

I raise my eyebrows.

"The first one is, 'do you believe in hard truths?' Not hard in the sense that there are harsh things that happen in the world, but hard in the sense that sin runs rampant, in people and structures and even in nature, and that if nothing is done about it, it will destroy everything."

"Okay. Yes." I say.

"That's the first step. That's the first basic difference between faith and non-faith, because as soon as sin is real, so is the battle."

I nod and shrug.

"The second question is, 'For whom are these truths hard?' If sin is rampant in your world, and if that sin must be fought, for whom is that truth a hard truth?" He waits for my quick reply.

"Me. I mean, it's also a hard truth for God because He's ultimately responsible, but it's a hard truth for me because it means the battle is one I have to engage. It means there is something for me to do in the fight."

"Okay. I'd say that's where you've been, working hard to fight the fight and all of that. But how do you feel today?"

I tear up. "Lost. I've failed, and I've proven that I'm totally full of shit, and

I'm angry with everyone who keeps insisting that everything I've tried is still the right way to go, and I'm just...exhausted."

"So do you still believe in hard truths, if the battle gets you nowhere?" Glenn asks.

"I don't know how to quit believing in them, but I guess it feels impossible to take them on because they're so much bigger than I am, and because I'm one of them when it comes down to it."

"So, let's go back to the second question again. For whom are the hard truths hard? If you have broken yourself against them and have seen that you are light years from being able to adequately address them, and you're a pretty capable guy, by whom could the hard things be overcome?"

"Jesus."

"Right. It sounds like such an obvious answer, such a church answer, doesn't it?"

"Yeah."

"But here's the most important thing that difference will do in your world. Do you want to know?"

I nod.

"It kills the word 'should.' It kills the phrase 'supposed to,' and the preamble, 'a Christian is' whatever. Think about your world and how different it would be if you could get past trying to do it right. You're a classic first-born child, running scared and trying to get it all right so you stay out of trouble and can get the praise. It doesn't work that way with God. You already are a Christian, and what makes you a Christian is not your works. You will do works because you are a follower of Jesus, but as soon as you turn it around and start looking to do things to define your Christianity, you cease to be a follower of Jesus. The hard truth is not yours. Jesus said that the yoke He would give us was easy and the burden light. Is that what you've experienced?"

"No." I snort. "Not even close."

"Then you have to ask yourself if He's the one who gave it to you. Maturity in the faith comes when a person is willing to admit that there are hard truths, and that they are hard for Jesus, not for us. I think that's where you've finally been led, after a remarkable effort to serve God on your terms, I might add. And I think you're ready to try trusting him for real."

49.

Easter

Pastor Tony has a term and a sort of game he plays. If there is a big decision to make about life, say something like whether or not to move home after five years of trying different ministry stuff, he does what he calls "putting it in the tomb." He prays about it and gives it to God during Lent. If the idea returns to him at Easter, it's alive and he acts upon it. If it doesn't come back, if it dies in the tomb, nothing comes of it. That's what I did this year.

Easter was 15 days ago. Loma and I attended Tony's thriving multiracial suburban church, where he has absolutely hit his stride. We sat in the front row. She wore a yellow sundress. As we sang the doxology, I wrapped my arm lightly around her waist, which is pretty much the only time I've ever touched her, other than once when she hugged me after I followed her to make sure she got home safely in a blizzard. As we stood there in the bright light, I knew it was time to leave Denver.

Loma cried when I told her, saying that once I left she truly would be alone. There's little point in analyzing her, but it would be fair to say that she'd keep me near to her for the comfort no matter what it cost me. And there's little point in analyzing me, but it made me feel good that she was sad about my departure.

My other friends understood and encouraged me, though they said they would miss me. I've run out of time to tell quite a few other friends, who will find out weeks and months from now that I've left town.

I gave notice the next day, and have been offered an interview at the plumbing distributor's Indianapolis branch, which I'll probably look into until I figure out what else I'm going to do.

My stuff is packed and ready to go. It took a Ryder truck, packed to the ceiling, to get me here. I'm returning home in my white sedan and will fill up part of an SUV too.

The SUV arrives. It is my father's. It is driven by my two brothers. My sister-in-law is in the back seat. After five years of misunderstanding, mocking, condemnation—all of these things going both directions—at the end of the day, when everything else has fallen apart, it is my brothers who have driven 20 hours to take me home. I am overcome by the moment. I did not know what was important until right now. My brothers look like me, fair and stocky, strong and loyal, nice guys who are well aware of their flaws, but are willing to love anyone willing to be loved. I am proud to be one of them.

We load my things into the SUV and pull away from my place an hour later. They don't even want to spend the night—they would rather push to make the round trip all at once. We do stop by the Coors brewery for a tour and samples, and lunch beneath the mountains in Golden, and then we hit the road.

They don't understand me. They have no idea what I'm talking about with most of the ideas I spray around. They have no interest in the version of myself I've sought to create. They have no desire to offer the prophet respect in his hometown. All they care about is that their brother is coming home.

What a relief.